SHELLS &
SHELLFISH
of the
PACIFIC
NORTHWEST

SHELLS & SHELLFISH

of the

PACIFIC NORTHWEST

A FIELD GUIDE

Rick M. Harbo

Third Printing, 2007

Harbour Publishing
P.O. Box 219
Madeira Park, BC
V0N 2H0 Canada

Cover, page design and composition by Martin Nichols
Map and figures by Nola Johnston

Printed and bound in Hong Kong by Prolong Press Limited

CANADIAN CATALOGUING IN PUBLICATION DATA

Harbo, Rick M., 1949-
    Shells & Shellfish of the Pacific Northwest

    Includes index.
    ISBN 13: 978-1-50017-146-4

    1. Shellfish—Northwest, Pacific. 2. Shells—Northwest, Pacific.
I. Title.
QL417.H37 1996 594.09795   C96-910088-4

Contents

Appendices

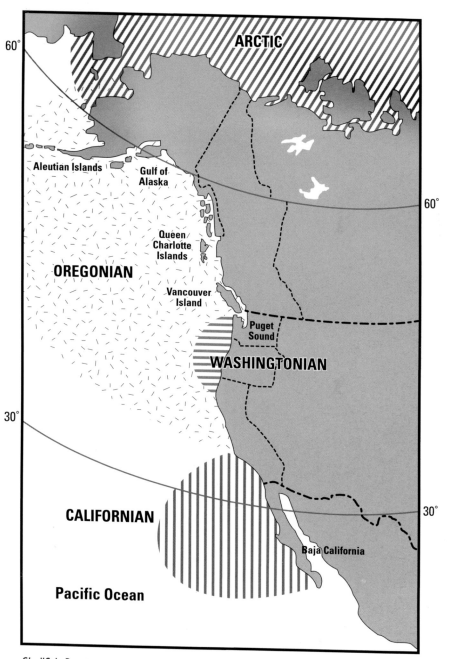

Shellfish Provinces of the Pacific Northwest Coast.

Introduction

The Pacific Northwest is one of the world's favourite outdoor recreation spots, known for its rugged natural beauty and its rich, abundant wildlife. Because of its temperate climate and warm ocean currents, the area is home to an especially rich variety of marine life, including hundreds of species of shellfish. Campers, hikers, swimmers, divers and beachcombers can find a cornucopia of intertidal and subtidal creatures, from the tiny Adanson lepton to the Giant Pacific chiton.

This guide introduces 225 of the most familiar species to be found along the Northwest Coast—the clams, oysters, mussels, abalone, snails, whelks, tusks, chitons and other common shellfish that inhabit the beaches, shallow waters and intertidal areas near salt water. All of them are members of the phylum Mollusca (the mollusks), and they are among the most abundant and interesting creatures in the world.

How to Use This Guide

This book will help you identify shells and shellfish in their natural settings, so that you can observe species without having to disturb them. You can identify your specimen by the look of its shell, or—a first in field guides to shells and shellfish!—by its siphons or "show" protruding from the sand or mud.

The common shells of the Pacific Northwest fall into four classes of mollusks: bivalves (two-shelled animals like clams and scallops), gastropods (single-shelled animals like snails and abalone), tuskshells, and chitons.

Identifying a Species by Shell

Go to the Colour Guide and find the class of mollusk your specimen belongs to, by looking for the icon at the top of the page:

Bivalves
(Class Bivalvia or Pelecypoda)

Two shells joined with a hinge. Clams, oysters, mussels, scallops, cockles and shipworms belong to this class, which has some 12,000 species that live in fresh and salt water.

Gastropods
(Class Gastropoda)

One shell, cap-shaped or whorled. Abalone, limpets, periwinkles, snails, whelks and olive shells belong to this class.

Tuskshells
(Class Scaphopoda)

Tubular, tusk-shaped shell open at both ends. There are about 500 living species of tuskshells, all of which live in salt water.

Chitons
(Class Polyplacaphora)

Thin shell of 8 overlapping plates set in a fleshy girdle. There are 500 to 600 species of chitons, all of which live in salt water.

Then narrow your search until you find your specimen.

Keep in mind that there are hundreds of subspecies and variations, and you may not find your exact shell. But with this guide you can identify all common species found on the Northwest Coast.

Identifying a Species by Siphon or "Show"

Some clams can be identified by their "shows," the visible exposed parts, particularly the siphons which protrude from the sand or mud. To identify a specimen by its show, go to the Siphons section, at the end of the Bivalves section.

This section includes an identification key as well as colour photographs.

Piddock siphons at the water's edge.

For More Information

To find more identification details and interesting facts about your specimen or its family, turn to the page indicated in each entry. The Field Guide, page 113, has lots of extra information.

For tips on how to find shells, how to clean and store specimens, how to start a scientific collection, or how to make sure certain species are safe to eat, see the Introduction, page 115.

A Checklist of all species listed in this book starts on page 234. You can use it to keep track of your specimen sightings, or to help organize your shell collection.

Appendices include a Recreational Harvest Information guide, a list of PSP (Red Tide) Marine Toxin Hotlines, a Glossary of Terms and Scientific Names, Further Reading (including seafood cookbooks), and an Index to common and scientific names.

Shellfish and the Environment

Like all living things, shellfish and even their empty shells play an important role in the ecology of the sea and the seashore. So please harvest your specimens carefully, taking only what you need and disturbing the habitat as little as possible. Check with your local Fish and/or Wildlife authorities for current quotas and restrictions on gathering methods.

Small dredge haul.

Bivalves

Bivalves (class Bivalvia) are mollusks whose shells have two halves, or valves. Another name for this class is Pelecypoda, which means "hatchet-footed." Bivalves do not have heads, and most species feed by filtering microscopic plant and animal particles from the water. A few are predatory.

There are about 10,000 living bivalve species in the world, all of which are aquatic, and a few of which live in fresh waters. In British Columbia 180 bivalve species have been described. About 70 of them are found in the intertidal zone or to depths of 165' (50 m). The 100 most common species are included in this guide.

AWNING-CLAMS
Family Solemyidae

GUTLESS AWNING-CLAM

Solemya reidi
Size: To 2¹/²" (60 mm).
Range: 50°N–33°N, Northern Vancouver Island and south to Point Loma, California.
Habitat: Often in areas rich in organics, sulphide; near effluent outfalls and in log storage areas, 130–200' (40–60 m) depth. Sometimes found in "cleaner" sediments.
Description: *Page 132*

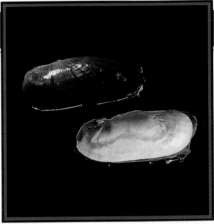

B-1

NUT SHELLS Family Nuculidae

DIVARICATE NUTCLAM

Acila castrensis
Size: To ⁵/8" (15 mm) length.
Range: 57°N–24°N; NE Bering Sea, Alaska south to Punta San Pablo, Baja, California, and in the Gulf of California.
Habitat: Mud–sand bottoms 16–725' (5–220 m).
Description: *Page 132*

B-2

YOLDIA CLAMS
Family Sareptidae (=Yoldiidae)

AXE YOLDIA

Megayoldia thraciaeformis
Size: To 2¹/²" (65 mm) length.
Range: 70°N–38°N; Circumpolar; southern Arctic, northern Bering Sea south to off San Francisco Bay, California.
Habitat: Mud–sand bottoms 80–2000' (25–600 m).
Description: *Page 133*

B-3

B-4

CRISSCROSS YOLDIA

Yoldia seminuda
Size: To 1 1/2" (40 mm) length.
Range: 71°N–34°N; Arctic, Beaufort Sea, Bering Sea south to San Diego, California.
Habitat: Mud–sand bottoms 50–500' (15–150 m).
Description: *Page 133*

BITTERSWEET CLAMS
Family Glycymerididae

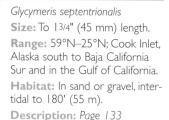

Glycymeris septentrionalis
Size: To 1 3/4" (45 mm) length.
Range: 59°N–25°N; Cook Inlet, Alaska south to Baja California Sur and in the Gulf of California.
Habitat: In sand or gravel, intertidal to 180' (55 m).
Description: *Page 133*

B-5

PHILOBRYAS Family Philobryidae

HAIRY PHILOBRYA

Philobrya setosa
Size: To 1/4" (5 mm) length.
Range: 60°N–23°N; Prince William Sound, Alaska and south to Baja California Sur, and possibly farther south to Costa Rica.
Habitat: Attaches to broken shells and coralline algae by byssus; found in the intertidal zone to 240' (73 m).
Description: *Page 134*

B-6

**SECTION I
BIVALVES**

PACIFIC BLUE MUSSEL

B-7

Mytilus edulis
Considered to be several species or subspecies.

Range: 71°N–19°N; Arctic to Alaska and south to Mexico.

Habitat: Quiet, sheltered locations, in the intertidal zone to 16'
(5 m) depths. They are a common and dominant species, forming
dense masses on hard surfaces attached by strong byssal threads.

Description: *Page 135*

BLUE MUSSEL

Mytilus edulis
Size: To 4 1/2" (110 mm).
Range: Unknown. Considered introduced to BC.
Description: *Page 135*

MEDITERRANEAN MUSSEL

Mytilus galloprovincialis
Size: To 6" (150 mm).
Range: Unknown. Found in a sheltered inlet in BC; found in south-
ern California to Mexico. Native to the Mediterranean, western
France, Britain and Ireland.
Habitat: Warmer waters.
Description: *Page 135*

FOOLISH MUSSEL

Mytilus trossulus
Size: To 3 1/2" (90 mm) length.
Range: Uncertain. Arctic to Alaska and south to Central California.
Habitat: Protected waters; intertidal on rocks and pilings.
Description: *Page 135*

B-8

CALIFORNIA MUSSEL

Mytilus californianus

Size: To 10" (255 mm) length.

Range: 60°N–18°N; Cook Inlet, Alaska to Punta Rompiente, Baja California Sur and Mexico.

Habitat: Extensive mussel beds are seen on surf-exposed rocks and wharves; from the intertidal zone to 330' (100 m), dominant on sea mounts.

Description: *Page 136*

California mussel beds

Horsemussels

STRAIGHT (FAN) HORSEMUSSEL

B-9

Modiolus rectus

Size: To 9" (230 mm) length.

Range: 54°N–5.1°S; Tow Hill, Queen Charlotte Islands, BC south to Baja and Gulf of California, and as far south as Paita, Peru.

Habitat: Solitary, buried in sand, anchored by byssal threads and sand or mud; white siphons show at surface (see page 62). Found in the intertidal zone to depths of 50' (15 m).

Description: *Page 136*
See also S-9.

NORTHERN HORSEMUSSEL

Modiolus modiolus

Size: To 7" (180 mm) length.

Range: 50°N–37°N; Bering Sea south to Monterey, California.

Habitat: In aggregations or mussel "mats" binding gravel and rocks, sometimes in the intertidal zone and to depths of 660' (200 m).

Description: *Page 137*
See also S-10.

B-10

Boring Datemussels

CALIFORNIA DATEMUSSEL

Adula californiensis

Size: To 2¹/2" (60 mm).

Range: 54°N–33°N; Graham Island, Queen Charlotte Islands, BC south to Point Loma, California.

Habitat: Intertidal to 65' (20 m), boring in clay, shale and other soft rocks.

Description: *Page 137*

B-11

Burrowing, Nestling or Attached Mussels

DISCORDANT MUSSEL

Musculus discors

Size: To 2¹/4" (55 mm).

Range: 71°N–47°N; Beaufort Sea, Cook Inlet, Alaska south to Aberdeen, Washington.

Habitat: Buried in fine sand or in a "nest" of agglutinated sand, attached to tunicates or stalks of seaweed washed up on beach; in depths of 16–500' (5–150 m).

Description: *Page 137*

B-12

B-13

BLACK MUSSEL

Musculus niger
Size: To 2¼" (57 mm).
Range: 71°N–48°N; Beaufort Sea, Aleutian Islands, Alaska south to Willapa Bay, Washington; also on Atlantic Coast.
Habitat: In muddy gravel. The adult may use its byssal threads to form a "cocoon" around its shell. At depths of 50–500' (15–150 m).
Description: *Page 138*

B-14

TAYLOR'S DWARF-MUSSEL

Musculus taylori
Size: To 3/8" (8 mm).
Range: 53°N–48°N; Hotspring Island, Queen Charlotte Islands, BC south to Victoria, BC.
Habitat: Intertidal.
Description: *Page 138*

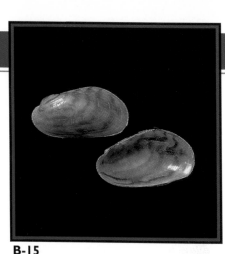

B-15

JAPAN MUSSEL

Musculista senhousia
Size: To 1½" (40 mm).
Range: Intermittent; 48°N–34°N; Strait of Georgia, BC, Puget Sound, Washington, and in California. Introduced from Japan along with oysters.
Habitat: Intertidal, in estuarine conditions to 65' (20 m).
Description: *Page 138*

BRITISH COLUMBIA CRENELLA

Solamen columbianum
Size: To 1/2" (11 mm)
Range: 60°N–33°N; Aleutian Islands, Alaska south to Point Loma, California.
Habitat: At depths of 65–180' (20–55 m).
Description: *Page 138*

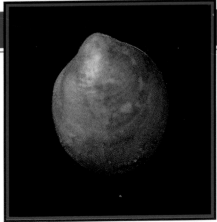

B-16

OYSTERS Family Ostreidae

OLYMPIA OYSTER

Ostrea conchaphila
Size: To 31/2" (90 mm) diameter.
Range: 57°N–9°N; Sitka, Alaska south to Panama.
Habitat: On mud–gravel flats, in splash pools and with fresh water seepage; in the intertidal zone to depths of 165' (50 m).
Description: *Page 139*

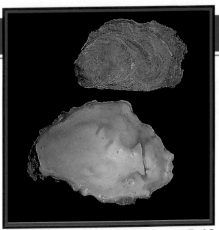

B-17

PACIFIC OYSTER

Crassostrea gigas
Size: To 12" (30 cm) length.
Range: 61°N–34°N; Prince William Sound, Alaska south to Newport Bay, California.
Habitat: Firm or rocky beaches, intertidally to 20' (6 m).
Description: *Page 139*

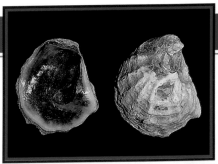

B-18

Pacific oyster pearls

Oystercatcher

Pacific Oysters

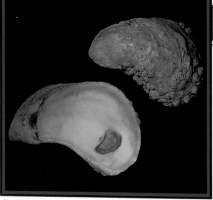

AMERICAN OYSTER

Crassostrea virginica

Size: To 8" (20 cm) length.

Range: Small population in BC on Boundary Bay flats at the mouth of the Nikomekl River.

Habitat: Intertidal on soft to firm substrates of sand–mud–gravel, usually in estuarine conditions.

Description: *Page 140*

B-19

EDIBLE FLAT OYSTER

Ostrea edulis

Size: To 3" (75 mm).

Range: Experimental culture sites in BC; not established in the wild.

Habitat: Soft to firm substrates in the intertidal zone.

Description: *Page 140*

B-20

JINGLE/ROCK OYSTERS
Family Anomiidae

GREEN FALSE-JINGLE

Pododesmus macroschisma

Size: To 5 1/4" (130 mm) length.

Range: 58°N–28°N; Bering Sea to Alaska and south to Baja California Sur; and in the Gulf of California.

Habitat: Attached to rocks and other solid objects, intertidal to 300' (90 m).

Description: *Page 141*

B-21

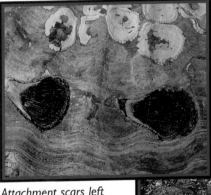

Attachment scars left behind from false-jingles.

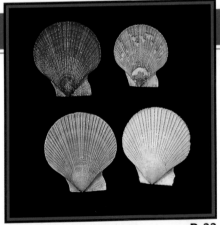

Green false-jingles eaten by painted sea star.

SCALLOPS Family Pectinidae

SMOOTH PINK SCALLOP

Chlamys rubida

Size: To 2 1/2" (66 mm) height.

Range: 57°N–33°N; Kodiak Island, Alaska south to San Diego, California; not common south of Puget Sound, Washington.

Habitat: On gravel–mud bottoms, at depths of 3–660' (1–200 m).

Description: *Page 142*

B-22

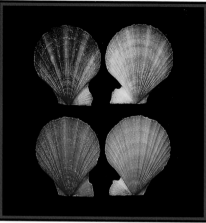

B-23

SPINY PINK SCALLOP

Chlamys hastata
Size: To 3 1/4" (83 mm) height.
Range: 60°N–33°N; Gulf of Alaska south to San Diego, California.
Habitat: On rocky reefs, sometimes in shallow water, 7–500' (2–150 m).
Description: *Page 142*

B-24

GIANT ROCK SCALLOP

Crassadoma gigantea
Size: To 10" (250 mm) or more height. It is a toss-up whether this or the weathervane scallop is the largest scallop in the world. Rock scallops have thicker shells and are heavier.
Range: 60°N–27°N; Prince William Sound, Alaska south to Baja California Sur.
Habitat: On rocky bottoms, intertidal in crevices or under boulders, to depths of 265' (80 m).
Description: *Page 143*
See also S-15.

Scallop eyes.

WEATHERVANE SCALLOP

Patinopecten caurinus
Size: To 11" (280 mm).
Range: 59°N–36°N; Northern Alaskan islands and south to Point Sur, California.
Habitat: In small depressions on sand or gravel, 33–660' (10–200 m).
Description: *Page 143*

B-25

JAPANESE WEATHERVANE SCALLOP

Mizuhopecten yessoensis
Size: To 9" (220 mm) height.
Range: Cultured species. No wild sets recorded to date.
Habitat: Have been held suspended in the water column in lantern nets. Some experimental bottom culture has been also been attempted in the subtidal zone.
Description: *Page 144*

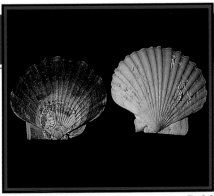

B-26

VANCOUVER SCALLOP

Delectopecten vancouverensis
Size: To 1/4" (6 mm).
Range: 60°N–28°N; Prince William Sound, Alaska south to Baja California.
Habitat: At 80–1500' (25–450 m) on sand–mud bottoms, usually attached in a nest to large sponges, large crustaceans and other objects.
Description: *Page 144*

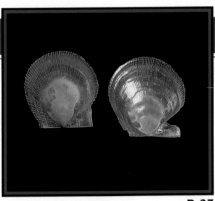

B-27

LUCINE CLAMS
Family Lucinidae

WESTERN RINGED LUCINE

Lucinoma annulatum
Size: To 3 1/4" (82 mm).
Range: 60°N–26°N; Prince William Sound and northern Alaskan islands south to the Gulf of California.
Habitat: Intertidal in sand–mud, to 2500' (750 m).
Description: *Page 145*

B-28

FINE-LINED LUCINE

Parvalucina tenuisculpta
Size: To 5/8" (15 mm).
Range: 60°N–28°N; Kodiak Island, Alaska south to Isla Cedros, Baja California Norte.
Habitat: Intertidal in sand–mud, to depths of 900' (275 m) and more, sometimes in dense numbers.
Description: *Page 145*

B-29

DIPLODON CLAMS
Family Ungulinidae

ROUGH DIPLODON

Diplodonta impolita
Size: To 1 1/2" (36 mm) length.
Range: 57°N–44°N; Kodiak Island, Alaska south to Oregon.
Habitat: Intertidal to 330' (100 m).
Description: *Page 146*

B-30

CLEFTCLAMS Family Thyasiridae

GIANT CLEFTCLAM

Conchocele bisecta
Size: To 4 1/2" (110 mm) length.
Range: 57°N–41°N; Bering Sea,
Alaska south to Humboldt Bay,
California.
Habitat: Common subtidal
species in mud at 165–1000'
(50–300 m).
Description: *Page 146*

B-31

FLEXUOSE CLEFTCLAM

Thyasira flexuosa
Size: To 1/2" (12 mm)
Range: 71°N–34°N;
Circumboreal; Panarctic; Beaufort
Sea south to San Pedro,
California.
Habitat: In sand–mud, 40–825'
(12–250 m).
Description: *Page 146*

B-32

NORTHERN AXINOPSID

Axinopsida serricata
Size: To 3/8" (8 mm).
Range: 60°N–28°N;
Circumboreal; Panarctic; Point
Barrow, Alaska south to Punta
San Pablo, Baja California Sur, and
in the Gulf of California.
Habitat: In sand–mud, intertidal
zone to 900' (275 m).
Description: *Page 147*

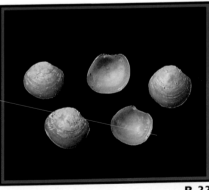

B-33

Family Astartida

ELLIPTICAL TRIDONTA

Astarte elliptica
Size: To 2" (50 mm).
Range: 71°N–48°N;
Circumboreal; arctic Alaska south
to Puget Sound, Washington.
Habitat: At depths of 65–825'
(20–250 m).
Description: *Page 147*

B-34

ESQUIMALT ASTARTE

Astarte esquimalti
Size: To 3/4" (18 mm).
Range: 71°N–48°N; Beaufort
Sea, Bering Sea and south to
Puget Sound, Washington.
Habitat: At depths of 33–660'
(10–200 m); also reported in the
intertidal zone in Alaska.
Description: *Page 147*

B-35

CARDITA CLAMS
Family Carditidae

CARPENTER'S CARDITA

Glans carpenteri
Size: To 1/2" (10 mm).
Range: 54°N–28°N; Frederick
Island, BC south to Punta
Rompiente, Baja California Sur.
Habitat: Nestling or attached to
the underside of rocks, intertidal
to 330' (100 m).
Description: *Page 148*

B-36

LASAEA CLAMS
Family Lasaeidae

ADANSON'S LEPTON

Lasaea adansoni
Size: To 1/8" (3 mm).
Range: 55°N–7°S; Sitka, Alaska south to Peru.
Habitat: Attached by byssus to algae, barnacles, *M. californianus* and other mussels; often at extreme high tide but to 33' (10 m).
Description: *Page 148*

B-37

KELLYCLAM

Kellia suborbicularis
Size: To 1/2" (13 mm).
Range: 60°N–4°S; Circumboreal; Prince William Sound, Alaska south to Peru.
Habitat: Intertidal to 65' (20 m), inside empty shells, empty pholad holes in crevices and among mussels.
Description: *Page 148*

B-38

NETTED KELLYCLAM

Rhamphidonta retifera
Size: To 5/8" (15 mm).
Range: 50°N–34°N; Very local and limited distribution at sites from Esperanza Inlet, Vancouver Island to Santa Rosa Island, California.
Habitat: Intertidal to depths of 80' (25 m).
Description: *Page 149*

B-39

B-40

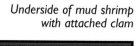

WRINKLED MONTACUTID

Neaeromya rugifera

Size: To 2" (50 mm) length.

Range: 50°N–28°N; Kodiak, Alaska to Punta Rompiente, Baja California Sur.

Habitat: Attached by byssus to underside of mud shrimp, *Upogebia pugettensis*, and to the "sea mouse" polychaete, *Aphrodite*. Intertidal to 16' (5 m) depths.

Description: *Page 149*

Underside of mud shrimp with attached clam

Mud Shrimp

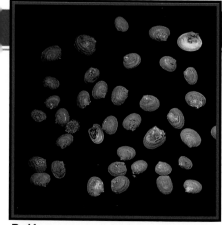

B-41

ROBUST MYSELLA

Rochefortia tumida

Size: To 3/16" (5 mm).

Range: 71°N–33°N; Beaufort Sea south to San Diego, California.

Habitat: Intertidal to 400' (120 m); often commensal with poly-chaete worms and other burrow-ing animals in mud and fine sand.

Description: *Page 149*

COCKLES Family Cardiidae

NUTTALL'S COCKLE

Clinocardium nuttallii
Size: To 5 1/2" (140 mm) length.
Range: 60°N–33°N; Southern Bering Sea, Alaska south to San Diego, California.
Habitat: Intertidal to 100' (30 m) depths, in sand–gravel in sheltered waters.
Description: *Page 150*
See also S-7.

B-42

SMOOTH COCKLE

Clinocardium blandum
Size: To 2" (50 mm).
Range: 54°N–39°N; Southern Bering Sea, Gulf of Alaska south to Sonoma County, California.
Habitat: In subtidal sand–mud at 33–165' (10–50 m).
Description: *Page 151*

B-43

ALEUTIAN COCKLE

Clinocardium californiense
Size: To 3" (75 mm) height.
Range: 60°N–58°N; Bering Sea and southeast into the Gulf of Alaska. Not found in California.
Habitat: Subtidal, 33–330' (10–100 m).
Description: *Page 151*

B-44

B-45

HAIRY COCKLE

Clinocardium ciliatum
Size: To 2³/4" (70 mm) length.
Range: 71°N–49°N;
Circumboreal; Panarctic; Beaufort
Sea, Bering Sea and south to
Barkley Sound, Vancouver Island.
Habitat: Found in subtidal mud
and sand, 33–500' (10–150 m).
Description: *Page 151*

B-46

FUCAN COCKLE

Clinocardium fucanum
Size: To 1¹/2" (40 mm).
Range: 55°N–48°N; Bering Sea
south to Puget Sound,
Washington.
Habitat: At depths of 65–265'
(20–80 m).
Description: *Page 151*

B-47

GREENLAND
COCKLE

Serripes groenlandicus
Size: To 4¹/2" (110 mm).
Range: 71°N–48°N;
Circumboreal; Panarctic; Point
Barrow, Alaska south to Puget
Sound, Washington.
Habitat: Intertidal to depths of
265' (80 m).
Description: *Page 152*

HUNDRED LINE COCKLE

Nemocardium centifilosum
Size: To 1" (25 mm).
Range: 59°N–28°N; Southern Bering Sea, Gulf of Alaska south to Punta Rompiente, Baja California Sur.
Habitat: At depths of 7–500' (2–150 m).
Description: *Page 152*

B-48

HORSE CLAMS – GAPER CLAMS – SURFCLAMS Family Mactridae

FAT GAPER

Tresus capax
Size: To 7" (180 mm) length.
Range: 55°N–35°N; Cook Inlet, Gulf of Alaska south to Oceano, California.
Habitat: More common at northern latitudes; mud–sand, intertidal to 100' (30 m).
Description: *Page 153*
See also S-5

B-49

PACIFIC GAPER

Tresus nuttallii
Size: To 9" (225 mm) length. Whole wet weight to 3 lbs (1.4 kg).
Range: 58°N–25°N; Kodiak Island, Alaska south to southern Baja California Sur.
Habitat: Intertidal to 165' (50 m). Buries deeper (12–36"/30–90 cm) in the sand or is lower on the tide than the fat gaper (*T. capax*), to avoid freezing. Usually in sandier substrate than *T. capax*.
Description: *Page 153*
See also S-4

B-50

B-51

HOOKED SURFCLAM

Simomactra falcata

Size: To 3¹/₂" (90 mm) length.

Range: 54°N–31°N; Rose Spit, Queen Charlotte Islands, BC south to Isla San Martin, Baja California Norte.

Habitat: Buried shallow in sand from intertidal to 165' (50 m) depths; often in protected waters.

Description: *Page 154*

B-52

ARCTIC SURFCLAM

Mactromeris polynyma

Size: To 5¹/₂" (140 mm) length. To 14 oz (400 g) whole wet weight.

Range: 65°N–46°N; Bering Sea, Alaska south to Neah Bay, Washington.

Habitat: In sand, mud or gravel, intertidal to 365' (110 m).

Description: *Page 154*

B-53

CALIFORNIA SURFCLAM

Mactrotoma californica

Size: To 2" (48 mm).

Range: Reports of *Mactrotoma californica* in BC have not been substantiated. Found 35°N–21°N, from Monterey, California south to Mexico.

Habitat: In sand or sand–mud, intertidal to 50' (15 m).

Description: *Page 154*

JACKKNIFE-CLAMS
Family Solenidae

SICKLE JACKKNIFE-CLAM

Solen sicarius
Size: To 5" (125 mm).
Range: 56°N–33°N; Queen Charlotte Islands, BC south to Baja California Norte.
Habitat: Buried in sand–mud in more sheltered habitats than the Pacific razor-clam (*Siliqua patula*); sometimes in eelgrass; intertidal to 130' (40 m).
Description: *Page 155*

B-54

RAZOR-CLAMS Family Pharidae

PACIFIC RAZOR-CLAM

Siliqua patula
Size: To 7" (180 mm) length.
Range: 59°N–35°N; Cook Inlet, Gulf of Alaska south to Morro Bay, California.
Habitat: On surf-exposed beaches; usually intertidal but to depths of 180' (55 m). See illustration #000 for hints on detecting these clams by siphon shows. Abundant in many locations along the Washington and Oregon coast.
Description: *Page 155*
See also S-11

B-55

TELLIN and MACOMA CLAMS
Family Tellinidae

BODEGA TELLIN

Tellina bodegensis
Size: To 2 1/2" (60 mm).
Range: 57°N–25°N; Sitka, Alaska south to Bahia Magdalena, Baja California Sur.
Habitat: On beaches exposed or partially exposed to open ocean; intertidal to 300' (100 m).
Description: *Page 156*

B-56

B-57

CARPENTER'S TELLIN

Tellina carpenteri
Size: To 1" (25 mm).
Range: 57°N–7°N; Sitka, Alaska south to Panama.
Habitat: In sand or sand–mud intertidal to 1450' (440 m).
Description: *Page 156*

B-58

PLAIN TELLIN

Tellina modesta
Size: To 1" (25 mm).
Range: 59°N–28°N; Cook Inlet, Alaska south to Baja California Sur.
Habitat: In sand, intertidal to 165' (50 m).
Description: *Page 156*

B-59

SALMON TELLIN

Tellina nuculoides
Size: To 3/4" (20 mm).
Range: 60°N–32°N; Bering Sea, Cook Inlet south to Baja California Sur
Habitat: In sand, intertidal to 330' (100 m).
Description: *Page 157*

Macoma clams

BALTIC MACOMA

Macoma balthica
Size: To 1 1/2" (38 mm) length.
Range: 70°N–38°N;
Circumboreal; Panarctic; Beaufort
Sea to San Francisco Bay,
California.
Habitat: Often abundant,
buried shallow to 8" (20 cm) in
sand–mud, intertidal to 130' (40
m), usually in bays and estuaries.
Description: *Page 157*

B-60

POINTED MACOMA

Macoma inquinata
Size: To 2 1/2" (63 mm) length.
Range: 57°N–34°N; Pribilof
Islands, Bering Sea south to Santa
Barbara, California.
Habitat: In sand–mud, intertidal
to 165' (50 m) depths in bays
and offshore.
Description: *Page 158*

B-61

BENT-NOSE
MACOMA

Macoma nasuta
Size: To 3" (75 mm) length.
Range: 60°N–22°N; Cook Inlet,
Alaska south to southern Baja
California Sur, reports to Cabo
San Lucas.
Habitat: Buried 4–6" (10–15
cm) beneath the surface, com-
mon in intertidal sand to depths
of 165' (50 m).
Description: *Page 158*

B-62

B-63

WHITE-SAND MACOMA

Macoma secta
Size: To 4" (100 mm) length.
Range: 54°N–25°N; Queen Charlotte Islands, BC south to Baja California Sur.
Habitat: Buried to 8–18" (20–45 cm) in sand, intertidal to depths of 165' (50 m) in sheltered waters.
Description: *Page 158*

B-64

HEAVY MACOMA

Macoma brota
Size: To 3" (75 mm) length.
Range: 71°N–48°N; Circumboreal; Arctic to Bering Sea and south to Puget Sound, Washington.
Habitat: In subtidal sand–mud at depths of 33–850' (10–260 m).
Description: *Page 159*

B-65

CHALKY MACOMA

Macoma calcarea
Size: To 2 1/2" (60 mm).
Range: 71°N–47°N; Circumboreal; Arctic to Bering Sea and south to Newport, Oregon.
Habitat: In sand, silt and gravel, intertidal to 1050' (320 m).
Description: *Page 159*

CHARLOTTE MACOMA

Macoma carlottensis
Size: To 1" (25 mm).
Range: 52°N–32°N; Gulf of Alaska south to Isla Los Coronados, Baja California Norte, and in the central Gulf of California.
Habitat: To depths of 16–5100' (5–1547 m).
Description: *Page 159*

B-66

FILE MACOMA

Macoma elimata
Size: To 1 1/2" (35 mm).
Range: 55°N–34°N; Aleutian Islands, Alaska south to Redondo Beach, California.
Habitat: In sand and silt, subtidal 30–1435' (9–435 m).
Description: *Page 159*

B-67

EXPANDED MACOMA

Macoma expansa
Size: To 2" (50 mm).
Range: 60°N–28°N; Aleutian Islands, Alaska to Oceano, California.
Habitat: In sand, exposed habitats, intertidal to 100' (30 m).
Description: *Page 160*

B-68

B-69

ALEUTIAN MACOMA

Macoma lama

Size: To 13/4" (45 mm).

Range: 71°N–53°N; Arctic, Bering Sea south to Queen Charlotte Islands, BC, possibly farther south.

Habitat: In clean sand along exposed coasts, intertidal to 600' (183 m).

Description: *Page 160*

B-70

SLEEK MACOMA

Macoma lipara

Size: To 3" (75 mm). One of the largest *Macoma* and generally larger and more oval than *M. brota*.

Range: 65°N–34°N; Northern Bering Sea south to Redondo Submarine Canyon, California.

Habitat: At depths of 65–850' (20–260 m).

Description: *Page 160*

B-71

FLAT MACOMA

Macoma moesta

Size: To 11/4" (30 mm) length.

Range: 71°N–43°N; Arctic to Bering Sea and south to off Coos Bay, Oregon.

Habitat: In silt and a variety of bottom types; intertidal to 1000' (300 m).

Description: *Page 160*

OBLIQUE MACOMA

Macoma obliqua
Size: To 1–2" (25–50 mm).
Range: 71°N–47°N; Point Barrow, Alaska south to Puget Sound, Washington.
Habitat: In gravel or sand, intertidal to 660' (200 m).
Description: *Page 161*

B-72

YOLDIA SHAPE MACOMA

Macoma yoldiformis
Size: To 1" (25 mm).
Range: 57°N–28°N; Sitka, Alaska south to Baja California Sur.
Habitat: In sand and silt, intertidal to 80' (25 m), protected waters.
Description: *Page 161*

B-73

SEMELE CLAMS Family Semelidae (includes Scrobiculariidae)

ROSE-PAINTED CLAM

Semele rubropicta
Size: To 2" (50 mm length).
Range: 60°N–28°N; Kenai Peninsula, northern Gulf of Alaska south to Baja California Sur, and in the Gulf of California.
Habitat: In gravel, intertidal to 330' (100 m).
Description: *Page 161*

B-74

B-75

SUNSETCLAMS Family
Psammobiidae (=Garidae)

CALIFORNIA SUNSETCLAM

Gari californica

Size: To 6" (149 mm).

Range: 60°N–25°N; Northern Gulf of Alaska south to Baja California Sur.

Habitat: Buried shallow (15–20 cm) in gravel, intertidal to 560' (170 m).

Description: *Page 161*

B-76

DARK MAHOGANY-CLAM

Nuttallia obscurata

Size: To 2¹/4" (55 mm).

Range: Strait of Georgia, BC. Originally from Japan, introduced to BC in 1980s–1990s.

Habitat: Buried to 8" (20 cm) in sand–gravel in the high- to mid-intertidal zone, often in areas of freshwater seepage.

Description: *Page 162*

B-77

VENUS CLAMS –
HARDSHELL–STEAMER CLAMS
Family Veneridae

BUTTER CLAM

Saxidomus gigantea

Size: To 5¹/4" (130 mm) length.

Range: 60°N–37°N; Southeast Bering Sea, Alaska south to central California; rarely to southern California.

Habitat: Buried to 12" (30 cm) in the mid- to lower intertidal zone, to depths of 130' (40 m).

Description: *Page 164*
See also *S-12*.

JAPANESE LITTLENECK

Venerupis philippinarum

Size: To 3" (75 mm) length.

Range: 54°N–37°N; Central northern coast of BC and south to Elkhorn Slough, California.

Habitat: In a variety of substrates from sand to mud to gravel. They have short siphons and are buried to only 4" (10 cm), high in the intertidal zone.

Description: *Page 165*

B-78

Variations of Japanese littleneck clams.

PACIFIC LITTLENECK

Protothaca staminea

Size: To 3" (75 mm) length.

Range: 54°N–23°N; Aleutian Islands, Alaska south to Baja California Sur.

Habitat: Buried to 4" (10 cm) or more in gravel, and in sand–mud bottoms in the mid-intertidal zone to 33' (10 m).

Description: *Page 166*

B-79

B-80

MILKY VENUS

Compsomyax subdiaphana
Size: To 3 1/2" (85 mm) length.
Range: 59°N–30°N; Cook Inlet and northern Gulf of Alaska, south to Baja California Norte, and in the Gulf of California.
Habitat: Subtidal; 7–1800' (2–550 m), often in soft mud.
Description: *Page 166*

B-81

THIN-SHELL LITTLENECK

Protothaca tenerrima
Size: To 4 1/2" (110 mm).
Range: 50°N–28°N; Kyuquot Sound, Vancouver Island, BC and south to Baja California Sur.
Habitat: Intertidal and subtidal to 33' (10 m), in gravel and sand.
Description: *Page 166*

B-82

RIBBED CLAM

Humilaria kennerleyi
Size: To 4" (100 mm) length.
Range: 60°N–34°N; Cook Inlet, Prince William Sound, south to Santa Rosa Island, California.
Habitat: In sand and gravel, intertidal to 150' (45 m). Common but not abundant.
Description: *Page 167*

LORD DWARF-VENUS

Nutricola lordi

Size: To 1/2" (10 mm) length.

Range: 59°N–26°N; Bering Sea, Gulf of Alaska and south to Baja California Sur.

Habitat: In sand and mud, often in the roots of eelgrass, intertidal to 230' (70 m).

Description: *Page 167*

B-83

PURPLE DWARF-VENUS

Nutricola tantilla

Size: To 1/4" (6 mm).

Range: 61°N–28°N; Prince William Sound, Alaska south to Isla Cedros, Baja California Norte.

Habitat: On sand–mud bottoms, often found among the roots of eelgrass; intertidal to 400' (120 m).

Description: *Page 167*

B-84

PETRICOLA CLAMS
Family Petricolidae

HEARTY PETRICOLID

Petricola carditoides

Size: To 21/4" (55 mm) length.

Range: 57°N–26°N; Sitka, Alaska south to Baja California Sur.

Habitat: Nestling in empty pholad holes and crevices; low intertidal zone to 165' (50 m).

Description: *Page 168*

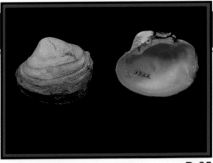

B-85

Family Turtoniidae

LITTLE MULLET SHELL

B-86

Turtonia minuta
Size: To 1/16" (2 mm).
Range: 60°N–49°N;
Circumboreal; Bering Sea and
south to Barkley Sound,
Vancouver Island, BC.
Habitat: Intertidal, attached by
byssus to coralline and other
algae, sessile animals and rocks.
Description: *Page 168*

SOFTSHELL CLAMS
Family Myidae

SOFTSHELL-CLAM

B-87

Chondrophore

Mya arenaria
Size: To 4" (100 mm).
Range: 70°N–37°N; Icy Cape,
Alaska south to Elkhorn Slough,
California.
Habitat: Intertidal, usually
buried 4–8" (10–20 cm) below
the surface in sand–mud, often in
estuarine conditions.
Description: *Page 169*

TRUNCATED SOFTSHELL-CLAM

B-88

Mya truncata
Size: To 3 1/4" (80 mm) length.
Range: 71°N–47°N;
Circumboreal; Panarctic; Beaufort
Sea, Bering Sea and south to
Neah Bay, Washington.
Habitat: Intertidal to 330' (100
m), in mud and sand of protected
bays.
Description: *Page 170*
See also S-3.

BORING SOFTSHELL-CLAM

Platyodon cancellatus
Size: To 3" (75 mm).
Range: 54°N–28°N; Tlell, Queen Charlotte Islands, BC and south to Isla Cedros, Baja California Sur.
Habitat: Burrowing in soft clay or rock, intertidal to 65' (20 m). Unlike most burrowing bivalves, this clam makes an elongated burrow, like the shape of its shell, rather than a round burrow.
Description: *Page 170*
See also S-18.

B-89

CALIFORNIA SOFTSHELL-CLAM

Cryptomya californica
Size: To 11/16" (28 mm) length.
Range: 59°N–6°S; Gulf of Alaska south to Peru.
Habitat: Burrows in intertidal mud–sand, often in estuaries, and at depths to 265' (80 m). Sometimes found deep in the substrate (20"/50 cm or more) with its short (1/32"/1 mm) siphons, feeding from the burrows of the burrowing shrimps *Callianassa* and *Upogebia* and the echiurid worm, *Urechis capo*.
Description: *Page 170*

B-90

GIANT CLAMS – GEODUCKS – NESTLING CLAMS Family Hiatellidae

PACIFIC GEODUCK

Panopea abrupta
Size: To 73/4" (195 mm) length.
Range: 58°N–34°N; Kodiak Island, Alaska south to Newport Bay, California.
Habitat: Buried in a variety of substrates from mud to sand to gravel, intertidal to 330' (100 m) or more.
Description: *Page 171*
See also S-1.

B-91

Pacific geoducks.

Juvenile pacific geoducks
are difficult to find.

Geoduck harvest.

False Geoducks—
Roughmya Clams

AMPLE ROUGHMYA

B-92

Panomya ampla
Size: To 2³/4" (70 mm).
Range: 71°N–47°N; Point Barrow, Alaska to Puget Sound, Washington.
Habitat: Body is buried to 6" (15 cm) or more below surface of substratum, mud–sand to gravel.
Description: *Page 173*
See also S-2.

ARCTIC ROUGHMYA

Panomya norvegica
Size: To 4¹/2" (110 mm).
Range: 71°N–45°N; Point Barrow, Alaska south to Tillamook, Oregon and occasionally Goleta, California.
Habitat: Has been found in mud, closer to the surface of the substrate, in Trincomali Channel and other locations in the Gulf Islands of BC.
Description: *Page 173*

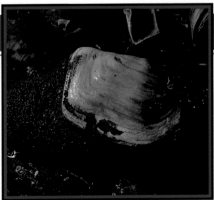

B-93

Nestling Saxicaves

ARCTIC HIATELLA

Hiatella arctica
Size: To 1¹/4" (33 mm).
Range: 71°N–10°N; Point Barrow, Alaska and south to Chile; considered to be found throughout the world.
Habitat: In algal holdfasts, mussel mats and burrows of other rock boring bivalves, attached by byssus; intertidal to 2650' (800 m).
Description: *Page 173*

B-94

NESTLING SAXICAVE

Hiatella pholadis
Size: To 2" (50 mm).
Range: 68°N–48°N; Bering Sea and south to Puget Sound, Washington.
Habitat: In burrows of pholads (piddocks), mussel beds and kelp holdfasts; intertidal to 33' (10 m).
Description: *Page 174*
See also S-17.

B-95

ROUGH PIDDOCK

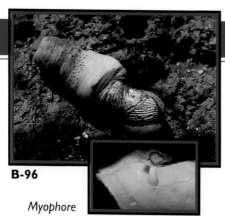

B-96

Myophore

Zirfaea pisbryii
Size: To 5³/4" (145 mm) length.
Range: 70°N–25°N; Arctic coast of Alaska and south to Baja California Sur.
Habitat: Buried to 20" (50 cm), intertidal in limestone, shale or hard clay; sand, mud to 412' (125 m).
Description: *Page 174*
See also S-6.

FLAT-TIP PIDDOCK

B-97

Penitella penita
Size: 1/8"–2³/4" (3–72 mm) length.
Range: 60°N–26°N; Prince William Sound, Alaska south to Baja California Sur.
Habitat: A very common species. Found in the mid-intertidal zone to 72' (22 m) in clay and soft rock; can be detected by small siphon holes relative to the size of the siphon and shell.
Description: *Page 174*
See also S-16.

ABALONE PIDDOCK

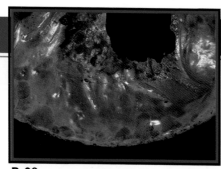

B-98

Penitella conradi
Size: To 1/2" (10 mm) in shells; to 1 1/4" (33 mm) in rock.
Range: 50°N–28°N; Port Neville, BC, probably Queen Charlotte Islands and south to Baja California Sur.
Habitat: Found in soft rock and shells in the intertidal zone to 65' (20 m) depth. This piddock bores into the shells of abalone, California mussels and old specimens of the turban snail, *Astraea* and the jingle shell, *Pododesmus*.
Description: *Page 175*

WOODBORERS – SHIPWORMS –
TEREDOS Family Teredinidae

SHIPWORM

Bankia setacea
Size: Shell to 1/4" (7 mm).
Range: 57°N–33°N; Bering Sea, Alaska south to San Diego, California.
Habitat: Found only in wood. Burrows are lined with a calcareous secretion. Intertidal to 300' (90 m).
Description: Page 175
See also S-14.

B-99

PANDORAS Family Pandoridae

PUNCTATE PANDORA

Pandora punctata
Size: To 2" (50 mm).
Range: 50°N–26°N; Esperanza Inlet, Vancouver Island south to Baja California Sur.
Habitat: In sand–mud on exposed coasts, 7–165' (2–50 m), often washed ashore.
Description: Page 176

B-100

THREADED PANDORA

Pandora filosa (Carpenter, 1864).
Size: To 1" (25 mm) length.
Range: 61°N–32°N; Northern Gulf of Alaska south to Ensenada, Baja California Sur.
Habitat: In gravel bottoms, 65–1000' (20–300 m).
Description: Page 177

B-101

BILIRATE PANDORA

Pandora bilirata
Size: To 5/8" (15 mm).
Range: 60°N–24°N; Prince William Sound, Alaska to Baja California Sur, and in the Gulf of California.
Habitat: In mud, subtidally in 16–825' (5–250 m).
Description: *Page 177*

B-102

WARD PANDORA

Pandora wardiana
Size: Largest of this family, to 21/4" (55 mm).
Range: 57°N–48°N; Point Barrow, Alaska, Bering Sea, Gulf of Alaska and south to Cape Flattery, Washington.
Habitat: At depths of 16–660' (5–200 m).
Description: *Page 177*

B-103

LYONSIA CLAMS – PAPER SHELLS
Family Lyonsiidae

ROCK ENTODESMA

Entodesma navicula
Size: To 4" (100 mm) length.
Range: 56°N–34°N; Southern Bering Sea south to Government Point, California.
Habitat: Nestled in crevices or under rocks; intertidal to 65' (20 m).
Description: *Page 177*
See also S-8.

B-104

BLADDERCLAM

Mytilimeria nuttalli

Size: To 13/4" (46 mm).

Range: 57°N–30°N; Sitka, Alaska to Baja California Norte.

Habitat: Found in the intertidal zone to 130' (40 m), protected in or under the thin mat of a compound ascidian such as *Aplidium* species or *Cystodes lobatus*.

Description: *Page 178*
See also S-13.

B-105

Lyonsia Clams

SCALY LYONSIA

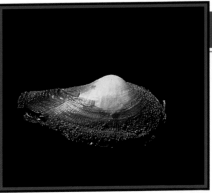

Lyonsia bracteata

Size: To 21/4" (55 mm).

Range: 56°N–48°N; Gulf of Alaska south to Cape Flattery, Washington.

Habitat: Sand bottoms, 165–925' (50–280 m).

Description: *Page 178*

B-106

CALIFORNIA LYONSIA

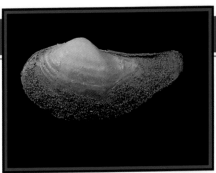

Lyonsia californica

Size: To 11/2" (38 mm).

Range: 57°N–17°N; Kodiak Island to Prince William Sound, Alaska and south to Acupulco, Mexico.

Habitat: Found in sand; intertidal to 330' (100 m).

Description: *Page 178*

B-107

Family Thraciidae

PACIFIC THRACIA

B-108

Thracia trapezoides
Size: To 2¹/₂" (65 mm).
Range: 57°N–28°N; Wide Bay, Alaska south to Isla Cedros, Baja California.
Habitat: In sand–mud, at 36–660' (11–200 m).
Description: *Page 179*

DIPPER SHELLS
Family Cuspidariidae

PECTINATE CARDIOMYA

B-109

Cardiomya pectinata
Size: ¹/₂–1¹/₂" (12–40 mm).
Range: 61°N–37°N; Prince William Sound, Alaska south to Monterey Bay, California.
Habitat: At 16–890' (5–270 m), in mud–sand.
Description: *Page 179*

LAMP SHELLS Phylum Brachiopoda (Brachiopods)

LAMP SHELL

BR-1

Terebratalia transversa
Size: To 1¹/₄" (30 mm) length.
Range: 57°N–33°N; Kodiak Island, Alaska to San Diego, California.
Habitat: Sometimes intertidal. Often abundant on subtidal rock faces.
Description: *Page 180*

Butter clam cannery, Sidney, BC, early 1900s.
Photo courtesy of Sidney Museum.

Bivalve Siphons & Shows
or "Eyes Looking Out"

Some clam species can be identified by their "shows," the visible exposed parts of the clam, particularly the siphons. Siphons, the tubes located at the posterior end of a bivalve, are formed from folds in the mantle. There are two siphons, an inhalant siphon for drawing in water and food (often the larger of the two), and an exhalant for expelling waste. Because siphons take a variety of forms, some bivalves can be recognized easily by their siphon shows, or "eyes looking out" as described by Native peoples.

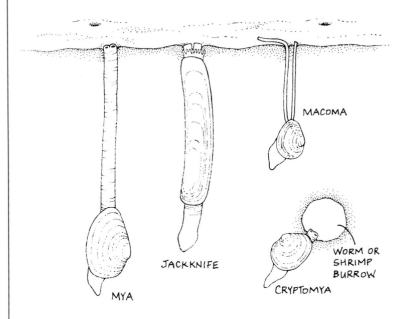

Figure 1: Bivalve Siphons and Burrowing

Local Native groups have for generations located clams in shallow waters by their shows, and sometimes wedged off chunks of clay to harvest them. They located cockles from shows, and gathered them by using a stick as thick as a man's thumb, cut flat at one end, to poke the sand to one side of the siphon show. When the cockle "bit," or clamped on the stick, it was pulled out of the sand and knocked off into a basket.

The shows provide a means to identify bivalves without having to harvest them. Siphons of intertidal species can even be observed in shallow water from a boat, or by snorkelling or diving at high tides.

The density of siphons visible on the surface of the substratum at any given time is called the "show factor," and it can be determined by repeated surveying and marking over time in a certain plot. Show factors can vary greatly among some species, such as geoduck clams, and shows can be affected by wave action from storms, currents, predators and other factors.

Identifying Clams by Siphons and Shows

A positive identification can often be made from the siphon show, or other exposed parts, of a clam. Clues can be found in the colour, size, shape and length of the siphon, as well as special features on the outside edge of the siphon, and whether the two siphons are fused or separate. The habitat of the show is also important. The type of substratum, the depth at which the clam is buried, the water depth and environmental conditions such as salinity or physical exposure, can all assist in identification.

Burrows of chubby mya (S-18).

In some bivalves, such as most mussels and oysters, the siphons are very short or nonexistent. Other siphons are long, muscular double tubes, so massive they cannot be retracted into the shell. Horse clams, geoducks and piddocks have this type of siphon. It allows the clam to burrow deep into the mud or sand, to depths as great as 3' (1 m) in the case of the geoduck, yet still feed at the surface of the substratum. The two siphons may be almost equal in diameter, but typically the excurrent siphon is smaller, to increase the velocity of the expelled water which carries wastes away from the clam.

The siphons often have fringes, as in horse clams and piddocks, or globules around the inner edge, as in cockles. These features may act to protect the animal from large unwanted debris. The siphons may be distinctly marked with exterior bumps, as in the piddocks. The tips of the siphons may be coloured, as in the piddocks, or they may have "pads," as in the horse clams or the boring softshell-clam (chubby mya), *Platyodon*.

A clam can also be identified by its "dimple," a visible indentation or mark in the substratum left by a burrowing bivalve. Sometimes small pellets of waste eliminated by the clam will signal its presence. But it is mainly commercial harvesters who are experienced enough to depend on these methods.

PACIFIC GEODUCK

Panopea abrupta

Siphon: Can be seen at the surface of sediments, sometimes extending 8" (20 cm) or more out of the substratum. Organisms seldom grow on it, but occasionally red algae and barnacles adhere. Outer surface is brown and rough; no plates at the tip. The two siphons are joined along their full length and each is 2–3" (5–7 cm) across when open. Siphon tip is smooth around the perimeter, does not

(B-91) S-I

have an inner ring of tentacles. Siphon interior is white, sometimes with tan-brown colour at the rim.

Dimple: Elliptical, in adults 2–3" (5–7 cm) across the longer diameter and 1–2" (2–3 cm) across the shorter diameter. May have numerous small pellets (pseudofeces), unusable particulate matter expelled through the incurrent siphon.

When retracted, dimple resembles impressions left by other clams, such as gaper or horse clams or the orange sea pen, *Ptilosarcus gurneyi*. The sea pen may completely retract into the substratum, leaving a dimple similar to that of a geoduck. When the hole is gently prodded, a geoduck will retract further into the substratum and often expel water. A sea pen is not capable of this behaviour.

The siphon shows and dimples of juvenile geoducks, less than 2 years old, are difficult to distinguish from those of smaller species, including the dimple of the sickle jackknife-clams *Solen sicarius*, the small siphon show of the truncated softshell-clam, *Mya truncata*, and the medium show of the false geoduck, *Panomya* species. However, juvenile geoducks are not found in high densities like *M. truncata* and other species.

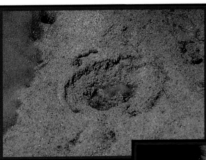

Geoduck dimple.

Geoduck siphon near sea pen.

S-2 (B-92)

Top: geoduck.
Bottom: false geoduck.

FALSE GEODUCK
(Ample Roughmya)

Panomya ampla

Medium-size clam, much smaller than full-size adult geoduck.

Siphon: Can be confused with siphon of juvenile geoducks, among which this species can often be found. When observed closely, siphon is different and so is retracting behaviour. Siphon to 6" (15 cm) or longer; exposed tip closes off in circular shape. Inhalant siphon is larger, sometimes vase-like; both siphons have rust-brown perimeters at the top and small "bumps" around the edges.

TRUNCATED
SOFTSHELL-CLAM

Mya truncata

Often found clumped together, usually buried shallow in mud–sand; easily dug up to confirm identity. Often found alongside adults, juvenile geoducks are buried much deeper.

Siphon: Small, fused; sometimes misidentified as juvenile geoduck siphons.

S-3 (B-88)

PACIFIC GAPER
(Horse clam)

Tresus nuttallii

Siphon: Rim and tentacles are often tan to pale orange, with heavier plates on siphon tips.

Dimple: According to commercial divers, dimples of both species can usually be distinguished from geoduck dimples because horse clams retract faster and the hard tips can felt with thin gloves.

(B-50) S-4

Tresus species

The two *Tresus* species may be found in separate populations or mixed (sympatric). Th shows are very similar but can be distinguished from each other. Can also be distinguished from other clams by growths of algae and other organisms on their siphon plates.

GAPER CLAMS (Horse clams)

FAT GAPER
(Horse clam)

Tresus capax

Siphon: Rim and tentacles often green in colour; siphon is generally smaller than that of *T. nuttallii*.

(B-49) S-5

Left: Fat gaper, right: Pacific gaper.

S-6 (B-96)

ROUGH PIDDOCK

Zirfaea pisbryii

Found in soft shale, clay and sticky mud, sometimes mixed with horse clams in lower inter-tidal areas and shallows below intertidal zone. Found in densities as high as 50 per square yard (m²) at some locations, to depths of 410' (125 m).

Siphon: Split siphons, unlike those of geoduck or gaper clams. Split may be very slight but sepa-ration is usually obvious. Siphon is similar in size to geoduck siphon; can protrude to 6" (15 cm) or more. Siphon has unique pattern of white bumps and ridges on exterior of dark maroon siphon tip. Siphon is pri-marily white with dark bumps when removed from the substra-tum; dark siphon tip is contract-ed. Interior of siphon is dark tan-brown and is pinched off, form-ing longitudinal ridges.

S-7 (B-42)

NUTTALL'S COCKLE
(Heart cockle)

Clinocardium nuttallii

A large, common cockle usually buried just below the surface on sand–mud beaches, sometimes forming a hump. Can be excavat-ed easily to confirm identity.

Siphon: When cockle is cov-ered with water, characteristic siphon shows at the surface. White hairs radiate from tip; inside rim of incurrent siphon has small white globules.

ROCK ENTODESMA
(Northwest ugly clam)

Entodesma navicula

Siphon: Split, orange-yellow siphon can often be seen protruding from rocks and crevices.

(B-104) S-8

STRAIGHT (FAN) HORSEMUSSEL

Modiolus rectus

A solitary species, buried shallow in sand but anchored firmly by a nest of byssal threads. Very difficult to excavate by hand.

Siphon: Unique white siphons show at surface of the sand–mud; posterior tip of shell may protrude as well. Tip of siphon is white-grey with small white spots; incurrent siphon is much larger than excurrent siphon.

(B-9) S-9

NORTHERN HORSEMUSSEL

Modiolus modiolus

A smaller mussel which forms clumps or aggregates partially buried in the substratum. Siphons are not fully developed, but a yellow mantle protrudes from the shell.

(B-10) S-10

S-11 (B-55)

PACIFIC RAZOR-CLAM

Siliqua patula

Seen on surf-beaten sandy beaches. Can burrow very quickly, making it difficult to catch. Adult clam densities are often less than 1 per square yard (m^2), but can exceed 2 per square yard (m^2)).

Siphon: Short, and fused except at the tips. Not always visible.

Dimple: A characteristic dimple or siphon show. Presence and number of shows depends on tide and weather; ideal conditions are on hot dry days with calm seas, at the lowest part of the beach.

S-12 (B-77)

BUTTER CLAM

Saxidomus gigantea

Siphon: Cream-coloured with black tips. Butter clams do not show on exposed tides but the dark siphon tips can sometimes be seen when snorkelling or diving in shallow water, or on shore when a large rock has been overturned.

BLADDERCLAM
(Bottle clam)

Mytilimeria nuttalli

Intertidal to 150' (45 m) depths; thin-shelled and fragile.

Siphon: Orange-brown, protruding from thin protective mat of the compound ascidian, *Cystodes* and *Aplidium*.

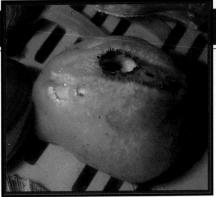

(B-105) S-13

SHIPWORM

Bankia setacea

Siphon: Many small, separate siphons protrude from wood, intertidal to 300' (90 m).

(B-99) S-14

Shipworm in fir log.

GIANT
ROCK SCALLOP

Crassadoma gigantea

Shell is large, almost circular, to 10" (25 cm); often completely covered by encrusting bushy growths of algae, bryozoans, tubeworms and other organisms. Can be detected and identified by its large size, and by orange mantle protruding from shell. Mantle edge bears numerous blue-green eyes and delicate sensory tentacles.

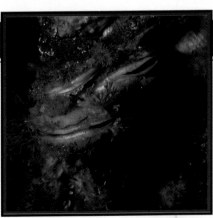

(B-24) S-15

These species, generally too small for the siphon shows to be seen and identified, are found in mussel beds, crevices or holes of other clams.

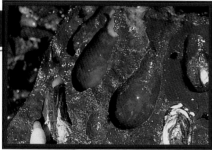

FLAT-TIP PIDDOCK

Penitella penita
Found in shallow waters, to 15' (5 m) depth, sometimes mixed with the rough piddock. It is found in hard clay or soft rock, in burrow rounded at the surface.
Siphon: White with bright orange-red tips.

S-16 (B-97)

(not illustrated) HEARTY PETRICOLID (Heart rock dweller)

Petricola carditoides

A relatively rare clam, found nestling in empty pholad holes and in crevices, low intertidal to 165' (50 m).
Siphon: Small, bright purple tips.

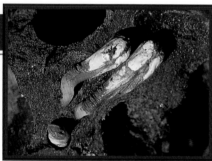

NESTLING SAXICAVE

Hiatella pholadis
Found in pholad holes, kelp holdfasts, wooden crevices and mussel mats.
Siphon: Tips are bright orange-red..

S-17 (B-95)

BORING SOFTSHELL-CLAM

Platyodon cancellatus
Also known as chubby mya and clay boring clam. Small clam which bores to 32" (13 cm) deep in soft rock (sandstone) and clay. Shape of burrow is elliptical, not circular like that of most boring mollusks. Mud or clay can be

S-18 (B-89)

found at the entrances to the burrow, whereas burrows of the piddock species, *Zirphaea*, have sand or shell at the entrance.
Siphon: Tips have 2 pointed pads; dark siphons close off in a cross pattern. Numerous tentacles around the siphon tip.

Siphon Identification Key

In this key, **small** means less than 1" (2.5 cm); **medium** means 1–2" (2.5–5 cm); **large** means more than 2" (5 cm).

1 a) Small white siphons protruding from wood, not just from a crevice in the wood. **Shipworm**, *Bankia setacea*.

b) Siphons not protruding from wood. Go to 2.

2 a) Small to medium siphons protruding from compound ascidian, Cystodes and Aplidium. **Bladderclam (Bottle clam)**, *Mytilimeria nuttalli*.

b) Siphons not protruding from compound ascidian. **Go to 3**.

3 a) Small to large siphons protruding from clay, rock, shale. **Go to 4**.

b) Siphons protruding from sand, mud, gravel, eelgrass beds. **Go to 9**.

4 a) Large siphons, tips dark maroon to brown with white bumps. **Rough piddock clam**, *Zirphaea pilsbryi*, usually high densities.

b) Small to medium siphons, in shale or clay. **Go to 5**.

5 a) Round siphon holes. **Go to 6**.

b) Elliptical siphon holes, siphons with 2 pointed pads at the tip, numerous tentacles around interior of siphon tip. **Boring softshell-clam**, *Platyodon cancellatus*. Not common.

6 a) Small to medium siphon tips, numerous in hard clay and rock. **Go to 7**.

b) Small to medium siphon tips, not common or numerous, found nestling in rocks or kelp holdfasts. **Go to 8**.

7 a) Siphons protruding, white with dark tips. **Flat-tip piddock**, *Penitella penita*.

b) Siphons protruding, white with orange bumps (less common in BC than farther south), in stiff clay or shale, hard rocks. **Oval piddock**, *Penitella richardsoni*.

8 a) Small red siphon tips. **Nestling saxicave**, *Hiatella pholadis*.

b) Small, bright purple siphon tips; in empty pholad holes and in crevices. **Hearty petrocolid**, *Petricola carditoides*.

c) Medium orange siphons, protruding from crevices or between rocks. **Rock entodesma**, *Entodesma saxicola*.

Siphon Identification Key

9 a) Unique round dimple or show of white siphon tips protruding from exposed, open coast beaches. **Pacific razor-clam**, *Siliqua patula*.

b) Dimples or siphons from sand, mud, gravel. **Go to 10.**

10 a) Large siphons. **Go to 11.**

b) Small to medium siphons. **Go to 13.**

11 a) Large siphons, fused at tip, 2 pads on each siphon, inner ring of tentacles on inside of siphon tip. **Go to 12.**

b) Large siphons, split at tip, 2 pads on each siphon, inner ring of tentacles on inside of siphon tip. **Go to 4.**

c) Large siphons, fused at tip, exterior brown, no pads or tentacles at tip, interior white, rim tan. Inhalant and exhalant siphons approximately equal in size. **Pacific geoduck**, *Panopea abrupta*.

12 a) Inner ring of tentacles dark green-blue. **Fat gaper clam (Horse clam)**, *Tresus capax*.

b) Larger siphons, heavier pads at tip, inner ring lighter, grey-peach. **Pacific gaper clam (Horse clam)**, *Tresus nuttallii*.

13 a) Siphon tips hairy, round openings with white globules on the rim. **Nuttall's cockle (Heart cockle)**, *Clinocardium nuttallii*.

b) Siphon tips not hairy. **Go to 14.**

14 a) Smooth, elliptical, white siphon tips, incurrent siphon much larger than inhalant. **Straight (fan) horsemussel**, *Modiolus rectus*.

b) Mussel mats with elliptical yellow siphons. **Northern horsemussel**, *Modiolus modiolus*.

c) Small to medium siphons, round to elliptical, similar to each other in size. **Go to 15.**

15 a) Small, fused siphons, dark exterior and white interior, single or in high densities. Inhalant and exhalant siphons approximately equal in size. **Truncated softshell-clam**, *Mya truncata*.

b) Medium siphons, tips separated, inner rim of round siphons red-orange, rim has very small tentacles, hardly visible. **False geoduck**, *Panomya* species.

Gastropods

An orange hermit crab takes up residence in the shell of the leafy hornmouth.

The gastropods ("stomach foot" or "belly foot") comprise the class Gastropoda—the largest class of mollusks with as many as 37,500 living species and 15,000 fossil species worldwide. Gastropods enjoy the widest distribution of any animal, from land snails on mountaintops to marine snails in the ocean depths. About 7,000 marine gastropod species live in North American waters.

(opposite) Northern abalone.

ABALONE Family Haliotidae

NORTHERN ABALONE

Haliotis kamtschatkana
Size: To 7" (175 mm) length.
Range: Sitka, Alaska south to Point Conception, California.
Habitat: In kelp and rocks, lower intertidal zone to 50' (15 m).
Description: *Page 184*

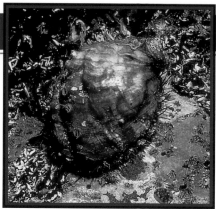

G-1

RED ABALONE

Haliotis rufescens
Size: To 10 1/2" (260 mm) length.
Range: Central BC to central Baja California
Habitat: On rocks, intertidal to 545' (165 m); most abundant from 20–40' (6–12 m).
Description: *Page 184*

G-2

KEYHOLE LIMPETS Family Fissurellidae

HOODED PUNCTURELLA

Cranopsis cucullata
Size: To 1 1/2" (40 mm).
Range: 57°N–30°N; Alaska to Cabo San Quintin, Baja California.
Habitat: On and under rocks from the low tide to 660' (200 m).
Description: *Page 185*

G-3

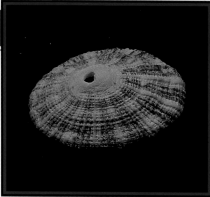

ROUGH
KEYHOLE LIMPET

Diodora aspera

Size: Shell to 2³/₄" (70 mm), body is larger than the shell.

Range: Alaska south to Baja California.

Habitat: Low intertidal and subtidal.

Description: *Page 185*

G-4

TWO-SPOT
KEYHOLE LIMPET

Fissurellidea bimaculata

Size: To ³/₄" (20 mm) shell length.

Range: Alaska to Baja California.

Habitat: On or under rocks on compound ascidians or sponges, and on holdfasts of kelp. Intertidal to shallow subtidal.

Description: *Page 186*

G-5

The shell is dwarfed by the large, colourful orange body.

TURBAN SNAILS
Family Turbinidae

RED TURBAN

G-6

Astraea gibberosa

Size: To 3" (75 mm) diameter, 2 1/4" (57 mm) height.

Range: SE Alaska, Queen Charlotte Islands south to Baja California; not common from Washington to northern California.

Habitat: On rocks on the open coast; sometimes shell is covered with coralline algae. Shallow subtidal to 200' (61 m) deep.

Description: *Page 190*

Red turban covered by pink coralline algae.

Red turban being consumed by a painted sea star.

DARK DWARF TURBAN

Homalopoma luridum

Size: To 1/2" (10 mm) height.

Range: Sitka, Alaska to northern Baja California.

Habitat: On rocks, intertidal and in shallows.

Description: *Page 191*

G-7

G-8

BLACK TURBAN

Tegula funebralis

Size: To 1 1/4" (30 mm) diameter.

Range: Vancouver Island south to Point Conception, California, and reports to central Baja California.

Habitat: Common and abundant aggregations under rocks in the intertidal zone.

Description: *Page 191*

G-9

BROWN TURBAN

Tegula pulligo

Size: To 1 1/2" (38 mm).

Range: Alaska south to Baja California; more common in the northern range.

Habitat: On kelp on rocky shores on the open coasts, not as common as black turbans. Intertidal to 10' (3 m).

Description: *Page 191*

G-10

BERING MARGARITE

Margarites beringensis

Size: To 1/2" (10 mm).

Range: Arctic to Alaska south to Hope Island, BC; also on Atlantic coast.

Habitat: On sand and mud.

Description: *Page 192*

HELICINA MARGARITE

Margarites helicinus
Size: To 1/2" (10 mm).
Range: Aleutian Islands, Alaska south to Washington.
Habitat: On kelp or under rocks; shallow water to 100' (30 m).
Description: *Page 192*

G-11

PUPPET MARGARITE

Margarites pupillus
Size: To 3/4" (17 mm).
Range: Alaska south to southern California; more common in the northern range.
Habitat: On sand, mud and rubble on sheltered beaches; intertidal to 300' (90 m).
Description: *Page 192*

G-12

LOVELY PACIFIC SOLARELLE

Solariella peramabilis
Size: To 3/4" (20 mm).
Range: 55°N–18°N; Japan, and Forrester Island, Alaska south to Mexico.
Habitat: On offshore rocky and soft bottoms; 330–2000' (100–600 m).
Description: *Page 193*

G-13

G-14

PEARLY TOPSNAIL

Lirularia lirulata

Size: To 1/4" (6 mm).

Range: Intertidal in BC and Washington; shallow subtidal species farther south to California.

Habitat: Under rocks and in gravel.

Description: *Page 193*

G-15

TUCKED TOPSNAIL

Lirularia succincta

Size: To 1/4" (6 mm).

Range: Alaska south to northern Baja California.

Habitat: Intertidal to shallow subtidal.

Description: *Page 193*

G-16

PURPLE-RING TOPSNAIL

Calliostoma annulatum

Size: To 1 1/4" (30 mm) height.

Range: Alaska south to Baja California.

Habitat: On the open coast, feeding on kelp and animals on rocks in the intertidal zone to 100' (30 m).

Description: *Page 193*

BLUE TOPSNAIL

Calliostoma ligatum
Size: To 1" (25 mm) diameter.
Range: Northern BC south to California.
Habitat: Common in rocky areas and kelp beds, intertidal to 100' (30 m) and deeper.
Description: *Page 194*

G-17

CHANNELLED TOPSNAIL

Calliostoma canaliculatum
Size: To 1 1/2" (35 mm) height.
Range: Alaska south to central California; not common north of California.
Habitat: In rocky areas and on kelp.
Description: *Page 194*

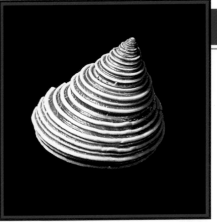

G-18

VARIABLE TOPSNAIL

Calliostoma variegatum
Size: To 1" (25 mm) height.
Range: 55°N–28°N; Forrester Island, Alaska south to Isla Cedros, Baja California.
Habitat: On rocks, subtidal in deep water.
Description: *Page 194*

Note juvenile to right on hydrocoral.

G-19

G-20

SILVERY TOPSNAIL

Calliostoma platinum
Size: To 1" (25 mm) height.
Range: 53°N–33°N; Moresby Island, Queen Charlotte Islands south to San Diego, California.
Habitat: In deep waters on soft bottoms, 600–2300' (180–700 m).
Description: *Page 194*

G-21

SPINY TOPSNAIL

Cidarina cidaris
Size: To 1 1/2" (40 mm) height.
Range: 60°N–28°N; Prince William Sound, Alaska south to Isla Cedros, Baja California.
Habitat: On offshore rocky–rubble bottoms; moderately deep.
Description: *Page 195*

"True" Limpets

G-22

WHITECAP LIMPET

Acmaea mitra
Size: To 1 1/2" (35 mm) length, 1 1/4" (30 mm) height.
Range: Aleutian Islands, Alaska south to Baja California.
Habitat: Intertidal and in shallow subtidal area, on rocks with encrusting coralline algae; shells often wash up on surf beaches.
Description: *Page 196*

SHIELD LIMPET

Lottia pelta

Size: To 2 1/4" (54 mm) length, arched to 5/8" (15 mm) height.

Range: Aleutian Islands, Alaska south to Baja California.

Habitat: Often associated with brown algae, including the sea palm *Postelsia*, and common in mussel beds.

Description: *Page 196*

G-23

Sea palm

PLATE LIMPET

Tectura scutum

Size: To 2" (50 mm) length; arched to 5/8" (15 mm) height.

Range: Aleutian Islands, Alaska south to California.

Habitat: Mid- to low intertidal and shallow subtidal.

Description: *Page 197*

G-24

Underside or "foot" of limpet.

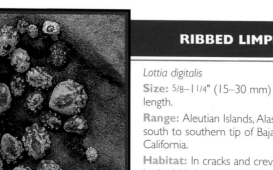

RIBBED LIMPET

Lottia digitalis

Size: 5/8–1 1/4" (15–30 mm) length.

Range: Aleutian Islands, Alaska south to southern tip of Baja California.

Habitat: In cracks and crevices in the high intertidal and splash zones, on vertical or overhanging rock faces, sometimes on shells of goose barnacles, *Pollicipes (Mitella) polymerus.*

Description: Page 197

G-25

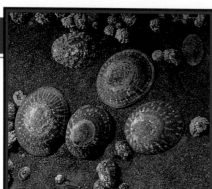

MASK LIMPET

Tectura persona

Size: To 2" (50 mm) length; arched to 5/8" (15 mm) height.

Range: Alaska south to Monterey.

Habitat: In deep cracks and depressions, high on beach, often in area of fresh water seepage, and in shade of overhanging trees; sheltered from the heaviest wave action.

Description: Page 197

G-26

FENESTRATE LIMPET

Tectura fenestrata

Size: To 1" (25 mm) length.

Range: Alaska south to California.

Habitat: On smooth boulders and rocks in the mid- and lower intertidal.

Description: Page 198

G-27

UNSTABLE LIMPET

G-28

Lottia instabilis
Size: To 1 1/2" (35 mm) length.
Range: Alaska south to San Diego.
Habitat: On the stipes of kelp and on holdfasts.
Description: *Page 198*

BLACK LIMPET

G-29

Lottia asmi
Size: To 1/2" (10 mm).
Range: Northern Vancouver Island south to Mexico.
Habitat: On black turban snail, *Tegula funebralis*, and sometimes on California mussel, *Mytilus californianus*.
Description: *Page 198*

SEAWEED LIMPET

G-30

Discurria insessa
Size: To 3/4" (20 mm).
Range: Southern Alaska south to Baja California.
Habitat: On algae at low tide, especially found feeding and eroding the brown feathery kelp, *Egregia menziesii*.
Description: *Page 199*

Feather boa kelp

G-31

SURFGRASS LIMPET

Tectura paleacea
Size: To 1/2" (10 mm).
Range: Vancouver Island south to northern Baja California.
Habitat: Found on the blades of open coast surfgrass, *Phyllospadix*.
Description: *Page 199*

G-32

EELGRASS LIMPET

Lottia alveus
Size: To 1/2" (12 mm).
Range: Alaska south to California, not common south of Washington.
Habitat: On the blades of eelgrass in protected waters.
Description: *Page 199*

PERIWINKLES – LITTORINES
Family Littorinidae

SITKA PERIWINKLE

Littorina sitkana
Size: To 7/8" (22 mm).
Range: Alaska south to Puget Sound.
Habitat: In sheltered waters on rocks among rockweed and other algae; in eelgrass from high to low intertidal.
Description: *Page 199*

G-33

CHECKERED PERIWINKLE

Littorina scutulata
Size: To 5/8" (15 mm) height.
Range: Alaska south to Baja California.
Habitat: In sheltered waters on rocks in the intertidal zone.
Description: *Page 200*

G-34

LACUNA SHELLS
Family Lacunidae

VARIABLE LACUNA

Lacuna variegata
Size: To 5/8" (16 mm) height.
Range: Alaska south to Puget Sound, some in California.
Habitat: On algae and conspicuous on eelgrass.
Description: *Page 200*

G-35

WIDE LACUNA

Lacuna vincta
Size: To 5/8" (16 mm).
Range: Circumpolar; Alaska south to Puget Sound, some in California.
Habitat: Intertidal on algae on rocky shores. Sometimes abundant.
Description: *Page 201*

G-36

NORTHERN COMPACT WORMSNAIL

G-37

Petalaconchus compactus

Size: Diameter of each small tube 1/8" (3 mm); mass of short, coiled tubes to 1" (25 mm) height.

Range: Vancouver Island south to California.

Habitat: On or under rocks, shallow subtidal to 165' (50 m).

Description: *Page 201*

THREADED BITTIUM

G-38

Bittium eschrichtii

Size: To 3/4" (20 mm), largest of the *Bittium* species.

Range: From Alaska south to central California.

Habitat: Common under rocks, often on oyster beds, sometimes on coralline algae in tidepools and sometimes on eelgrass. Intertidal to 180' (55 m).

Description: *Page 201*

SLENDER BITTIUM

G-39

Bittium attenuatum

Size: To 5/8" (15 mm) height.

Range: Southern Alaska south to northern Baja California.

Habitat: Rocky beaches, common and abundant among the roots of eelgrass. Intertidal to 230' (70 m).

Description: *Page 202*

HORNSNAILS Family Batillariidae
(formerly Potamididae)

MUDFLAT SNAIL

Batillaria cumingi
Size: To 1 1/4" (30 mm) length.
Range: Introduced from Japan along with oyster seed, British Columbia south to California.
Habitat: Sand–mud shores, mid- to high intertidal.
Description: *Page 202*

G-40

HOOFSNAILS
Family Hipponicidae

FLAT HOOFSNAIL

Hipponix cranioides
Size: To 3/4" (20 mm).
Range: BC south to California and possibly farther south, most common in California.
Habitat: Common in groups, intertidal and subtidal on the open coast, often overgrown with algae and other organisms.
Description: *Page 203*

G-41

CUP-AND-SAUCER SNAILS – SLIPPERSNAILS
Family Calyptraeidae

CUP-AND-SAUCER SNAIL

Calyptraea fastigiata
Size: To 1" (25 mm).
Range: Alaska south to California.
Habitat: Sometimes intertidal, usually subtidal, 60–450' (18–137 m) deep, on rocks, on dead shells or sometimes attached to crabs.
Description: *Page 203*

G-42

G-43

HOOKED SLIPPERSNAIL

Crepidula adunca

Size: To 1" (25 mm).

Range: Queen Charlotte Islands south to Baja California.

Habitat: Often stacked up on snail shells, especially the Black Turban, *Tegula funebralis*, and top shells, *Calliostoma*. Intertidal and deeper.

Description: *Page 203*

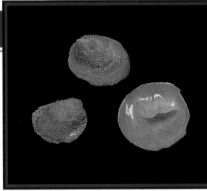

G-44

WRINKLED SLIPPERSNAIL

Crepipatella dorsata

Size: To 1" (25 mm) length.

Range: 60°N–14°S; Bering Sea, Alaska south to Peru.

Habitat: On rocks and snail shells. Intertidal and deeper.

Description: *Page 204*

G-45

WESTERN WHITE SLIPPERSNAIL

Crepidula perforans

Size: To 1 1/2" (38 mm).

Range: Vancouver Island south to Baja California.

Habitat: On rocks, but often on insides of shells, or in holes of boring clams. Intertidal and deeper.

Description: *Page 204*

NORTHERN WHITE SLIPPERSNAIL

Crepidula nummaria
Size: To 1 1/2" (40 mm).
Range: Alaska to Panama.
Habitat: Intertidal and in shallow water on rocks and dead shells, sometimes in holes of boring clams.
Description: *Page 204*

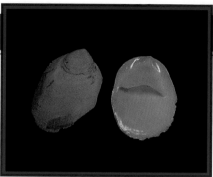

G-46

Family Trichotropididae

CHECKERED HAIRYSNAIL

Trichotropis cancellata
Size: To 1 1/4" (30 mm) height.
Range: Alaska south to Oregon.
Habitat: Subtidal in rocky areas, often among sea squirts and tube worms and overgrown with other organisms. Found on tube worms up off the bottom, where currents are stronger and more food is carried by.
Description: *Page 205*

G-47

Family Ranellidae (=Cymatiidae)

OREGON TRITON

Fusitriton oregonensis
Size: Largest intertidal snail, to 6" (150 mm) height.
Range: Bering Sea, Alaska south to San Diego, California.
Habitat: Intertidal to 300' (90 m).
Description: *Page 205*

G-48

Oregon triton eggs

VELUTINA SNAILS
Family Velutinidae

SMOOTH VELVET SNAIL

G-49

Velutina prolongata
Size: Shell to 3/4" (20 mm) length.
Range: Aleutian Islands, Alaska south to central California.
Habitat: On rocks in the intertidal and shallows to 330' (100 m).
Description: *Page 206*

SPIRAL VELVET SNAIL

G-50

Velutina velutina
Size: Shell to 3/4" (20 mm).
Range: Aleutian Islands, Alaska south to central California.
Habitat: On rocks, often associated with the solitary stalked tunicate, *Styela gibbsii,* in shallow waters to 65' (20 m).
Description: *Page 206*

MOONSNAILS Family Naticidae

ALEUTIAN MOONSNAIL

G-51

Cryptonatica aleutica
Size: To 1 1/4" (30 mm) height.
Range: Circumpolar; Arctic south to northern California.
Habitat: In or on the sand; shallow subtidal to 1650' (500 m).
Description: *Page 206*

LEWIS'S MOONSNAIL

Euspira lewisii
Size: To 5 1/2" (140 mm) height.
Range: Southeastern Alaska to southern California.
Habitat: On sand, intertidal to 165' (50 m).
Description: *Page 207*

G-52

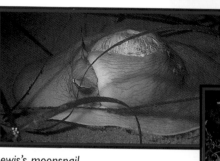

Lewis's moonsnail.

Shells drilled by moonsnails.

Moonsnail egg case.

WENTLETRAPS
Family Epitoniidae

TINTED WENTLETRAP

Epitonium tinctum
Size: To 5/8" (15 mm).
Range: 55°N–25°N; Forrester Island, Alaska south to Magdalena Bay, Baja California.
Habitat: Found near or feeding on the tentacles of sea anemones, *Anthopleura elegantissima* and giant green anemone, *A. xanthogrammica.* Intertidal to 150' (45 m). When exposed at low tide, the snail burrows into the sand.
Description: *Page 208*

G-53

Sea anemones.

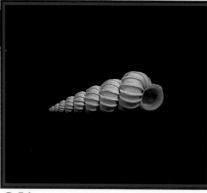

G-54

MONEY WENTLETRAP

Epitonium indianorum
Size: To 1 1/2" (35 mm).
Range: 55°N–25°N; Alaska south to Baja California.
Habitat: Often found associated with and feeding on tealia anemones, *Urticina crassicornis* and *U. lofotensis*. this snail is attracted by the "scent" of the anemone. Intertidal and subtidal to 400' (120 m).
Description: *Page 208*

Money wentletrap.

Tealia anemones.

G-55

BOREAL WENTLETRAP

Opalia borealis
Size: To 1" (25 mm).
Range: Aleutian Islands, Alaska south to Puget Sound, Washington.
Habitat: Intertidal and subtidal.
Description: *Page 208*

SHINING BALCIS SNAILS
Family Eulimidae (=Melanellidae)

SHINING BALCIS

Balcis micans
Size: To 1/2" (13 mm) height.
Range: 57°N–27°N; Kodiak Island, Alaska south to Baja California.
Habitat: Subtidal, 100–330' (30–100 m).
Description: *Page 209*

G-56

ROCKSNAILS – DWARF TRITONS – WHELKS AND DOGWINKLES Family Muricidae

LEAFY HORNMOUTH

Ceratostoma foliatum
Size: To 31/2" (85 mm).
Range: Alaska south to San Pedro, California.
Habitat: On barnacles and bivalves, intertidal to 200' (60 m).
Description: *Page 209*

G-57

Leafy hornmouth.

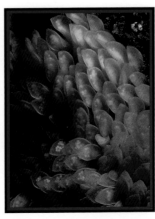

Leafy hornmouth eggs.

LURID ROCKSNAIL

Ocinebrina lurida
Size: To 1 1/2" (38 mm) height.
Range: 57°N–32°N; Sitka, Alaska south to northern Baja California.
Habitat: On rocky beaches in the intertidal and to 180' (55 m); found on and known to attack giant chitons, *Cryptochiton*.
Description: *Page 210*

G-58

SCULPTURED ROCKSNAIL

Ocinebrina interfossa
Size: To 3/4" (20 mm) height.
Range: Alaska south to northern Baja California.
Habitat: On rocks in sheltered areas, intertidal to 20' (6 m).
Description: *Page 210*

G-59

JAPANESE ROCKSNAIL

Ceratostoma inornatum
Size: To 1 1/4" (30 mm) height.
Range: Introduced to BC and Puget Sound.
Habitat: Gravel, mud and sand beaches.
Description: *Page 210*

G-60

ATLANTIC OYSTER DRILL

Urosalpinx cinerea
Size: To 3/4" (20 mm).
Range: Found at Boundary Bay, BC along with a small population of Atlantic oysters; also found from Washington south to California in areas of oyster culture.
Habitat: In oyster beds and among barnacles, on which it feeds; buried in mud during the winter.
Description: *Page 210*

G-61

WHELKS – DOGWINKLES
Family Muricidae (continued)

FRILLED DOGWINKLE

Nucella lamellosa
Size: 2–3 1/4" (50–80 mm) height.
Range: Aleutian Islands, Alaska south to central California.
Habitat: On rocks and in crevices, intertidal to shallow subtidal.
Description: *Page 211*

G-62

Dogwinkle eggs.

CHANNELLED DOGWINKLE

Nucella canaliculata
Size: To 1 1/2" (40 mm).
Range: Aleutian Islands, Alaska south to central California.
Habitat: On rocks and barnacles.
Description: *Page 211*

G-63

G-64

STRIPED DOGWINKLE

Nucella emarginata
Size: To 1 1/16" (28 mm).
Range: Bering Sea, Alaska south to northern Baja California.
Habitat: Feeds on mussels on semi-protected and exposed rocky beaches.
Description: *Page 212*

G-65

FILE DOGWINKLE

Nucella lima
Size: To 1 1/4" (30 mm).
Range: Aleutian Islands, Alaska and BC; not common below the northern end of Vancouver Island to northern California.
Habitat: On rocky beaches.
Description: *Page 212*

G-66

SANDPAPER TROPHON

Scabrotrophon maltzani
Size: To 1" (25 mm).
Range: Bering Sea, Alaska south to Baja California.
Habitat: Intertidal in Alaska; on rocky bottoms to 1000' (330 m).
Description: *Page 212*

STUART'S TROPHON

Boreotrophon stuarti
Size: To 2¹/2" (60 mm).
Range: 58°N–33°N; Pribilof Islands, Bering Sea south to Newport Beach, California.
Habitat: Rocky bottoms, intertidal in Alaska, to depths of 330' (100 m).
Description: *Page 213*

G-67

CORDED TROPHON

Boreotrophon orpheus
Size: To 1" (25 mm).
Range: Gulf of Alaska south to Washington.
Habitat: Subtidal, 0 to165' (50 m), gravel and rock bottoms.
Description: *Page 213*

G-68

WHELKS Family Buccinidae

DIRE WHELK

Lirabuccinum dirum
Size: To 2" (50 mm) height.
Range: Alaska south to central California; particularly abundant in Washington.
Habitat: Intertidal on wave-washed rocks.
Description: *Page 213*

G-69

G-70

LYRE WHELK

Buccinum plectrum
Size: To 2 1/2" (60 mm).
Range: Circumpolar; Alaska south to Puget Sound.
Habitat: Common offshore, 100–2000' (30–600 m).
Description: *Page 214*

G-71

RIDGED WHELK

Neptunea lyrata
Size: To 6 1/2" (165 mm) height.
Range: Alaska south to northern California.
Habitat: On sand and mud, from shallow shores, occasionally intertidal, to 330' (100 m).
Description: *Page 214*

G-72

PHOENICIAN WHELK

Neptunea phoenicia
Size: To 4 1/2" (110 mm) height.
Range: Alaska south to Oregon.
Habitat: In deep water, on soft and rocky bottoms. This snail is commonly taken in prawn traps.
Description: *Page 215*

TABLED WHELK

Neptunea tabulata
Size: To 4 1/2" (110 mm).
Range: 57°N–33°N; Petersburg, Southeast Alaska south to San Diego, California.
Habitat: On mud, subtidal.
Description: *Page 215*

G-73

CHOCOLATE WHELK

Neptunea smirnia
Size: To 4 1/2" (110 mm).
Range: Japan and Alaska south to Puget Sound, Washington.
Habitat: Common soft-bottom species; shallows to 1000' (300 m).
Description: *Page 215*

G-74

AMPHISSA SHELLS DOVE SHELLS Family
Columbellidae (=Pyrenidae)

WRINKLED AMPHISSA

Amphissa columbiana
Size: To 1" (25 mm).
Range: Alaska south to Oregon; not common in California.
Habitat: On rocky beaches and mud, in shallows.
Description: *Page 215*

G-75

JOSEPH'S COAT AMPHISSA

Amphissa versicolor
Size: To 5/8" (15 mm) height.
Range: BC to Baja California.
Habitat: Intertidal to 65' (20 m).
Description: *Page 216*

G-76

DOVESNAIL

Astyris gausapata
Size: To 1/2" (13 mm).
Range: 55°N–33°N; Alaska south to San Diego, California.
Habitat: On rocks, subtidal to 660' (200 m).
Description: *Page 216*

G-77

CARINATE DOVESNAIL

Alia carinata
Size: To 1/2" (10 mm).
Range: Southern Alaska south to Baja California.
Habitat: Among eelgrass and algae, often on giant kelp, *Macrocystis.* Intertidal to 16' (5 m).
Description: *Page 216*

G-78

DOGWHELKS – NASSA MUD
SNAILS Family Nassariidae

WESTERN LEAN NASSA

Nassarius mendicus

Size: To 7/8" (22 mm).

Range: Alaska south to central Baja California.

Habitat: On sand, mud and rocks, intertidal to 60' (18 m). Seen more often on the surface of the sand or rocks than other Nassas, which often burrow.

Description: *Page 216*

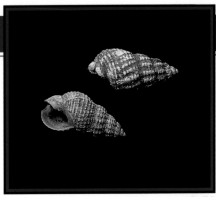

G-79

GIANT WESTERN NASSA

Nassarius fossatus

Size: To 2" (50 mm).

Range: Queen Charlotte Islands, BC south to Baja California.

Habitat: On sand–mud, inter-tidal to 60' (18 m), buried in sand.

Description: *Page 217*

G-80

OLIVE SHELLS Family Olividae

PURPLE OLIVE

Olivella biplicata

Size: To 1 1/4" (30 mm) height.

Range: Vancouver Island, BC south to Baja California.

Habitat: In sand, on open coast. They burrow into the sand quickly when the tide goes out.

Description: *Page 217*

G-81

G-82

BAETIC OLIVE

Olivella baetica

Size: To 3/4" (20 mm); smaller than purple olive, *O. biplicata*, above.

Range: Alaska south to Baja California.

Habitat: In sandy bays and beaches, often in same areas as purple olive. Also found in more protected waters.

Description: *Page 217*

TURRID SNAILS Family Turridae

LORA

G-83

Oenopota levidensis

Size: To 3/4" (20 mm) shell length.

Range: East Bering Sea south to northern California.

Habitat: Common in the shallows, in brown kelp (*Agarum*) beds, and on muddy sands to 660' (200 m).

Description: *Page 218*

TABLE LORA

Oenopota tabulata

Size: To 5/8" (15 mm) height.

Range: Sitka, Alaska south to Puget Sound, Washington.

Habitat: In sand–shell mix, on rocks in the shallows, under the broad-bladed kelp canopy of *Agarum*.

Description: *Page 218*

G-84

CANCELLATE SNAKESKIN-SNAIL

Ophiodermella cancellata
Size: To 1/2" (13 mm).
Range: Outer coast of BC and San Juan Islands to Puget Sound, Washington.
Habitat: Sandy to silty areas, 165–1650' (50–500 m).
Description: *Page 218*

G-85

GRAY SNAKESKIN-SNAIL

Ophiodermella inermis
Size: To 1 1/2" (40 mm); largest of local species.
Range: Northern BC to central California.
Habitat: Sometimes intertidal, to 230' (70 m) and more, feeding on polychaete worms, usually in shallow water.
Description: *Page 219*

G-86

VIOLET-BAND MANGELIA

Kurtziella crebricostata
Size: Seldom over 1/2" (10 mm); maximum recorded 3/4" (20 mm).
Range: Cook Inlet, Alaska south to northern Washington.
Habitat: Sandy areas in shallow subtidal, and deeper in sand–mud. Intertidal to 280' (85 m).
Description: *Page 219*

G-87

PYRAMID SHELLS
Family Pyramidellidae

PYRAMID SNAIL

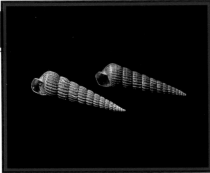

Turbonilla species
Size: To 1/2" (12 mm) height.
Range: Alaska south to California; often dredged.
Habitat: Soft bottoms.
Description: *Page 219*

G-88

Family Haminoeidae

WHITE BUBBLE SHELL

Haminoea vesicula
Size: Body to 3/4" (20 mm) length.
Range: Ketchikan, Alaska south to Magdalena Bay, Gulf of California.
Habitat: In bays, on mudflats and on eelgrass.
Description: *Page 220*

G-89

BUBBLE SHELLS
Family Acteonidae

BARREL SHELL

Rictaxis punctocaelatus
Size: Shell to 3/4" (20 mm) height.
Range: Alaska south to central Baja California.
Habitat: In tidepools or on sand among eelgrass, feeding on sand-dwelling worms; to 300' (90 m).
Description: *Page 220*

G-90

INTERNAL BUBBLE SHELL
Family Aglajidae

SPOTTED AGLAJA

Aglaja ocelligera
Size: To 1" (25 mm).
Range: Sitka, Alaska south to Santa Barbara, California.
Habitat: On mud–sand bottoms, shallow subtidal to 65' (20 m).
Description: *Page 221*

G-91

SIPHON SHELL or FALSELIMPET
Family Siphonariidae

CARPENTER'S FALSELIMPET

Siphonaria thersites
Size: To 1 1/4" (31 mm).
Range: Not commmon; Aleutian Islands, Alaska south to Puget Sound, Washington; more common in northern range.
Habitat: Mid-intertidal, on rocky ocean beaches, often among rockweed, *Fucus*.
Description: *Page 221*

G-92

Tuskshells

North American aboriginal people traditionally used tuskshells for decoration, and for currency and trade.

The class Scaphopoda comprises about 500 living species of burrowing mollusks commonly known as tuskshells or toothshells. The common name comes from the tusk-like appearance of the single curved and tapered shell, which is open on both ends. Tuskshells, or scaphopods, are found buried in the top few inches down to 16" (40 cm) deep in marine mud-sand, from the shallows to great depths in the ocean.

TUSKSHELLS Family Dentaliidae

WAMPUM TUSKSHELL

Antalis pretiosum
Size: To 2" (50 mm) length.
Range: Alaska south to Baja California.
Habitat: Common offshore in coarse shell–gravel.
Description: *Page 224*

T-1

WESTERN STRAIGHT TUSKSHELL

Rhabdus rectius
Size: To 5 1/4" (130 mm) length.
Range: Alaska south to Panama.
Habitat: Offshore in mud and silt.
Description: *Page 224*

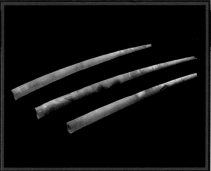

T-2

Chitons

Hairy chiton.

Chitons (pronounced *KY-tons*), also known as "sea cradles," are members of the class Polyplacophora ("bearing many plates"). They are slow-moving marine animals that have lived on earth for some 500 million years. Scientists have identified as many as 500–600 species of chitons worldwide. In BC there are some 20 intertidal species of chitons in as many as 8 families, and more than 100 intertidal and subtidal species can be found along the Pacific coast from the Aleutian Islands, Alaska south to Baja California.

Family Lepidochitonidae

LINED (Red) CHITON

C-1

Tonicella lineata

Size: To 2" (50 mm).

Range: 60°N–34°N; Aleutian Islands, Gulf of Alaska south to central California.

Habitat: Often on rocks, grazing on encrusting coralline algae, *Lithothamnion* and others. Often in depressions under purple sea urchins, *Strongylocentrotus purpuratus*.

Description: *Page 227*

A lined chiton falls victim to a sea star.

BLUE-LINE CHITON

C-2

Tonicella undocaerulea

Size: Often misidentified as the lined chiton, *T. lineata.*

Size: To 2" (50 mm).

Range: 57°N–34°N; Kodiak Island, Alaska south to central California.

Habitat: Often on rocks, grazing on coralline algae, from intertidal to shallow subtidal.

Description: *Page 227*

WHITE-LINE CHITON

Tonicella insignis
Size: To 2" (50 mm).
Range: 60°N–43°N; Alaska south to Oregon.
Habitat: Intertidal but mostly subtidal, to 170' (52 m).
Description: *Page 227*

C-3

Family Ischnochitonidae

MERTEN'S CHITON

Lepidozona mertensii
Size: To 1 1/2" (38 mm).
Range: 59°N–28°N; Cook Inlet, Alaska south to northern Baja California.
Habitat: Often under rocks, intertidal to 300' (90 m).
Description: *Page 228*

C-4

THREE-RIB CHITON

Lepidozona trifida
Size: To 2 1/2" (60 mm).
Range: 60°N–47°N; Aleutian Islands, Gulf of Alaska south to Puget Sound, Washington.
Habitat: On rocks, intertidal to 365' (110 m).
Description: *Page 228*

C-5

Family Mopaliidae

HAIRY CHITON

C-6

Mopalia ciliata
Size: To 3" (75 mm).
Range: 60°N–28°N; Gulf of Alaska south to northern Baja California.
Habitat: Protected areas, under rocks or sometimes in mussel beds, mid- to low intertidal.
Description: *Page 228*

MOSSY CHITON

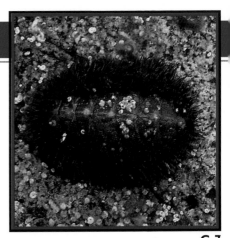

C-7

Mopalia muscosa
Size: To 23/4" (70 mm).
Range: 57°N–28°N; Alaska south to Isla Cedros, northern Baja California.
Habitat: Often in tidepools and on top of rocks; not affected by accumulations of silt.
Description: *Page 229*

WOODY CHITON

C-8

Mopalia lignosa
Size: To 23/4" (70 mm).
Range: 59°N–34°N; Alaska south to Point Conception, California.
Habitat: Intertidal and deeper. Found feeding on algae, especially sea lettuce, *Ulva*.
Description: *Page 229*

C-9

HIND'S MOPALIA

Mopalia hindsii
Size: To 4" (100 mm).
Range: 57°N–34°N; Kodiak, Alaska south to Ventura County, California.
Habitat: In shallow bays, protected waters, often on pilings and rocks with deposits of silt.
Description: *Page 229*

C-10

SWAN'S MOPALIA

Mopalia swanii
Size: To 2 1/2" (60 mm).
Range: 55°N–34°N; Aleutian Islands, Alaska south to Malibu, California.
Habitat: On bottoms of rocks, in crevices or under ledges; intertidal.
Description: *Page 229*

RED-FLECKED MOPALIA

Mopalia spectabilis
Size: To 2³/4" (70 mm).
Range: 60°N–32°N; Prince William Sound, Alaska south to Ensenada, northern Baja California.
Habitat: On bottoms of rocks, in crevices and under ledges; intertidal to 33' (10 m).
Description: *Page 230*

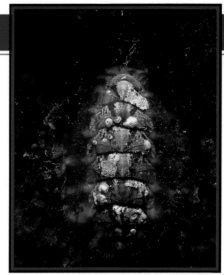

C-11

SMOOTH MOPALIA

Mopalia vespertina
Size: To 3¹/4" (80 mm).
Range: 57°N–35°N; Sitka, Alaska south to Morro Bay, central California.
Habitat: Common subtidal species.
Description: *Page 230*

C-12

BLACK KATY CHITON

Katharina tunicata
Size: To 3" (75 mm).
Range: 57°N–37°N; Alaska south to Monterey, California.
Habitat: Mid-intertidal, in exposed wave-swept situations.
Description: *Page 230*

C-13

C-14

RED VEILED-CHITON

Placiphorella rufa
Size: To 2" (50 mm).
Range: 60°N–43°N; Aleutian Islands to Prince William Sound, Alaska, south to southern Oregon.
Habitat: Common subtidal species, to 150' (45 m). In areas of strong currents.
Description: *Page 231*

C-15

Family Acantitochitonidae

GIANT PACIFIC CHITON

Cryptochiton stelleri
Size: To 13" (330 mm). This is the largest chiton in the world.
Range: 60°N–34°N; Alaska south to Channel Islands, California.
Habitat: Intertidal to 65' (20 m).
Description: *Page 231*

Underside of giant Pacific chiton.

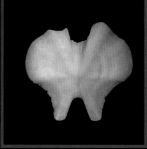

"Butterfly shell," a plate of giant Pacific chiton.

The
Mollusks

The phylum Mollusca ("soft bodied") is a large group of animals—in number of species, second only to the Arthropoda (insects, crabs, shrimp). Experts estimate that there are 50,000–100,000 living species of mollusks, many of which have yet to be described. Most of them live in marine waters, but many species live on land and in fresh waters.

The body of a mollusk is usually not segmented, and it is protected by a shell. The animal has a head, often with a rasping tonguelike "radula," a muscular foot, and a mass of tissue containing the gut and other organs. The mantle, a sheet of skin which envelops a mollusk's body, performs many protective functions including the secretion of the shell.

The shell gland develops at the edge of the mantle in the larval stage. Gradually this gland secretes the shell, in gastropods at the outer margin of the shell opening (the aperture), and in bivalves and chitons at the margins. The juvenile shell is usually a "miniature" of the adult shell, with some difference in proportions. Throughout its life, the shell will protect the animal from desiccation, predation and the physical forces of waves.

A mollusk shell has three layers, which provide great structural strength. The periostracum, the "horny" outer layer, is rich in protein and may be smooth or hairy. It grows only at the margin of the shell and is often worn off as the shell grows out. This protein material, conchiolin, also forms the "trap door" (operculum) of a gastropod that closes off the shell and protects the inner soft body. The hard middle layer of the shell expands out from the outer margin edge. This layer is made of densely packed calcium carbonate and other minerals. From the growing edge it may develop colours, spines or other growths that form patterns over time. Shells grow at different rates in different seasons, and growth patterns or rings (sometimes annual) are often visible on the outer surface of the shell. The third, inner layer of the shell lies over the mantle and is secreted continuously by the mantle. It is often pearly and increases in thickness over the life of the shell.

Since the first civilizations, mollusks and their shells have been useful to human beings in a wide variety of ways. They are most important as a source of nutritious food, but the shells have been essential also in making tools, money, ornaments, containers, weapons, trading tokens, paints and even works of art. Over the centuries hundreds of other uses have been found for mollusk shells, ranging from chicken feed to concrete filler. Another important use of shells, apparently dating as far back as people gathered them, was in games and sports—a tradition that persists to this day.

Not all authorities agree, but generally the mollusks are divided into seven classes. Four of those classes are described in this guide.

Class Bivalvia, marine and freshwater (about 12,000 living species): The bivalves ("two shells") are exclusively aquatic and are found in a variety of environments from moist sediments and river and lake bottoms to the abyssal depths of the oceans.

Class Gastropoda, marine, freshwater and terrestrial (about 50,000 species, 37,500 living and 15,000 fossil): The gastropods, mollusks that travel on a "stomach foot," are a large and diverse group. A gastropod has a single shell that is typically coiled or cone-shaped. The common snails, abalone and limpets are some members of this class. Gastropods without shells, such as sea slugs (nudibranchs, etc.), are not covered in this guide.

Class Scaphopoda, marine (about 500 living species): This is the least diverse class of mollusks. The scaphopods, "plow- or shovel-footed" mollusks known as tuskshells, have tusk-like or tooth-like shells which are tapered, tubular and open at both ends.

Class Polyplacophora, marine (500 to 600 living species): The chitons' class name, Polyplacophora, means "bearing many plates," a reference to the chiton's shell which has eight overlapping plates (valves) set into a surrounding fleshy "girdle." In several species the plates and the girdle are coloured and decorated.

There are three other classes of mollusks which do not appear in this guide. The class Cephalopoda, which has about 600 species, all marine, includes octopus and squid, as well as some species with external shells, such as the Nautilus, and some species with internal shells. The primitive, limpet-like class Monoplacophora ("one shell" or "one plate") has many fossil species but only about 10 living species, and they are extremely rare, being found in abyssal depths. The class Aplacophora ("without shell"), or "solengasters," comprises approximately 250 living species. These small, worm-like mollusks do not have shells, are strictly marine animals and are found worldwide. The skin is embedded with spicules.

There is no standard for the order of presentation of the classes of mollusks. If appearance in geological time were used, the order would likely be Gastropoda or Monoplacophora first; then Bivalvia, Cephalopoda and Polyplacophora which lived at about the same time; followed by Scaphopoda. The origin of the Aplacophora is unknown since these animals did not have shells.

Looking for Specimens

Every species listed in this book can be found on the BC coast, and many of them have much wider ranges, from Alaska to Baja California and even farther south. A few species are circumpolar, being found along both coasts and in the Arctic.

Some general patterns that are controversial among the experts, but interesting to note:

- Shells are more colourful and decorative in more southern latitudes.

- The number of species declines as one moves north.

- Species found in more northern latitudes show more extensive distribution patterns.

The best place to find shells is on any stretch of beach, where specimens are washed in naturally by tides or storms and left on the shore, and in tidepools or shallow waters. Snorkellers and scuba divers find a wonderful variety of shells in deeper waters.

Many living bivalves can be found in the intertidal zone (or littoral zone—the area between the high- and low-water marks), and can be collected from a wide variety of habitats, from sand to mud and gravel to rock. Look for specimens attached to rocks, beach debris, pilings and wharves, or buried in the soil. Some clams bury themselves only a few inches down, while others such as the geoduck clam dig down as deep as a few feet.

Specimens may be raked or dug, and sometimes they can be uncovered in the holdfast of seaweed. Take along a shovel, a rake and a turning tool, and tweezers and magnifying glass for handling tiny specimens. Some fortunate collectors have access to dredges that scoop up sediments from both shallow and deep waters. You may also be able to obtain rare specimens from commercial fishers who harvest shrimp or groundfish by dragging nets across the bottom.

It's advisable to get some information about the tides in any area you wish to explore, because finding shells is much easier at low tide. Wear appropriate clothing and footwear, and be aware of incoming tides, breaking waves or periodic "rogue" waves that can wash you off the rocks. Find out in advance about any special hazards around your collecting site.

Cleaning and Storing Specimens

The easiest way to clean a shell is to boil it in water for 5–15 minutes. A bivalve shell will open and you can easily pull off the tissue with forceps or scrape it off with a small knife or scalpel. For univalves, extract tissue with a hook or a bit of wire.

Small and fragile shells can be soaked in water for a few days to rot and release the tissue. Change the water several times each day.

Although the two valves of most bivalves are equal in size and shape, you may want to save a set of two shells, either separated or closed. Clean the inside thoroughly, then the two shells can be closed and tied together until the hinge ligament has dried.

Becoming a Collector

To make a scientific collection, clean the shells as described above. Then label and organize your specimens showing date of collection, area and specific location, depth of harvest, species, collector's name, and remarks such as the method of collection or notes on associated animals. You may also want to number your specimens and prepare an information card on each one.

Museums and other collectors protect the colours of the shells by storing them in cabinets or drawers, away from direct sunlight. To protect some specimens from drying and cracking, you can apply a light coat of glycerin with your finger or a brush.

A pair of tweezers is useful for handling small specimens, and you can examine them carefully with a hand lens or magnifying glass. To make chitons easier to examine, brush off the silt with a soft-bristle toothbrush.

Gathering Edible Shellfish

All the species in this book are edible if you are adventurous, but if you are gathering bivalves for food, you must be aware of certain poisonous effects from pollution and from naturally occurring toxins such as red tide. These conditions are unique to bivalves, which are "filter feeders"—that is, they pump large volumes of water through their bodies in order to filter out food particles. Abalone, snails, limpets and other single-shelled organisms are grazers, not filter feeders, so they are not affected by red tides. Avoid harbours or areas posted for contamination. Even in apparently unpolluted areas, it is best to gather food carefully. See page 246 for more details and a list of marine toxin hotline telephone numbers from Alaska to California.

Information on commercial fisheries can be found in relevant sections of the Field Guide. A few of my favourite cookbooks and guides are listed in Further Reading, page 244. The Recreational Harvest Information section lists contact numbers for Alaska, BC, Washington, Oregon and California.

Working with Nature

Whether you are gathering shells to decorate your home, to use them in arts or crafts, or to create a scientific collection, please harvest your specimens carefully. Shellfish populations can be depleted seriously even by beach-combers. At all stages of life, shellfish play an important part in the ecology of the sea and seashore. Even the empty shells play a role, serving as homes for other animals and hard surfaces to which a variety of life forms attach themselves.

BC, Washington, Oregon and California all have restrictions on the quantities and sizes of shells you can gather, and on methods of gathering them. Find out about current regulations before you start to collect shells.

Keep these five basic rules in mind:

1. Collect only what you need. Take time to examine your material. Do not take immature or imperfect shells that you may not keep.

2. Replace rocks, soils, beach debris or other materials you have disturbed while gathering your specimens. Some experts estimate that a rock overturned and not replaced can disrupt the life on that rock for as long as *ten years!*

3. Look out for shells that protect egg masses of other marine animals, and do not disturb them.

4. Keep proper records and label your collection. A shell collection with correct data is very valuable to science. Record the name of each specimen, the location and date you found it. Other data such as depth and habitat are important.

5. Comply with outdoor recreation codes. Pack out what you pack in, take care of public property, and build fires carefully and legally.

A Word About Scientific and Common Names

Unique scientific names are assigned to living things according to a procedure of classification developed in the eighteenth century by Carolus Linnaeus, a Swedish naturalist. In this system, each creature has a two-part name, and it is organized in groupings that relate it to similar animals. Scientists classify specimens by examining both living animals and fossil records. They use Latin words because Latin is an early written language used by many scholars to record names. Since Linnaeus, about 1.5 million species have been named.

The approximate meaning of names from root words in Latin, Greek and other languages are shown in the Glossary of Scientific Names, page 250. Linnaeus's system was designed to be used and understood by every scientific community in the world, and it is widely accepted as the standard for classification. International organizations monitor changes and maintain the official current version of the system. Inevitably, names and groupings evolve and change as authorities review information new and old, and as animal populations increase, decrease and migrate. Shellfish are grouped and differentiated on the basis of shell characteristics, internal anatomy and ecology, but the experts do not always agree on naming, renaming or classifying, and impassioned debates on the subject can go on for years.

Most species have local or common names as well as Latin names, which can confuse anyone who is not a specialist. For example, the term "littleneck clam" is used for numerous species of clams throughout the world, but only one littleneck clam bears the scientific name *Protothaca staminea*. Many of the mollusks do not have "recognized" common names, which allows for some poetic (I'd like to think) licence used in this guide. Different common and scientific names appear throughout the literature and in lists published by the American Fisheries Society (1988). I have been as consistent and up-to-date as possible, and when several names are in use for a species, I have included them under "Alternate names." While not all of these names are still considered "correct," some are likely to resurface in the literature.

Parentheses appear around the author of a species' name and the publication date, such as "(Carpenter, 1864)," only when the species is no longer placed in the genus in which it was originally described.

Bivalves

B ivalves (class Bivalvia) are mollusks whose shells have two halves, or valves. Another name for this class is Pelecypoda, which means "hatchet-footed." Bivalves do not have heads, and most species feed by filtering microscopic plant and animal particles from the water. A few are predatory.

There are about 10,000 living bivalve species in the world, all of which are aquatic, and a few of which live in fresh waters. In British Columbia 180 bivalve species have been described. About 70 of them are found in the intertidal zone or to depths of 165' (50 m). The 110 most common species are included in this guide.

Bivalves are among the world's oldest living animals. The *Guinness Book of Records* (1993) reports that a thick-shelled specimen of Atlantic clam, the ocean quahog (*Arctica islandica*), collected in 1982, was found to have about 220 annual growth rings. The oldest living clams in the Pacific Northwest area are the geoduck clams, *Panopea abrupta*, which have been aged to 146 years in a sample from Kyuquot on the west coast of Vancouver Island. Other large clams such as horse clams (*Tresus* species) and butter clams (*Saxidomus giganteus*) reach estimated ages of 20 years or more.

The most common method for calculating the age of bivalve shells is to count the lines or ridges that form during the winter when growth slows down. But there are many "false checks" laid by different events through the season. Ages and growth patterns of shells can be judged more accurately by tagging live specimens and recovering them many times over a period of years. For very long-lived species such as the geoduck clam, more elaborate procedures are required. The shells are cut and the layers of shell at the hinge area are read with a microscope or by projection, like the growth rings of a tree.

The Shell

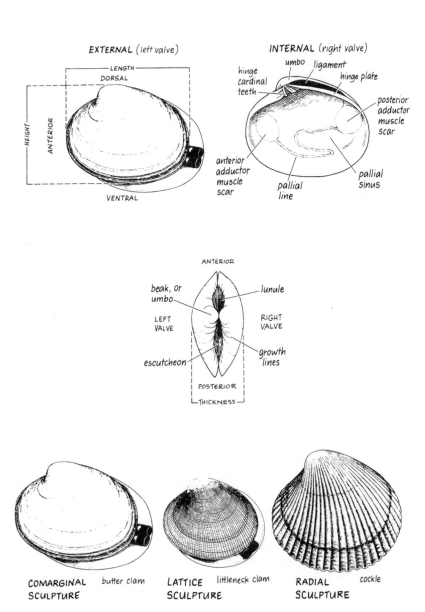

Figure 2: Bivalve Shell Features and Measurements

Spiny pink scallop.

A bivalve is identified most often by the special characteristics of its shell.

- **Size, length, height and thickness**
  Standard shell measurements are usually based on length of the shell, except for scallops and cockles which are typically measured by height.

- **Shape**
  The shell may be round, oval, elongated, wing-shaped, worm-like, compressed, globular, etc.

- **Equal or unequal valves**
  The two halves of a bivalve's shell are usually equal in size and shape, but some species, such as scallops and jingle oysters, have very different left and right shells. A shell is oriented as a left or right valve. There are anterior, posterior, dorsal and ventral orientations.

- **Hinge and teeth**
  The two shells are often hinged by an internal or external **ligament** and **teeth**. The number, shape and placement of the teeth (cardinal or lateral) are often key identifying features. Prominent spoon-shaped projections (**myophores**) or sockets (**chondrophores**) may be present in the hinge section. This area may also include depressions, the **lunule** and **escutcheon** for attachment of the hinge ligament.

The interior margin of the shell is often smooth but sometimes has fine teeth (taxodont dentition) in the hinge area and marginal teeth or crenulations.

■ **Beak**

The **umbo** or beak is the juvenile start of the shell. Its location and prominence can help identify a species.

■ **External colour**

Many bivalves have a **periostracum**, an outer shell covering that may be a different colour than the shell itself. The periostracum is often cracked, weathered, or abraded and flaked off. It may be thick, thin or transparent, light or dark in colour, smooth or rough. Some bivalves, such as the geoduck clam, have only a thin, partial periostracum, usually at the ventral margins.

■ **External sculpturing**

Comarginal (concentric) growth lines are typical, as in the butter clam. Other identifying marks include ridges, grooves, radial ribs, posterior ridges (keels) and other marks. The piddocks have a rasp-like radial sculpture that changes in sections across the shells. Some species such as the cleftclam (*Thyasira*) have a distinctive groove across the shell.

■ **Internal colour**

The interior of a bivalve shell is typically white but many are stained with colours (e.g. manila clam, bittersweet) and some are pearly (e.g. mussels, nut clams, tellins).

■ **Internal markings**

Most shells have internal lines and **scars** from the attachment of muscles and other body parts. Hard-shell clams bear anterior and posterior scars, but on scallops and oysters there may only be one scar where the muscles are united. A **pallial line** and **pallial sinus** may also be present.

■ **Other physical features**

Some bivalves attach to hard surfaces with a byssus ("beard") of organic threads that are secreted by a gland in the foot. The byssus is most commonly seen in species of mussels. The rock or jingle oyster has a short, thick, plug-like byssus that leaves a characteristic calcified "scar" on surfaces to which it attaches (see page 22).

Some species can repair their shells when they are damaged. New shell material is secreted by the mantle, filling holes or cracks with repeats of the basic shell pattern and colour. The repairs are known as growth scars or healed breaks.

The Soft Body

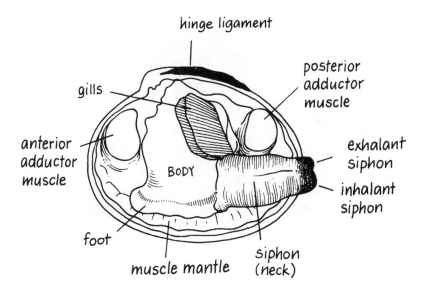

Figure 3: Internal Anatomy of a Butter Clam

The hinge ligament that joins a bivalve's shells may be internal or external. One or two large interior **adductor muscles** hold the valves together and allow them to spring apart at the hinge. The **mantle**, an interior sheet of tissue, typically is drawn out into two siphons, an **inhalant** (incurrent) and an **exhalant** (excurrent) **siphon**, usually located at the posterior end.

Feeding

Most bivalves are "filter feeders": they feed by pumping in sea water through the **inhalant siphon** and filtering out small organisms. The bivalve's lips or palps select food particles, mainly by size, and these particles are trapped by masses of mucous, which is secreted by the **gills**. Excess food or particles (pseudofeces) are expelled from the **inhalant siphon**, see photo S-9, page 62. In the stomach, digestion is aided by a rotating gelatinous rod called the crystalline style.

Pacific gaper clam siphons. Note that the siphons are joined and that inhalant siphon is much larger.

Not all bivalves filter the water. The *Macoma* and other members of the Family Tellinidae are deposit feeders, ingesting sediment from the sea bottom and siphoning off food particles. The shipworm is unique among bivalves, as it ingests wood in the process of boring elaborate burrows in docks, pilings and ships' hulls. Prey capture has been observed in only a few bivalves, the septibranchs (Order Septibranchia). The inhalant siphon can be dramatically extended and withdrawn to capture small living prey. The gutless awning-clam (*Solemya reidi*), a relatively large clam that grows to 2 1/2" (60 mm), has neither a gut nor a digestive system but is sustained by intracellular bacteria. This clam is found in large concentrations in sediments rich in sulphide, such as below wood-fibre beds in log booming and log storage areas.

Respiration and Circulation

A bivalve's respiration takes place primarily in the mantle and the gills. The circulatory system is simple but efficient, with colourless blood and a heart, veins and arteries to pump it through the body. The nervous system has numerous centres, with processes to determine water quality, an area in the foot that helps the bivalve orient itself and move around, and, in some species such as scallops, eyes on the mantle edge that detect changes in light intensity. The mantle and sometimes the siphons have slender sensory tentacles that detect movement and particles in the water.

Attachment and Locomotion

Most bivalves are relatively sessile (sedentary), attaching to hard objects or burrowing into the floor of the sea and moving only small distances. Almost all clams bury themselves very slowly, but a few species move faster. The razor-clam, for example, has a smooth, thin shell and a strong foot to pull the clam down into the sand quickly. Boring into clays and rocks requires a rasping, abrasive action of the elaborate shell and, in species such as the date-mussel, a chemical secretion from the mantle as well.

A few bivalves such as the oyster and the rock scallop can cement their shells directly to a hard surface by secreting calcareous material. Other species such as mussels attach themselves with the byssus or "beard." The jingle or rock oyster (*Pododesmus*) attaches by a single muscle byssus, and leaves a distinctive scar where it was attached. The byssal threads from the noble pen shell (*Pinna nobilis*), a Mediterranean species, were so plentiful and strong that they were once woven into fabric.

But some non-burrowing bivalves do move around. Scallops can open and close their valves rapidly, propelling themselves through the water in a swimming motion. Other bivalves move by extending the muscular foot from between the valves. The kellyclam (*Kellia*), which attaches by a single byssal thread, moves by throwing out a new thread, breaking the old one and drawing itself forward.

Reproduction

Most bivalve species have separate sexes which reproduce by releasing gametes, eggs and sperm, into the water to be fertilized externally. The larvae may be widely distributed as they develop. Eventually they settle, growing shells and attaching to hard surfaces or burrowing into the substrate.

In many of the smaller bivalves, such as small nestling clams, brooding takes place entirely in the mantle cavity. Eggs are fertilized there, and larvae develop until they can survive on their own, at which point they "crawl" out and settle nearby (see kellyclam, page 28).

In most bivalves, the gonads of males and females are difficult to distinguish without dissection. But in many scallops, the male gonad is coloured white and the female gonad orange-red, and in the milky venus clam (*Compsomyax subdiaphana*), the male gonad is white and the female gonad red.

Some individuals such as the cockle may be hermaphroditic (having both male and female gonads), and species such as oysters may rhythmically alternate sexuality, being male and then female.

Predators

A number of predators feed on bivalves, including worms, shore birds, ducks and many sea stars, notably the pink star (*Pisaster brevispinus*), the ochre star (*Pisaster ochraceus*), the sunflower star (*Pycnopodia helianthoides*), the mottled star (*Evasterias troschelli*) and the painted sea star (*Orthasterias koehleri*). Several species of crabs feed on clams, including the Dungeness (*Cancer magister*) and red rock crab (*C. productus*). Moonsnails (*Polinices lewisii*) bore into the shells of many different clams, and carnivorous whelks (*Nucella canaliculata* and *N. emarginata*) bore into mussels.

Sea otters are known to dive and dig to feed on intertidal and subtidal bivalves along the Pacific shore from Alaska to California. They prefer larger clams which live in the intertidal or shallow subtidal zones, and in the shallow substrate. They take a number of species, most commonly butter clams (*Saxidomus gigantea*), littleneck clams (*Protothaca staminea*) and horse clams or "otter clams" (*Tresus* species). Sea otters have been observed diving for up to 2 minutes to forage on horse clams. They open the shells by biting, twisting or prying them open with their teeth. A sea otter may also smash the two shells together or hold a rock on its chest and break the clam against the rock. Castoff "otter shells" can be distinguished by a newly broken edge on one of the two valves, and the remains of the adductor muscle or mantle. A shell may have holes from the otter's teeth.

Sea otters also harvest geoduck clams (*Panopea abrupta*) that have been buried as deep as 3' (1m) in the substrate. Geoducks that have been broken open by otters typically have the cardinal tooth of the shell hinge broken.

Bivalves are mostly quiet and sedentary, but they do have ways of repelling predators. Scallops can "swim" away. Several species of mussels (*Mytilus edulis*) engage in gaping, twisting shell movements to ward off predatory snails. Mussels can also slow or immobilize snails by attaching byssal threads to them. Razor-clams (*Siliqua patula*) may shed the tips of their siphons to escape predators. Cockles and jackknife-clams respond to predators such as the sunflower star and pink star by leaping. The animal extends a worm-like foot and then contracts it suddenly so that the body is thrown forward.

Commensals

A number of bivalves live in association with other organisms, protecting them in some manner and thereby being allowed to inhabit certain locales. For example, the California softshell-clam (*Cryptomya californica*) burrows deep in the substrate to avoid predators, but it can feed with its short (1/32"/1 mm) siphons, which stick into the burrows of burrowing shrimp and echiurid worms. The bladderclam (*Mytilimeria nuttallii*) lives in the protective covering of an encrusting marine animal, a compound tunicate, which protects the thin, fragile shell of the clam. The wrinkled montacutid, or mud shrimp clam (*Pseudopythina rugifera*), attaches by a byssus to the underside of the mud shrimp and the polychaete sea mouse; small sea cucumber clams (*Scintillona bellerophon*) can be found in the intertidal zone commensal with the sea cucumber; the small robust mysella (*Rochefortia tumida*) is commensal with burrowing animals.

Many bivalves in turn host other animals, such as commensal pea crabs. The pea crabs can cause mild damage to their host while feeding. A number of bivalves are known to host male, immature female or juvenile pea crabs, and only the gaper or horse clams host mature pairs of adult pea crabs.

Parasites

Parasitic flatworms and copepods (small crustaceans) attack and kill oysters, scallops and mussels. Blue mussels and oysters are sometimes parasitized by a small (1/32"/1 mm long) red copepod (*Mytilicola orientalis*), which lives in the animal's digestive tract. This parasite has been found in lesser numbers in butter clams and cockles. The copepod was likely introduced from Japan along with oyster seed.

Horse clams host a nemertean worm, *Malacobdella grossa,* that is sometimes considered commensal or parasitic. This nemertean is also found in the mantle of the white-sand macoma (*Macoma secta*) and the razor-clam (*Siliqua patula*). The littleneck clam (*Protothaca staminea*) and gapers (*Tresus nuttallii*) sometimes contain larval tapeworms.

None of these parasites is harmful to human beings when the shellfish are cooked and eaten.

Distribution and Habitat

Most bivalves living in this region occupy what most experts call the Oregonian Province of the Eastern Pacific Ocean (the area we think of as the Northwest Coast), and many are found from the Bering Strait (66°N), including the Aleutian Archipelago in Alaska, to Point Conception, California (34.5°N). See map on page 7 for an overview.

Bivalves can live in a vast range of depths, from the intertidal zone to the sea bottom far below the water surface. One population of clams was found at 21,000' (6366 m), close to hydrothermal vents near Japan. Most specimens in this guide are found from intertidal areas to moderate depths (400'/120 m). Typical ranges are given for each species, but the depths at which a bivalve lives are determined by a number of physical, chemical and biological factors.

Species found in the intertidal zone must be tolerant to extreme changes in the environment due to tidal action that covers and uncovers the beach. Some species are only found in exposed oceanic conditions while others can tolerate the low salinities of estuaries. Predation limits the range of many of the larger intertidal bivalves. The more abundant and larger species in shallow waters may be a result of larval behaviour and the greater availability of food. The number of intertidal species generally decreases in more northern latitudes, as the animals are exposed to colder temperatures and scouring by ice.

Fisheries and Other Uses

Because they are so abundant in the intertidal zone, clams, mussels and oysters are readily harvested from the wild, so they have been an important source of food for human beings for centuries. Middens found throughout the Northwest Coast show that aboriginal groups in the area regularly harvested clams both at permanent village sites and in summer settlements. The favoured species were butter clams, littleneck clams, cockles and, in the Masset area of Haida Gwaii (the Queen Charlotte Islands), razor-clams. Horse clams, called "summer clams," were dried and used for trade as well as a staple food.

From the early 1800s on, clams were important to early European settlers as well. Commercial clam and other bivalve fisheries never reached the production levels of salmon, herring and other fin fish, but they have provided significant quantities of food for export and domestic use, and the fisheries have been important economically for both seasonal and full-time workers.

Commercial clam production in British Columbia began in 1882 at Rivers Inlet. Whole butter clams were put up by "solid pack," the salmon canning process used at that time. By the late 1800s and early 1900s, several small canneries in the area were processing clams, using wooden retorts and hand-soldering each can. Most of the plants were primarily salmon canneries which canned clams seasonally. The Saanich Canning Company at Sidney, also canned berries and fruit in the summer and fall. Clam canning was a seasonal activity, carried out from November to April, because if the meat was canned later than that, it was discoloured by the "green feed" of the spring phytoplankton blooms. The summer and fall were salmon-canning seasons.

Most of the clams processed were butter clams, packed whole or minced. The highest landings of butter clams on record were 7.7 million lbs (3476 mt) in 1938. Pacific littleneck clams, labelled the "Very Tender Little Neck Clams" were also packed in smaller tins (1s) and clam nectar was sold in cans (1s) and bottles (120 mL/4 oz). Razor-clams were first canned in 1923 at Tow Hill, near Masset, Queen Charlotte Islands, and in 1925 1.7 million lbs (757 mt)

Clam Cannery, Bag Harbour, Queen Charlotte Islands, c. 1914.

were landed. Current annual harvest levels of razor-clams are less than 330,000 lbs (150 mt), and the clams are sold fresh or frozen for crab bait.

Since the fisheries were established, their output has fluctuated, and the favoured species have changed over time. From the 1920s to the 1970s, the products of choice were butter clams and razor-clams. In the 1980s the market shifted to live steamers, in particular the manila and to a lesser extent the native littleneck clam. Landings of manila clams peaked in 1988 at 8.6 million lbs (3909 mt). In the late 1970s, subtidal fisheries for geoducks and small quantities of horse clams were established. These species are harvested by divers. Peak landings of geoducks were 12.6 million lbs (5735 mt) in 1987. Horse clams have not been fully exploited due to slower markets, so peak landings were 783,200 lbs (356 mt) in 1987.

Fisheries for other bivalves, including oysters and scallops, operate in the Northwest Coast area, and several species of oysters, clams and scallops are cultured.

Shellfish and their shells have played other important roles in the lives of human beings. For First Nations people in the area, bivalves have been profoundly important for centuries in daily life and culture—a tradition reflected in many myths and legends. The Haida tell a story of Raven setting the first people free from a gigantic clam shell. The Manhousaht on the west coast of Vancouver Island tell about Heron using a mussel shell knife to scrape his fat clumsy legs, turning them into long, slender ones and becoming successful at fishing.

Shells have also been used traditionally for clothing, ornaments and works of art. Thick shells such as the native oyster and rock scallop were used as pendants, and clams and mussels were cut into sections and ground into beads, powdered into paint, or made into ornaments to be attached to clothing and headdresses. Shells have been sharpened and used as tools, weapons and hunting implements. Larger shells have served as containers and cooking implements. Some aboriginal groups dried part of the clam harvest and strung the meat on strips of cedar bark, then stored it in baskets and boxes to be used as currency for trade.

Paralytic Shellfish Poison (PSP) and Other Biotoxins

Bivalves feed on several species of planktonic algae that contain natural toxins (biotoxins). These toxins do not appear to harm the bivalves, but they render certain shellfish toxic to humans. **Always check with the local fisheries or wildlife department before harvesting shellfish for food.** Governments maintain intensive monitoring and testing programs all along the coast, and closures should not be ignored. A list of PSP (Red Tide) Marine Toxin Hotlines from Alaska to California appears on page 246.

Paralytic Shellfish Poison

The most commonly known toxin is paralytic shellfish poison (PSP), which is caused by blooms of various algae. PSP outbreaks occur throughout the world, and are common along the east and west coasts of North America. On the Pacific coast, poisonings have been recorded from Mexico to Alaska, and some outbreaks have been serious enough to cause deaths.

PSP is not a new phenomenon. Even the early European explorers documented deaths and illnesses. The Russian Baranoff expedition lost 100 men in 1799, after they ate mussels near Sitka, Alaska, subsequently named Peril Strait. In British Columbia, the first recorded incident was chronicled by Captain George Vancouver in June 1793. Four of his crew became ill and one died, poisoned by mussels gathered from the central coast. The dead men are remembered to this day by the names Carter Bay, Mussel Cove and Poison Inlet. Since that time hundreds of people have been poisoned and many have died from eating filter-feeding bivalve mollusks.

The species affected include butter clams, bay mussels, sea mussels, native littlenecks, manila clams, cockles, smooth pink and spiny scallops and rock scallops. But all bivalves concentrate the toxin and can be poisonous at times. Most oysters and commercial clam species retain toxins for 4–6 weeks, but some, such as butter clams, may remain toxic for as long as 2 years.

Red Tides

"Red tides" are so named because the toxic algae that bloom are often so concentrated that they discolour the water, turning it a reddish colour. The west coast species, *Alexandrium catenella* and *A. acatenella*, are pale in colour, clear or with an orange tint. This can create confusion because red tides are often caused by other non-toxic species, while blooms of the toxic species may not discolour the water at all.

The *Alexandrium* algae are single-cell organisms that propel themselves around with tiny whip-like tails. They produce a poison, saxitoxin, which can be 10,000 times more deadly than cyanide. An adult human being can be poisoned to death by ingesting a single clam.

Amnesic Shellfish Poison

A different red tide toxin was identified in late 1987, after several people were poisoned by eating cultured blue mussels from eastern Prince Edward Island. The poisoning symptoms were gastric and neurological distress, with memory loss. Demoic acid, a poison produced by a phytoplankton, *Pseudonitzschia pugens*, has been found in razor-clams, mussels and other species on the Pacific coast.

Contamination from Pollution

Many Northwest Coast area shellfish closures have been posted because of sewage contamination or industrial pollution. Certain stretches of beach in rural, urban and agricultural areas are sometimes closed because of contamination from wastes of wild or domestic animals. Other causes of closure include direct discharge of sewage from moored or anchored boats, municipal or industrial waste discharges, and seepage from foreshore septic tank and tile field disposal systems. To make sure the shellfish you are gathering for food is safe, consult with local fisheries authorities and watch for posted signs along the beach.

Class
Bivalvia

Subclass Protobranchia (Paleotaxodonta)

AWNING-CLAMS Family Solemyidae

These clams live in U-shaped burrows in the mud. Their shells have a thick, polished periostracum.

GUTLESS AWNING-CLAM *(Illustration #B-1)*

Species: *Solemya reidi* Bernard, 1980.
Size: To 2½" (60 mm).
Range: 50°N–33°N, Northern Vancouver Island and south to Point Loma, California.
Habitat: Often in areas rich in organics, sulphide; near effluent outfalls and in log storage areas, 130–200' (40–60 m) depth. Sometimes found in "cleaner" sediments.
Description: Exterior dark brown. Thick periostracum extends beyond the shell margin; interior has radial rib.
Comments: This clam feeds from the nutrients provided by bacteria that live within the tissue of the clam.

NUT SHELLS Family Nuculidae

These are small clams with an oval shape, pearly interiors and sharp, distinctive teeth along the hinge (taxodont dentition). They do not have siphons.

DIVARICATE NUTCLAM *(Illustration #B-2)*

Species: *Acila castrensis* (Hinds, 1843).
Alternate names: Tent nutshell, nut clam.
Size: To ⅝" (15 mm) length.
Range: 57°N–24°N; NE Bering Sea, Alaska south to Punta San Pablo, Baja, California, and in the Gulf of California.
Habitat: Mud–sand bottoms 16–725' (5–220 m).
Description: Anterior beaks; shell exterior olive to dark brown with a ·radial pattern that forms chevron-like or tent shaped patterns; interior pearly with distinct hinge teeth.

YOLDIA CLAMS Family Sareptidae (=Yoldiidae)

Most of these clams are small with the exception of the Axe Yoldia, which grows to a length of 2¹/2" (60 mm). Yoldia clams have multiple distinctive teeth along the margins.

AXE YOLDIA *(Illustration #B-3)*

Species: *Megayoldia thraciaeformis* (Storer, 1838).
Alternate names: Broad yoldia.
Size: To 2¹/2" (65 mm) length.
Range: 70°N–38°N; Circumpolar; southern Arctic, northern Bering Sea south to off San Francisco Bay, California.
Habitat: Mud–sand bottoms 80–2000' (25–600 m).
Description: Broad shell with posterior broadly truncate; oblique fold from the umbo to posterior third of shell; large spoon-like chondrophore holds ligament, hinge area with 12 prominent teeth on either side. Exterior yellow to tan shiny periostracum to dull black in larger specimens; interior chalky white.

CRISSCROSS YOLDIA *(Illustration #B-4)*

Species: *Yoldia seminuda* Dall, 1871.
Alternate names: *Yoldia scissurata* (Dall, 1897).
Size: To 1¹/2" (40 mm) length.
Range: 71°N–34°N; Arctic, Beaufort Sea, Bering Sea south to San Diego, California.
Habitat: Mud–sand bottoms 50–500' (15–150 m).
Description: Elongated shell with fine concentric lines that cross the growth lines; posterior pointed. Shiny, yellow to tan periostracum.

Subclass Pteriomorphia

BITTERSWEET CLAMS Family Glycymerididae

These are sturdy oval clams with an arched hinge and small, fine teeth. They are generally only found in shallow warm waters.

WESTERN BITTERSWEET *(Illustration #B-5)*

Species: *Glycymeris septentrionalis* (Middendorff, 1849).
Alternate names: Northern bittersweet, California bittersweet; several species have been assigned, including *G. subobsoleta* (Carpenter, 1864).
Size: To 1³/4" (45 mm) length.

Range: 59°N–25°N; Cook Inlet, Alaska south to Baja California Sur and in the Gulf of California.

Habitat: In sand or gravel, intertidal to 180' (55 m).

Description: Shell pale brown to white, often with zigzag patterns, flattened ribs often worn smooth. Periostracum worn, sometimes heavy at the margins. Interior with yellow and often purple-brown stains; margin of shell has numerous teeth; hinge has numerous (15–16) small teeth.

Comments: At first look, this clam has been misidentified by divers as the littleneck clam, *Protothaca staminea*. A closer examination shows the hinge and shell sculpture vary greatly.

PHILOBRYAS Family Philobryidae

These very small shells are strong and inflated.

HAIRY PHILOBRYA *(Illustration #B-6)*

Species: *Philobrya setosa* (Carpenter, 1864).

Size: To 1/4" (5 mm) length.

Range: 60°N–23°N; Prince William Sound, Alaska and south to Baja California Sur, and possibly farther south to Costa Rica.

Habitat: Attaches to broken shells and coralline algae by byssus; found in the intertidal zone to 240' (73 m).

Description: Triangular in shape. Exterior white to orange, radial ribs with hair; interior pearly with single adductor muscle scar.

Comments: There may be more than one species; further study of this group is required.

MUSSELS Family Mytilidae

There are two common intertidal mussels and several less common, subtidal mussels found in the Northwest Coast region. Mussels have equal shells, are typically elongated and attach by strong, thin threads called the "byssus" (the "beard" or "byssal threads"), which are produced by a gland in the foot. There are no hinge teeth and the hinge ligament is both internal and external.

The common mussels form "mussel beds" by attaching to rocks, pilings and other hard surfaces. Some mussels nestle in rock burrows or bore into rock or clay. Others are found in sand and gravel anchored by a mat of byssal threads, and some form agglutinated nests on the sand.

Because of their wide distribution, and because they typically absorb certain shellfish toxins faster than other commercial species, mussels are used in pollution monitoring programs. A series of mussel stations is maintained, at which regular checks are made for occurrences of red tide and other toxic algae blooms. The "mussel watch" has been a critically important program for shellfish growers and harvesters to ensure that their clams, oysters, scallops and other bivalves are safe to eat.

PACIFIC BLUE MUSSEL *(Illustration #B-7)*

Species: *Mytilus edulis* complex, Linnaeus, 1758.
Alternate names: At this writing, the mussel known as the Pacific blue mussel, edible mussel or bay mussel is considered to be several species or subspecies that cannot be easily distinguished by the shells alone.
Range: 71°N–19°N; Arctic to Alaska and south to Mexico.
Habitat: Quiet, sheltered locations, in the intertidal zone to 16' (5 m) depths. They are a common and dominant species, forming dense masses on hard surfaces and attached by strong byssal threads.
Description: Various. See species below.
Comments: Blue mussels live only 1–2 years in BC, but in other parts of the world they may live longer (up to 17 years in Sweden, for example) and their shells may grow to lengths of 41/2" (110 mm).
As with most common names, the term "blue mussel" is not always accurate. The mussels are blue to black and sometimes tan to brown.
Currently the blue mussel species in BC are considered to include:

Blue Mussel, *Mytilus edulis* Linnaeus, 1758.

Size: To 41/2" (110 mm).
Range: Unknown. Considered introduced to BC.
Description: Triangular to elongated; beak blunt, usually not curved.

Mediterranean Mussel, *Mytilus galloprovincialis* Lamarck, 1819.

Size: To 6" (150 mm).
Range: Unknown. Found in a sheltered inlet in BC; found in southern California to Mexico. Native to the Mediterranean, western France, Britain and Ireland.
Habitat: Warmer waters.
Description: Triangular, flared; pointed curved beaks.

Foolish Mussel, *Mytilus trossulus* A.A. Gould, 1850.

Size: To 31/2" (90 mm) length.
Range: Uncertain. Arctic to Alaska and south to Central California.
Habitat: Protected waters; intertidal on rocks and pilings.
Description: Thin elongated shells, anterior pointed and posterior rounded. Smooth exterior with fine concentric lines; periostracum black, blue or brown. Interior dull blue with dark margin.

CALIFORNIA MUSSEL *(Illustration #B-8)*

Species: *Mytilus californianus* Conrad, 1837.
Alternate names: Sea mussel, ribbed mussel.
Size: To 10" (255 mm) length.
Range: 60°N–18°N; Cook Inlet, Alaska to Punta Rompiente, Baja California Sur and Mexico.
Habitat: Extensive mussel beds are seen on surf-exposed rocks and wharves; from the intertidal zone to 330' (100 m), dominant on sea mounts.
Description: Shells thick and pointed at anterior end; strong radial ribs often worn on larger specimens. Heavy blue-black periostracum; interior blue-grey, iridescent at margins. Shells are held fast by byssal threads. Meat colour is bright orange.
Comments: Often hosts pea crabs. Often contains several tiny pearls of various shapes. Open-coast aboriginal people in the Northwest Coast area used these mussels extensively for food, and for chisels, knives and harpoon heads.

Horsemussels

There is some confusion in the taxonomy of the horsemussels, because scientists disagree on the number of species. In BC there are two or more distinct types. One, *Modiolus rectus*, is found solitary in sand–mud. Some consider *M. rectus* to be synonymous with *M. flabellatus*, which has a unique siphon show. The other type is *Modiolus modiolus*, which is found in aggregations attached to rocks, shell or gravel, or at the surface of sediments with the posterior tip of the shell exposed. *M. modiolus* is found intertidally at some locations and is also brought up in trawls and dredges.

STRAIGHT (FAN) HORSEMUSSEL *(Illustration #B-9, #S-9)*

Species: *Modiolus rectus* (Conrad, 1837).
Alternate names: Fan-shaped horsemussel; *Modiolus flabellatus*.
Size: To 9" (230 mm) length.
Range: 54°N–5.1°S; Tow Hill, Queen Charlotte Islands, BC south to Baja and Gulf of California, and as far south as Paita, Peru.
Habitat: Solitary, buried in sand, anchored by byssal threads and sand or mud; white siphons show at surface (see page 62). Found in the intertidal zone to depths of 50' (15 m).
Description: Elongated shells, length about 3 times the height; exterior smooth with some concentric ridges; thin-shelled, hairy periostracum, pale on hind two-thirds and dark brown on the front one-third.

NORTHERN HORSEMUSSEL *(Illustration #B-10, #S-10)*

Species: *Modiolus modiolus* (Linnaeus, 1758).
Size: To 7" (180 mm) length.
Range: 50°N–37°N; Bering Sea south to Monterey, California.
Habitat: In aggregations or mussel "mats" binding gravel and rocks, sometimes in the intertidal zone and to depths of 660' (200 m).
Description: Oval, inflated, thicker shell; length about 2 times the height and width. Shell is purple beneath the periostracum. A visible yellow mantle may protrude from the shell.
Comments: Often hosts pea crabs.

Boring Datemussels
Species of mussel that bore in shale have been described from a few locations in BC. Several species are found in Washington, Oregon and California.

CALIFORNIA DATEMUSSEL *(Illustration #B-11)*

Species: *Adula californiensis* (Philippi, 1847).
Alternate names: Pea-pod borer.
Size: To 2¹⁄2" (60 mm).
Range: 54°N–33°N; Graham Island, Queen Charlotte Islands, BC south to Point Loma, California.
Habitat: Intertidal to 65' (20 m), boring in clay, shale, other soft rocks.
Description: Elongated, cylindrical, curved shell; brownish-black shiny periostracum with a hairy mat that binds mud and debris on the posterior slope; interior bluish-grey.

Burrowing, Nestling or Attached Mussels
Several species of small- to medium-size mussels can be found in intertidal and shallow subtidal areas, attached or buried in sand–mud and gravel, often forming nests of byssal threads and particles of sand. *Musculus* species brood their young.

DISCORDANT MUSSEL *(Illustration #B-12)*

Species: *Musculus discors* (Linnaeus, 1767).
Size: To 2¹⁄4" (55 mm).
Range: 71°N–47°N; Beaufort Sea, Cook Inlet, Alaska south to Aberdeen, Washington.
Habitat: Buried in fine sand or in a "nest" of agglutinated sand, attached to tunicates or stalks of seaweed washed up on beach; in depths of 16–500' (5–150 m).
Description: Elongated, radial riblets on the front end, shallow groove across the shell. Exterior dark brown on the anterior, posterior olive; interior is whitish-bluish-grey.

BLACK MUSSEL *(Illustration #B-13)*

Species: *Musculus niger* (Gray, 1824).
Alternate names: Little black mussel.
Size: To 2¼" (57 mm).
Range: 71°N–48°N; Beaufort Sea, Aleutian Islands, Alaska south to Willapa Bay, Washington; also on Atlantic Coast.
Habitat: In muddy gravel. The adult may use its byssal threads to form a "cocoon" around its shell. At depths of 50–500' (15–150 m).
Description: Oval-elongated, thin shell. Exterior light tan to dark black-brown with many fine, low ribs; beaded radial riblets. Interior light blue, iridescent.

TAYLOR'S DWARF-MUSSEL *(Illustration #B-14)*

Species: *Musculus taylori* (Dall, 1897).
Size: To 3/8" (8 mm).
Range: 53°N–48°N; Hotspring Island, Queen Charlotte Islands, BC south to Victoria, BC.
Habitat: Intertidal.
Description: Oval-elongated shell, smooth except for a few lines on the anterior slope. Thick periostracum, green to brown to red.
Comments: This is one bivalve whose distribution is reported to be limited to BC.

JAPAN MUSSEL *(Illustration #B-15)*

Species: *Musculista senhousia* (Benson, 1842).
Size: To 1½" (40 mm).
Range: Intermittent; 48°N–34°N; Strait of Georgia, BC, Puget Sound, Washington, California. Introduced from Japan along with oysters.
Habitat: Intertidal, in estuarine conditions to 65' (20 m).
Description: Elongated shell; exterior covered with a greenish periostracum (sometimes to red), often with wavy brown markings.

BRITISH COLUMBIA CRENELLA *(Illustration #B-16)*

Species: *Solamen columbianum* (Dall, 1897).
Alternate names: *Crenella columbianum.*
Size: To 1/2" (11 mm).
Range: 60°N–33°N; Aleutian Islands, Alaska south to Point Loma, California.
Habitat: At depths of 65–180' (20–55 m).
Description: Shell is subquadrate, inflated. Periostracum thin, light to dark brown. Interior margin with fine notches or crenulations.

OYSTERS Family Ostreidae

There are more than 200 species of oysters worldwide. Less than a dozen, from the two genera *Ostrea* and *Crassostrea*, are cultured or harvested commercially. Common culture methods include placing seed on beaches, on longlines and in floating trays.

Four species of oysters may be found in this region: the native or Olympia oyster, and three introduced species, the Pacific or Japanese oyster, the Atlantic oyster and the European flat oyster.

Pododesmus cepio, the rock or jingle oyster, is a member of the Family Anomiidae, and differs greatly from the true oysters.

Oysters have unequal valves. The lower left valve is cupped and often cemented to a hard object, or sometimes found lying free. The hinge ligament is internal or semi-internal. There is no adult foot or byssus.

OLYMPIA OYSTER *(Illustration #B-17)*

Species: *Ostrea conchaphila* Carpenter, 1857.
Alternate names: *Ostrea lurida.*
Size: To 31/2" (90 mm) diameter.
Range: 57°N–9°N; Sitka, Alaska south to Panama.
Habitat: On mud–gravel flats, in splash pools and with fresh water seepage; in the intertidal zone to depths of 165' (50 m).
Description: Irregular to oval shape. The top (right) valve is usually flattened; exterior is grey; interior white or iridescent green. The margins near the hinge are notched; triangular ligament.
Comments: It is believed that populations have been reduced or eliminated due to toxic pulp mill effluent.

PACIFIC OYSTER *(Illustration #B-18)*

Species: *Crassostrea gigas* (Thunberg, 1793).
Alternate names: Japanese oyster.
Size: To 12" (30 cm) length.
Range: 61°N–34°N; Prince William Sound, Alaska south to Newport Bay, California.
Habitat: Firm or rocky beaches, intertidally to 20' (6 m).
Description: Variable shape, long-thin to round and deep; shell is fluted; exterior grey-white with new growth often purple-black; smooth white interior. Lower (left) valve is usually cupped; upper valve is flattened and smaller than other valve.
Comments: This oyster, introduced as seed from Japan in the early 1900s, is the most important culture species on the West Coast. It lives

20 years or longer, and often harbours irregular pearls, without lustre. It is preyed upon by snails or oyster drills, sea stars and even a bird named after it, the oyster catcher.

AMERICAN OYSTER *(Illustration #B-19)*

Species: *Crassostrea virginica* (Gmelin, 1791).
Alternate names: Atlantic oyster, eastern oyster.
Size: To 8" (20 cm) length.
Range: Small population in BC on Boundary Bay flats at the mouth of the Nikomekl River.
Habitat: Intertidal on soft to firm substrates of sand–mud–gravel, usually in estuarine conditions.
Description: Thick, pear-shaped shells; smooth with concentric sculpture. Light brown exterior; smooth white interior. The top (right) valve is flatter.
Comments: This is the common edible oyster of the east coast of North America. It has been introduced to several West Coast sites but few populations have persisted in the wild.

EDIBLE FLAT OYSTER *(Illustration #B-20)*

Species: *Ostrea edulis* Linnaeus, 1758.
Alternate names: Belon oyster, European flat oyster.
Size: To 3" (75 mm).
Range: Experimental culture sites in BC; not established in the wild.
Habitat: Soft to firm substrates in the intertidal zone.
Description: Round shell with flat lower (left) shell and inflated upper valve. Exterior beige to grey, with rough radiating ridges and scales; interior white.
Comments: In North America this species was first been cultured in Maine and California; recently attempts have been made to establish populations in BC.

JINGLE/ROCK OYSTERS
Family Anomiidae

Shells of this family are typically anchored with a plug-like byssus. The shells are flattened and fit to the contours of the substrate on which they rest. Scientists' opinions differ on whether there are two species or two subspecies, *Pododesmus machrochisma cepio* and *P. machrochisma machrochisma*. Opinions also differ on the distribution of the two.

GREEN FALSE-JINGLE *(Illustration #B-21)*

Species: *Pododesmus macroschisma* (Deshayes, 1839).
Alternate names: Rock oyster, jingle shells, blister shell.
Size: To 51/4" (130 mm) length.
Range: 58°N–28°N; Bering Sea to Alaska and south to Baja California Sur, and in the Gulf of California.
Habitat: Rocks and other solid objects, intertidal to 300' (90 m).
Description: The circular shell forms to shape of substrate; exterior of upper (left) shell is grey-white with light radiating lines; lower shell has a pear-shaped hole near the hinge for a short, thick byssus with a calcareous attachment. Interior of shell is polished, upper valve often iridescent green.
Comments: The byssus leaves a distinctive calcareous "scar" to 25 mm long, as shown on a weathervane scallop shell. Painted sea star, *Orthasterias koehleri*, have been observed feeding on the abundant jingle oysters on a shallow, rocky reef.

SCALLOPS Family Pectinidae

Four larger common scallop species are encountered in shallow waters: the pink, spiny, rock and weathervane scallops. The Japanese scallop has been cultured in BC. Numerous other species of scallops live in the area, many of them small and found only in deep waters.

Most scallops have strong radial ribs. The hinges have a characteristic wing-like shape, called "ears," which are not always equal in length. When the shells gape, eyes are found between sensory tentacles, around the edge of the mantle. The eyes do not perceive images, but they can detect shadows.

Scallops typically lie with the right valve (more rounded; usually lighter in colour) to the bottom; many attach temporarily by a byssus. The top (left) valve is coloured to camouflage the shell against the bottom. The lower lighter valve is less visible against a watery background when the scallop is swimming and exposed to fish predators.

Some scallops, unlike most bivalves, are capable of swimming through the water by clapping their shells to expel water. An exception is the rock scallop. After a juvenile free swimming stage, this species cements its shell to a hard object for the rest of its life.

The free-swimming scallops, *Chlamys hastata* and *C. rubida*, are typically encrusted with sponges, the yellow-orange rough sponge, *Myxilla incrustans*, and the smooth, light-brown to violet sponge, *Mycale adhaerans*. The thick shells of the rock scallop, *Crassadoma gigantea*, are often infested with the yellow boring sponge, *Cliona celata*.

Scallop Fisheries

The commercial scallop fishery on the Pacific coast is a minor one, consisting of a small drag fishery for weathervane scallops in Oregon and Alaska, and a small dive and drag fishery for spiny and pink scallops—sometimes marketed as "singing scallops" and "swimming scallops." Rock scallops are protected for Native and sports fishermen.

SMOOTH PINK SCALLOP *(Illustration #B-22)*

Species: *Chlamys rubida* (Hinds, 1845).
Alternate names: Reddish scallop, swimming scallop.
Size: To 2¹/₂" (66 mm) height.
Range: 57°N–33°N; Kodiak Island, Alaska south to San Diego, California; not common south of Puget Sound, Washington.
Habitat: On gravel–mud bottoms, at depths of 3–660' (1–200 m).
Description: Circular shell with prominent radial ridges, front ears about 2 times length of hind ears; byssal notch almost triangular. Exterior of upper (left) valve is pink to red-purple, white, or yellow; lower (right) valve is paler. Smooth, prominent radial ribs, about 30 (more than *C. hastata*), with small narrower ribs between and many fine, scaly ribs.
Comments: This species is not as large or abundant as *C. hastata*, but is found mixed in the catches of commercial and sport fishers. The shells are typically encrusted with sponges (see above).

SPINY PINK SCALLOP *(Illustration #B-23)*

Species: *Chlamys hastata* [*hericia*] (Sowerby, 1842).
Alternate names: Pink scallop, Pacific pink scallop, swimming scallop.
Size: To 3¹/₄" (83 mm) height.
Range: 60°N–33°N; Gulf of Alaska south to San Diego, California.
Habitat: On rocky reefs, sometimes in shallow water, 7–500' (2–150 m).
Description: Shells are almost circular; margin broadly fluting or undulating. Byssal notch deep, squarish. Typically encrusted with sponges.
Comments: These scallops can swim when disturbed and when avoiding predators.
Edibility: Spiny scallops are abundant on rocky reefs at 65' (20 m) and more, and are fished commercially by divers and fishers using drags from a small vessel. The scallop is usually steamed open and served whole like a clam, and its meat is very rich. Some people just remove the small single white muscle that holds the shells together—it is delicious fried or baked. Check with the local fisheries department for pollution or PSP closures.

GIANT ROCK SCALLOP *(Illustration #B-24, #S-15)*

Species: *Crassadoma gigantea* (Gray, 1825).
Alternate names: Purple-hinged or giant scallop, *Hinnites giganteus* (Gray, 1825).
Size: To 10" (250 mm) height. It is a toss-up whether this or the weathervane scallop is the largest scallop in the world. Rock scallops have thicker shells and are heavier.
Range: 60°N–27°N; Prince William Sound, Alaska south to Baja California Sur.
Habitat: On rocky bottoms, intertidal in crevices or under boulders, to depths of 265' (80 m).
Description: Thick, irregular round shells often infested with a boring sponge or encrusted with various plants and animals (see above). The shell has ribs, many with spiny projections. Orange mantle bears numerous blue eyes.
Comments: At low tide there is sometimes a sharp clapping noise as the rock scallop suddenly closes its upper valve. The **juvenile rock scallop**, to 1³/4" (45 mm), has orange, sometimes cream and brown exterior (Fig. B-24). It is initially free-swimming, then the lower (right) valve attaches permanently. The juvenile shape and pattern are retained at the umbo but the colours are lost. Scientists believe this species can live as long as 50 years.
Lip plugs and nose rings made from the shell of this species, and dating back 2000 years, have been found in middens in the Northwest Coast area. Aboriginal people also ground burnt shells and used them in preparing white paint, or mixed them with other colours in making masks, face paint, totems and images on canoes.
Edibility: This is one of my favourite seafoods. The large muscle that holds the shells together is delicious fried or baked. But please remember the rock scallop is slow-growing and can live longer than 20 years. An area can quickly be depleted of large scallops. Be aware of bag limits and marine protected areas or marine parks where harvest is prohibited.

WEATHERVANE SCALLOP *(Illustration #B-25)*

Species: *Patinopecten caurinus* (A.A. Gould, 1850).
Alternate names: Giant Pacific scallop, *Pecten caurinus.*
Size: To 11" (280 mm). Often reported as the largest scallop in the world but the rock scallop may be even larger.
Range: 59°N–36°N; Northern Alaskan islands and south to Point Sur, California.
Habitat: In small depressions on sand or gravel, 33–660' (10–200 m).
Description: Shells are almost circular. Left valve reddish-pinkish grey,

about 17 rounded ribs; right valve usually near white with about 24 broad, flattened square ribs.

Comments: The shells are sometimes encrusted with barnacles or jingle oysters. It was a tradition among some coast aboriginal groups to gather the shells of this species after storms washed them ashore, and to make the shells into shaman's rattles and noisemakers for dancers. A hole was cut near the hinge and several shells were threaded on one wooden hoop.

Fisheries: This scallop is abundant in a few locations and some years can support a commercial fishery in Alaska and Oregon. Populations are limited in BC and have not been able to support a commercial fishery.

Edibility: As with other scallops, yum!

JAPANESE WEATHERVANE SCALLOP *(Illustration #B-26)*

Species: *Mizuhopecten yessoensis* (Jay, 1857).
Alternate names: *Patinopecten yessoensis.*
Size: To 9" (220 mm) height.
Range: The first outplants of this species in BC waters occurred in 1985, for aquaculture. No wild sets have been recorded to date.
Habitat: Have been held suspended in the water column in lantern nets. Some experimental bottom culture has been also been attempted in the subtidal zone.
Description: Left (upper) valve has flattened ribs, purple-grey with interior margin dark purple; right valve rounded, white, thick rounded ribs.
Comments: This species was imported after unsuccessful attempts to culture the local weathervane scallop. It is generally harvested at a smaller size, at 2–3 years.

VANCOUVER SCALLOP *(Illustration #B-27)*

Species: *Delectopecten vancouverensis* (Whiteaves, 1893).
Alternate names: Transparent scallop.
Size: To 1/4" (6 mm).
Range: 60°N–28°N; Prince William Sound, Alaska south to Baja California.
Habitat: At 80–1500' (25–450 m) on sand–mud bottoms, usually attached in a nest to large sponges, large crustaceans and other objects.
Description: Delicate shell with long hinge line; exterior with small, irregular, densely crowded radial lines; almost transparent, tinge of yellowish-grey.

Indian clam-digger's canoe and baskets, c. 1912.

Subclass Heterodonta

LUCINE CLAMS Family Lucinidae

These clams are typically circular and compressed. They have short siphons and, as a result, no pallial sinus scars on the interior of the shell. They reside in sand–mud.

WESTERN RINGED LUCINE *(Illustration #B-28)*

Species: *Lucinoma annulatum* (Reeve, 1850).
Size: To 31/4" (82 mm).
Range: 60°N–26°N; Prince William Sound and northern Alaskan islands south to the Gulf of California.
Habitat: Intertidal in sand–mud, to 2500' (750 m).
Description: Shell compressed, dorsal margins flat; evenly spaced, sharp concentric ridges; thin greenish-brown periostracum.

FINE-LINED LUCINE *(Illustration #B-29)*

Species: *Parvalucina tenuisculpta* (Carpenter, 1864).
Alternate names: *Lucina tenuisculpta.*
Size: To 5/8" (15 mm).
Range: 60°N–28°N; Kodiak Island, Alaska south to Isla Cedros, Baja California Norte.
Habitat: Intertidal in sand–mud, to depths of 900' (275 m) and more, sometimes in dense numbers.
Description: Shell is nearly circular, umbones near the middle, slightly inflated. Exterior is chalky white with faint radial ribs, light brown/grey periostracum along lower margin; inner margin has fine teeth.

DIPLODON CLAMS Family Ungulinidae

Members of this family are found in tropical and temperate waters world-wide. They live in sand or gravel, or nestle or build nests of sand under rocks or in crevices.

ROUGH DIPLODON *(Illustration #B-30)*

Species: *Diplodonta impolita* S.S. Berry, 1953.
Alternate names: Round diplodon, orb diplodon. Most texts refer to *Diplodonta orbella* (Gould, 1851), but *D. orbella* is limited to more southern ranges.
Size: To 11/2" (36 mm) length.
Range: 57°N–44°N; Kodiak Island, Alaska south to Oregon.
Habitat: Intertidal to 330' (100 m).
Description: Plump circular shell with central umbones. Exterior polished with thin brown periostracum; interior dull white, no pallial sinus.
Comments: Considered to be less inflated than *D. orbella*.

CLEFTCLAMS Family Thyasiridae

GIANT CLEFTCLAM *(Illustration #B-31)*

Species: *Conchocele bisecta* (Conrad, 1849).
Alternate names: *Thyasira bisecta*.
Size: To 41/2" (110 mm) length.
Range: 57°N–41°N; Bering Sea, Alaska to Humboldt Bay, California.
Habitat: Common subtidal species in mud at 165–1000' (50–300 m).
Description: Anterior truncated; both valves have a rounded posterior with a deep groove; ventral margin curved.

FLEXUOSE CLEFTCLAM *(Illustration #B-32)*

Species: *Thyasira flexuosa* (Montagu, 1803).
Alternate names: Gould's thyasira, cleft clam, *Thyasira gouldii* (Philippi, 1845).
Size: To 1/2" (12 mm).
Range: 71°N–34°N; Circumboreal; Panarctic; Beaufort Sea south to San Pedro, California.
Habitat: In sand–mud, 40–825' (12–250 m).
Description: Shells may vary, resulting in a number of different names assigned to this species. Generally shells are inflated, relatively thick and solid. Both valves have a deep posterior groove, prominent umbones towards the centre. Exterior chalky white with light, worn brown periostracum; interior somewhat glossy with radiating lines.

NORTHERN AXINOPSID *(Illustration #B-33)*

Species: *Axinopsida serricata* (Carpenter, 1864).
Alternate names: Silky axinopsid.
Size: To 3/8" (8 mm).
Range: 60°N–28°N; Circumboreal; Panarctic; Point Barrow, Alaska south to Punta San Pablo, Baja California Sur, and in the Gulf of California.
Habitat: In sand–mud, intertidal zone to 900' (275 m).
Description: Smooth, inflated shell. The prominent beaks overhang the anterior-dorsal margin; neither valve has a groove. Exterior white to pale green; interior hinge has one small tooth in the right valve and a socket in the right.

Family Astartidae

These small but solid clams are important to bottom-feeding fishes. Because of the short siphons there is no pallial sinus scar on the interior of the shell. Several species of *Astarte* can be found in BC waters, most in deeper waters to 165' (50 m).

ELLIPTICAL TRIDONTA *(Illustration #B-34)*

Species: *Astarte elliptica* (Brown, 1827).
Alternate names: Alaska astarte, *Tridonta alaskensis* (Dall, 1903), *Astarte alaskensis.*
Size: To 2" (50 mm).
Range: 71°N–48°N; Circumboreal; arctic Alaska south to Puget Sound, Washington.
Habitat: At depths of 65–825' (20–250 m).
Description: Rounded-triangular shell; broad and regular comarginal ribs; prominent beaks. Exterior covered with yellow to dark brown periostracum that peels off.

ESQUIMALT ASTARTE *(Illustration #B-35)*

Species: *Astarte esquimalti* (Baird, 1863).
Size: To 3/4" (18 mm).
Range: 71°N–48°N; Beaufort Sea, Bering Sea and south to Puget Sound, Washington.
Habitat: At depths of 33–660' (10–200 m); also reported in the intertidal zone in Alaska.
Description: Rounded-triangular shell; the prominent beaks are inclined toward posterior end, which is unusual. Unique fine broken or discontinuous comarginal ridges well separated. Exterior yellow to dark brown.

CARDITA CLAMS Family Carditidae

Small, solid clams that have strong radial ridges and resemble small cockles. Several species are found in BC waters. Most species brood their young.

CARPENTER'S CARDITA *(Illustration #B-36)*

Species: *Glans carpenteri* (Lamy, 1922).
Alternate names: Little heart clam, *Cardita carpenteri*.
Size: To 1/2" (10 mm).
Range: 54°N–28°N; Frederick Island, BC south to Punta Rompiente, Baja California Sur.
Habitat: Nestling or attached to the underside of rocks, intertidal to 330' (100 m).
Description: Subquadrate, length about 1.5 times height; exterior mottled brownish, grey; 14–15 radial ribs. Interior of valves usually purplish.
Comments: This clam broods its young.

LASAEA CLAMS Family Lasaeidae

This family has recently been considered to include the kellyclams, the lasaea clams, the mud shrimp clam (previously *Family Montacutidae*) and the mysella clams.

ADANSON'S LEPTON *(Illustration #B-37)*

Species: *Lasaea adansoni* (Gmelin, 1791).
Alternate names: Red lasaea, *Lasaea subviridis* Dall, 1899, *Lasaea rubra*.
Size: To 1/8" (3 mm).
Range: 55°N–7°S; Sitka, Alaska south to Peru.
Habitat: Attached by byssus to algae, barnacles, *Mytilus californianus* and other mussels; often at extreme high tide but to 33' (10 m).
Description: Exterior grey-white with wavy concentric lines; tinged with purple-red near upper margin and umbones.
Comments: This clam broods its young in the gill chamber. When they are ready, the young crawl out and settle nearby.

KELLYCLAM *(Illustration #B-38)*

Species: *Kellia suborbicularis* (Montagu, 1803).
Alternate names: Suborbiculate kellyclam, considered to include *Kellia laperousi*.
Size: To 1/2" (13 mm).
Range: 60°N–4°S; Circumboreal; Prince William Sound, Alaska to Peru.
Habitat: Intertidal to 65' (20 m), inside empty shells, empty pholad holes

in crevices and among mussels.

Description: Small globular shell; olive green or yellow periostracum sometimes eroded to white shell at the hinge; interior dull white. Unusual siphon arrangement: short inhalant at anterior end, short exhalant siphon at posterior end.

Comments: *Kellia* uses a byssus thread to move, by throwing a new thread ahead of itself and pulling to break the old one. This clam broods its young and releases numerous small clams. It is often found in discarded beer or pop bottles.

NETTED KELLYCLAM *(Illustration #B-39)*

Species: *Rhamphidonta retifera* (Dall, 1899).
Size: To 5/8" (15 mm).
Range: 50°N–34°N; Very local and limited distribution at sites from Esperanza Inlet, Vancouver Island to Santa Rosa Island, California.
Habitat: Intertidal to depths of 80' (25 m).
Description: Elliptical; translucent with fine comarginal lines. Netted appearance is not always obvious, even under magnification.

WRINKLED MONTACUTID *(Illustration #B-40)*

Species: *Neaeromya rugifera* (Carpenter, 1864).
Alternate names: Mud shrimp clam, rough wrinkled lepton. *Neaeromya rugifera, Orobitella rugifera.*
Size: To 2" (50 mm) length.
Range: 50°N–28°N; Kodiak, Alaska to Punta Rompiente, Baja California Sur.
Habitat: Attached by byssus to underside of mud shrimp, *Upogebia pugettensis*, and to the "sea mouse" polychaete, *Aphrodite*. Intertidal to 16' (5 m) depths.
Description: Shell has yellow periostracum, rough irregular concentric lines. Lower (ventral) margin is slightly indented.

ROBUST MYSELLA *(Illustration #B-41)*

Species: *Rochefortia tumida* (Carpenter, 1864).
Alternate names: Fat Pacific lepton, *Mysella tumida*.
Size: To 3/16" (5 mm).
Range: 71°N–33°N; Beaufort Sea south to San Diego, California.
Habitat: Intertidal to 400' (120 m); often commensal with polychaete worms and other burrowing animals in mud and fine sand.
Description: Chalky under a smooth, light brown periostracum. Umbones are close to posterior, and inclined toward posterior end, which is atypical.

Native woman digging for cockles, c. 1912. The stick was used to feel around for the hard shells.

COCKLES Family Cardiidae

Cockles have strong, radiating ribs. One large common cockle is found in the intertidal zone and several less common species are found subtidally. There are several hundred living species of cockles, found worldwide.

NUTTALL'S COCKLE *(Illustration #B-42, #S-7)*

Species: *Clinocardium nuttallii* (Conrad, 1837).
Alternate names: Basket cockle, heart cockle.
Size: To 5 1/2" (140 mm) length.
Range: 60°N–33°N; Southern Bering Sea, Alaska south to San Diego, California.
Habitat: Intertidal to 100' (30 m) depths, in sand–gravel in sheltered waters.
Description: Shell as high or slightly higher than long; 34–38 strong ribs with wavy lines across ribs at the margins. Short siphons show at surface (see illustration #S-7). Yellow-brown colour, young often mottled with russet and brown patterns.
Comments: This cockle exhibits a stunning, leaping escape response to the sunflower star *Pycnopodia* and the pink spiny sea star, *Pisaster brevispinus*. The species can live as long as 16 years. It often hosts pea crabs.

SMOOTH COCKLE *(Illustration #B-43)*

Species: *Clinocardium blandum* (Gould, 1850).
Alternate names: Difficult to distinguish from *C. fucanum*; some authorities consider them to be the same.
Size: To 2" (50 mm).
Range: 54°N–39°N; Southern Bering Sea, Gulf of Alaska south to Sonoma County, California.
Habitat: In subtidal sand–mud at 33–165' (10–50 m).
Description: As many as 45 rounded, closely spaced ribs. More inflated than Aleutian cockle (*C. californiense*).

ALEUTIAN COCKLE *(Illustration #B-44)*

Species: *Clinocardium californiense* (Deshayes, 1839).
Alternate names: California cockle. Here is an example of the problem of using a location as a common name. Over time, it was found that this cockle was a different species from those in California, but although it does not live in California it retains the original name *californiense*.
Size: To 3" (75 mm) height.
Range: 60°N–58°N; Bering Sea and southeast into the Gulf of Alaska. Not found in California.
Habitat: Subtidal, 33–330' (10–100 m).
Description: Shell is longer than high, 45–50 ribs or more; one or more furrows in the posterior-dorsal margin are obvious in larger specimens.

HAIRY COCKLE *(Illustration #B-45)*

Species: *Clinocardium ciliatum* (Fabricius, 1780).
Alternate names: Iceland cockle.
Size: To 2 3/4" (70 mm) length.
Range: 71°N–49°N; Circumboreal; Panarctic; Beaufort Sea, Bering Sea and south to Barkley Sound, Vancouver Island.
Habitat: Found in subtidal mud and sand, 33–500' (10–150 m).
Description: Shell slightly longer than high, with about 40 ribs; exterior whitish, covered with grey, fibrous periostracum with dark concentric bands.

FUCAN COCKLE *(Illustration #B-46)*

Species: *Clinocardium fucanum* (Dall, 1907).
Alternate names: May be the same as *C. blandum*.
Size: To 1 1/2" (40 mm).
Range: 55°N–48°N; Bering Sea south to Puget Sound, Washington.
Habitat: At depths of 65–265' (20–80 m).

Description: Shell slightly longer than high; 45–50 ribs often with distinct concentric lines from rest periods during shell growth.
Comments: Separate species may have been designated on the basis of small specimens gathered from a few sites.

GREENLAND COCKLE *(Illustration #B-47)*

Species: *Serripes groenlandicus* (Mohr, 1786).
Size: To 41/2" (110 mm).
Range: 71°N–48°N; Circumboreal; Panarctic; Point Barrow, Alaska south to Puget Sound, Washington.
Habitat: Intertidal to depths of 265' (80 m).
Description: Shell length greater than height; low radial ribs often worn away in the middle of the shell; posterior end partially truncate. Tan or light green to brown periostracum; interior white to pale yellow.

HUNDRED LINE COCKLE *(Illustration #B-48)*

Species: *Nemocardium centifilosum* (Carpenter, 1864).
Size: To 1" (25 mm).
Range: 59°N–28°N; Southern Bering Sea, Gulf of Alaska south to Punta Rompiente, Baja California Sur.
Habitat: At depths of 7–500' (2–150 m).
Description: Almost round shell, slightly longer than high; posterior quarter with prominent concentric ridges and low radial ribs; exterior white with yellow to brown markings.

HORSE CLAMS – GAPER CLAMS – SURFCLAMS
Family Mactridae

These large, smooth clams are recognized by the chondrophore, a spoon-shaped socket holding the interior ligament in the centre of the hinge.

Horse clams were known traditionally by Native peoples as the "summer-clam," because they were harvested in summer, then cooked and dried (skewered on waxberry stems), and stored in large cedar boxes or baskets to be used for food and trade. Horse clams were also known as "otter shell" or "otter clams" to the sea otter hunters. Shells with the fresh muscles still attached were signs of sea otters feeding in the area (Ellis and Wilson, 1981). The larger empty shells were used as bowls and ladles, and shells of various shapes and sizes were used to measure, dispense and mix potions or medicines.

Horse Clam Fishery
The horse clams or gaper clams, *Tresus* species, are fished commercially by divers in BC and taken by recreational diggers. The surf clam, *Mactromeris*

polynyma, is harvested by drags in Alaska. An Atlantic surf clam, *Spisula soldissima*, is fished commercially on the east coast.

FAT GAPER *(Illustration #B-49, #S-4)*

Species: *Tresus capax* (Gould, 1850).
Alternate names: Horse clam, Alaskan gaper, summer clam, otter clam.
Size: To 7" (180 mm) length.
Range: 55°N–35°N; Cook Inlet, Gulf of Alaska south to Oceano, California.
Habitat: More common at northern latitudes; mud–sand, intertidal to 100' (30 m).
Description: Oval shell, typically 1.5 times the height; lower margin more deeply rounded than Pacific horse clam (*T. nuttallii*).
Comments: When exposed at low tide, the fat horse clam spits jets of water when disturbed. It almost always has a pair of pea crabs (*Pinnixia faba* or *P. littoralis*) in its mantle.
Edibility: This clam was traditionally harvested and dried by Natives. It is taken for sport by digging with a fork in the intertidal zone. Commercial divers harvest this clam using a high-pressure jet of water to loosen the sand so they can pull the clams free (see illustration for geoducks). There is little body meat in this large clam. The neck meat is frozen, but even when it is steamed or blanched, it is difficult to remove the skin from the neck. This clam is best minced and pounded for chowders.

PACIFIC GAPER *(Illustration #B-50, #S-5)*

Species: *Tresus nuttallii* (Conrad, 1837).
Alternate names: Pacific horse clam, summer clam, otter clam.
Size: To 9" (225 mm) length. Whole wet weight to 3 lbs (1.4 kg).
Range: 58°N–25°N; Kodiak Island, Alaska south to southern Baja California Sur.
Habitat: Intertidal to 165' (50 m). Buries deeper (12–36"/30–90 cm) in the sand or is lower on the tide than the fat horse clam (*T. capax*), to avoid freezing. Usually in sandier substrate than *T. capax*.
Description: Large, elongated shell, length 1.5 times the height. The shells gape and are not able to contain the large siphon. Siphon has leather-like plates at the tip.
Comments: Rarely hosts pea crabs.
Edibility: See fat gaper, above. The Pacific gaper often grows larger and is more sought after in the limited commercial fishery.

HOOKED SURFCLAM *(Illustration #B-51)*

Species: *Simomactra falcata* (A. A. Gould, 1850).
Alternate names: *Spisula falcata* (Gould, 1850).
Size: To 31/2" (90 mm) length.
Range: 54°N–31°N; Rose Spit, Queen Charlotte Islands, BC south to Isla San Martin, Baja California Norte.
Habitat: Buried shallow in sand from intertidal to 165' (50 m) depths; often in protected waters.
Description: Shell anterior elongated and narrower than posterior. Thin, shiny, light brown periostracum.

ARCTIC SURFCLAM *(Illustration #B-52)*

Species: *Mactromeris polynyma* (Stimpson, 1860).
Alternate names: Northern clam, Stimpson surfclam, *Spisula polynyma*.
Size: To 51/2" (140 mm) length. To 14 oz (400 g) whole wet weight.
Range: 65°N–46°N; Bering Sea, Alaska south to Neah Bay, Washington.
Habitat: In sand, mud or gravel, intertidal to 365' (110 m).
Description: Thick shell, oval to triangular. Exterior whitish with thin brown periostracum; interior white, spoon-shape depression in hinge of both valves.
Comments: This clam is long-lived, to 25 years and more. It has been harvested commercially by dragging in Alaska.

CALIFORNIA SURFCLAM *(Illustration #B-53)*

Species: *Mactrotoma californica* (Conrad, 1837).
Alternate names: California mactra, *Mactra californica*.
Size: To 2" (48 mm).
Range: There have been reports of *Mactrotoma californica* from BC, but these have not been substantiated. Found 35°N–21°N, from Monterey, California south to Mexico.
Habitat: In sand or sand–mud, intertidal to 50' (15 m).
Description: Oval, thin-shelled; low flattened ridge runs from umbones to narrow, square posterior. Umbones have comarginal undulations. Exterior white with fibrous grey-brown periostracum; interior white.

JACKKNIFE-CLAMS Family Solenidae

SICKLE JACKKNIFE-CLAM *(Illustration #B-54)*

Species: *Solen sicarius* A.A. Gould, 1850.
Alternate names: Blunt razor-clam.
Size: To 5" (125 mm).
Range: 56°N–33°N; Queen Charlotte Islands, BC south to Baja California Norte.
Habitat: Buried in sand–mud in more sheltered habitats than the Pacific razor-clam (*Siliqua patula*); sometimes eelgrass; intertidal to 130' (40 m).
Description: Elongated, slightly curved but almost rectangular; anterior end blunt. Smooth, shiny periostracum: greenish-yellow to brown (sometimes worn down to the white shell). Siphons joined; shows can be confused with other juvenile clams. Forms a permanent vertical burrow.
Comments: This species often hosts pea crabs.

RAZOR-CLAMS Family Pharidae

PACIFIC RAZOR-CLAM *(Illustration #B-55, #S-11)*

Species: *Siliqua patula* (Dixon, 1789).
Alternate names: Northern razor-clam.
Size: To 7" (180 mm) length.
Range: 59°N–35°N; Cook Inlet, Gulf of Alaska south to Morro Bay, California.
Habitat: On surf-exposed beaches; usually intertidal but to depths of 180' (55 m). See illustration #S-11 for hints on detecting these clams by siphon shows. Abundant in many locations along the Washington and Oregon coast. The four major beaches in Washington are Long Beach, Twin Harbours, Copalis and Mocrocks, comprising over 50 miles (80 km) of digging area.
Description: Thin, brittle, long and narrow shells, rounded at the anterior end, slightly truncated at the posterior. Shiny, smooth olive to brown periostracum. Short, white siphons, fused except at the tips. Interior white with purple; has a rib slanting to the anterior end.
Comments: This species often hosts pea crabs. The razor-clam's strong muscular foot, and the smooth, streamlined shell, allow it to burrow rapidly to depths of 24" (60 cm) within a minute.
Edibility: The meat is cleaned from the shell and fried—mmmm! The razor-clam supports Native, commercial and sports fisheries, but many landed in BC are used for crab bait. Some beaches in Washington have been closed for conservation reasons and also because of naturally occurring toxins. Check with the local fisheries office before harvesting.

TELLIN and MACOMA CLAMS Family Tellinidae

This family is known worldwide for its colourful clams. Many of the species are abundant in the intertidal zone and shallow waters, and their distribution extends to deeper waters (660'/200 m). The shells often have a twist at the posterior end. The pallial line and pallial sinus are key characters of the Macoma clams, but are difficult to show in photographs.

BODEGA TELLIN *(Illustration #B-56)*

Species: *Tellina bodegensis* Hinds, 1845.
Alternate names: *Tellina (Peronidia) bodegensis.*
Size: To 21/2" (60 mm).
Range: 57°N–25°N; Sitka, Alaska south to Bahia Magdalena, Baja California Sur.
Habitat: On beaches exposed or partially exposed to open ocean; intertidal to 300' (100 m).
Description: Elongated white shell, smooth with fine concentric lines on exterior; rounded anterior, posterior pointed and bent slightly to the right. Interior often has yellow-orange blush.

CARPENTER'S TELLIN *(Illustration #B-57)*

Species: *Tellina carpenteri* Dall, 1900.
Size: To 1" (25 mm).
Range: 57°N–7°N; Sitka, Alaska south to Panama.
Habitat: In sand or sand–mud intertidal to 1450' (440 m).
Description: Thin, elongated shell, almost oblong. Exterior greyish-white to dark pink; fine concentric grooves near lower margin and front end. Interior white, sometimes blushed with pink or yellow.

PLAIN TELLIN *(Illustration #B-58)*

Species: *Tellina modesta* (Carpenter, 1864).
Alternate names: Modest tellin, button tellin.
Size: To 1" (25 mm).
Range: 59°N–28°N; Cook Inlet, Alaska south to Baja California Sur.
Habitat: In sand, intertidal to 165' (50 m).
Description: Oval, flattened shell; exterior white, shiny with fine, regular concentric grooves in the front two-thirds, hind end smooth; interior shiny. Both shells with a thickened rib from the umbone, between anterior adductor muscle and pallial sinus.

SALMON TELLIN *(Illustration #B-59)*

Species: *Tellina nuculoides* (Reeve, 1854).
Alternate names: *T. salmonea.*
Size: To 3/4" (20 mm).
Range: 60°N–32°N; Bering Sea, Cook Inlet south to Baja California Sur.
Habitat: In sand, intertidal to 330' (100 m).
Description: Small, solid shell, subtrigonal with both ends rounded; exterior polished yellow or white with growth checks coloured reddish-brown or dark greyish-purple; interior white to salmon colour.
Comments: This species leaves tracks in the sand as it moves just below the surface.

Macoma clams

There are numerous species of *Macoma*, most found in the intertidal zone. The most common and abundant are Baltic Macoma (*M. balthica*), stained (polluted, fouled) Macoma (*M. inquinata*), bent-nose clam (*M. nasuta*) and white sand clam (*M. secta*). Less common intertidal species of *Macoma* are chalky Macoma (*M. calcarea*), expanded Macoma (*M. expansa*), Aleutian Macoma (*M. lama*), flat (doleful) Macoma (*M. moesta*), oblique Macoma (*M. obliqua*) and yoldia shape Macoma (*M. yoldiformis*). Subtidal Macoma species in BC include the Pacific brota (*M. brota*), Charlotte Macoma (*M. carlottensis*), file Macoma (*M. elimata*) and large Pacific Macoma (*M. lipara* or, according to some authorities, *M. brota*).

BALTIC MACOMA *(Illustration #B-60)*

Species: *Macoma balthica* (Linnaeus, 1758).
Alternate names: *M. inconspicua.*
Size: To 11/2" (38 mm) length.
Range: 70°N–38°N; Circumboreal; Panarctic; Beaufort Sea to San Francisco Bay, California.
Habitat: Often abundant, buried shallow to 8" (20 cm) in sand–mud, intertidal to 130' (40 m), usually in bays and estuaries.
Description: Small, oval shells of varying colour: pink, blue, yellow or orange.
Comments: This small, colourful clam is commonly encountered on sand beaches. It is believed that many populations in the southern range were introduced from the Atlantic. The Baltic Macoma is too small to eat.

POINTED MACOMA *(Illustration #B-61)*

Species: *Macoma inquinata* (Deshayes, 1855).
Alternate names: Polluted Macoma, fouled Macoma.
Size: To 2¹/2" (63 mm) length.
Range: 57°N–34°N; Pribilof Islands, Bering Sea south to Santa Barbara, California.
Habitat: In sand–mud, intertidal to 165' (50 m) depths in bays and offshore.
Description: Posterior of shell is wedge-shaped with slight distinctive indentation. Exterior cream with concentric striations; marginal brown periostracum. External ligament large and prominent. Hind end rounder than *M. nasuta*. Internal pallial line and pallial sinus joined at muscle scar.
Comments: This species often hosts pea crabs.

BENT-NOSE MACOMA *(Illustration #B-62)*

Species: *Macoma nasuta* (Conrad, 1837).
Size: To 3" (75 mm) length.
Range: 60°N–22°N; Cook Inlet, Alaska south to southern Baja California Sur, reports to Cabo San Lucas.
Habitat: Buried 4–6" (10–15 cm) beneath the surface, common in intertidal sand to depths of 165' (50 m).
Description: Thin, white shells; valves bend sharply to the right, near the pointed posterior end. Separate orange-coloured siphons collect detritus off the surface of the sea bed.
Comments: This clam is often drilled and eaten by the moonsnail. The empty shell can be found on the surface with a perfect small hole in it, usually near the hinge. This species often hosts pea crabs.

WHITE-SAND MACOMA *(Illustration #B-63)*

Species: *Macoma secta* (Conrad, 1837).
Size: To 4" (100 mm) length.
Range: 54°N–25°N; Queen Charlotte Islands, BC south to Baja California Sur.
Habitat: Buried to 8–18" (20–45 cm) in sand, intertidal to depths of 165' (50 m) in sheltered waters.
Description: Thin, white shell; ridge from umbo to posterior ventral margin. Separate white siphons.
Comments: This species often hosts pea crabs.

HEAVY MACOMA *(Illustration #B-64)*

Species: *Macoma brota* Dall, 1916.
Alternate names: Pacific brota.
Size: To 3" (75 mm) length.
Range: 71°N–48°N; Circumboreal; Arctic to Bering Sea and south to Puget Sound, Washington.
Habitat: Found in subtidal sand–mud at depths of 33–850' (10–260 m).
Description: Large solid shell, moderately inflated; posterior is squared off with a slight flex. Exterior smooth white, yellow to orange satin; interior white.

CHALKY MACOMA *(Illustration #B-65)*

Species: *Macoma calcarea* (Gmelin, 1791).
Size: To 2¹/₂" (60 mm).
Range: 71°N–47°N; Circumboreal; Arctic to Bering Sea and south to Newport, Oregon.
Habitat: In sand, silt and gravel, intertidal to 1050' (320 m).
Description: Subovate shell; posterior end slightly pointed and flexed to the right. Exterior chalky with dark, grey, peeling periostracum at margin.

CHARLOTTE MACOMA *(Illustration #B-66)*

Species: *Macoma carlottensis* Whiteaves, 1880.
Size: To 1" (25 mm).
Range: 52°N–32°N; Gulf of Alaska south to Isla Los Coronados, Baja California Norte, and in the central Gulf of California.
Habitat: To depths of 16–5100' (5–1547 m).
Description: Elongated shell, beaks at centre. Exterior glossy with thin periostracum that may be greenish; interior glossy.

FILE MACOMA *(Illustration #B-67)*

Species: *Macoma elimata* Dunhill & Coan, 1968.
Size: To 1¹/₂" (35 mm).
Range: 55°N–34°N; Aleutian Islands, Alaska south to Redondo Beach, California.
Habitat: In sand and silt, subtidal 30–1435' (9–435 m).
Description: Subovate shell; rounded anterior, blunt posterior section. Ligament deep in the escutcheon.

EXPANDED MACOMA *(Illustration #B-68)*

Species: *Macoma expansa* Carpenter, 1864.
Size: To 2" (50 mm).
Range: 60°N–28°N; Aleutian Islands, Alaska to Oceano, California.
Habitat: In sand, exposed habitats, intertidal to 100' (30 m).
Description: Oval shell; anterior end slightly shorter than posterior. Exterior glazed, often with yellow-tinted periostracum.

ALEUTIAN MACOMA *(Illustration #B-69)*

Species: *Macoma lama* Bartsch, 1929.
Size: To 13/4" (45 mm).
Range: 71°N–53°N; Arctic, Bering Sea south to Queen Charlotte Islands, BC, and possibly farther south.
Habitat: In clean sand along exposed coasts, intertidal to 600' (183 m).
Description: Pointed, slightly twisted posterior end. Exterior periostracum glossy and adherent.
Comments: This species is heavier than the flat Macoma (*M. moesta*), and the shell is more pointed at the siphon (posterior) end.

SLEEK MACOMA *(Illustration #B-70)*

Species: *Macoma lipara* Dall, 1916.
Size: To 3" (75 mm). One of the largest *Macoma* and generally larger and more oval than *M. brota*.
Range: 65°N–34°N; Northern Bering Sea south to Redondo Submarine Canyon, California.
Habitat: At depths of 65–850' (20–260 m).
Description: Large, oval solid shell; exterior shiny, white to straw yellow; periostracum olive-green to grey, eroded.

FLAT MACOMA *(Illustration #B-71)*

Species: *Macoma moesta* (Deshayes, 1855).
Size: To 11/4" (30 mm) length.
Range: 71°N–43°N; Arctic to Bering Sea and south to off Coos Bay, Oregon.
Habitat: In silt and a variety of bottom types; intertidal to 1000' (300 m).
Description: Elongated oval shell; thin and polished periostracum. Pallial sinus deep in left valve, moderate in right.
Comments: Two subspecies have been described. The southern subspecies, Alaska–Oregon, has a less rounded posterior end than specimens from farther north.

OBLIQUE MACOMA *(Illustration #B-72)*

Species: *Macoma obliqua* (Sowerby, 1817).
Size: To 1–2" (25–50 mm).
Range: 71°N–47°N; Point Barrow, Alaska south to Puget Sound, Washington.
Habitat: In gravel or sand, intertidal to 660' (200 m).
Description: Rounded shell, slightly squared at lower posterior. Exterior dull-chalky, periostracum at margin.

YOLDIA SHAPE MACOMA *(Illustration #B-73)*

Species: *Macoma yoldiformis* Carpenter, 1864.
Size: To 1" (25 mm).
Range: 57°N–28°N; Sitka, Alaska south to Baja California Sur.
Habitat: In sand and silt, intertidal to 80' (25 m), protected waters.
Description: Elongated shell with pointed posterior end; white, shiny, adherent periostracum.

SEMELE CLAMS
Family Semelidae (includes Scrobiculariidae)

Many members of this family are known for their brightly coloured shells. Most species are tropical, but a few are found in colder waters.

ROSE-PAINTED CLAM *(Illustration #B-74)*

Species: *Semele rubropicta* Dall, 1871.
Alternate names: Rose petal Semele.
Size: To 2" (50 mm length).
Range: 60°N–28°N; Kenai Peninsula, northern Gulf of Alaska south to Baja California Sur, and in the Gulf of California.
Habitat: In gravel, intertidal to 330' (100 m).
Description: Oval shell with pink rays similar to sunset shell (see below). Thin, dark to tan periostracum sometimes in patches over the shell, most along the ventral edge. Interior has deep, broad pallial sinus.

SUNSETCLAMS Family Psammobiidae (=Garidae)

CALIFORNIA SUNSETCLAM *(Illustration #B-75)*

Species: *Gari californica* (Conrad, 1849).
Size: To 6" (149 mm).
Range: 60°N–25°N; Northern Gulf of Alaska to Baja California Sur.
Habitat: Buried 6–8" (5–20 cm) in gravel, intertidal to 560' (170 m).

Description: Large, smooth, elongated shells, rounded at both ends. Yellowish-white, often with pink rays; concentric sculpture. Thin, brown periostracum, usually at edges; separate siphons.
Comments: This species often hosts pea crabs.

DARK MAHOGANY-CLAM *(Illustration #B-76)*

Species: *Nuttallia obscurata* (Reeve, 1857).
Alternate names: Varnish clam.
Size: To 2 1/4" (55 mm).
Range: Strait of Georgia, BC. Originally from Japan, introduced to BC in 1980s–1990s.
Habitat: Buried to 8" (20 cm) in sand–gravel in the high- to mid-intertidal zone, often in areas of freshwater seepage.
Description: Thin, flat, oval shells; shiny brown periostracum, worn white at the hinge; interior purple; long separate siphons.
Comments: This clam has spread quickly in the protected waters of the Strait of Georgia. The species often hosts pea crabs.

VENUS CLAMS – HARDSHELL–STEAMER CLAMS
Family Veneridae

Hardshell butter and steamer clams (manila and littleneck clams) all occur intertidally in BC, but some subtidal stocks have been found and exploited in Washington. Extensive sport and commercial fisheries for these clams have been developed.

Figure 4 illustrates the key identifying characteristics of common and abundant hardshell clams taken in the fisheries. **It is very important to be able to separate butter clams from other species, because of their tendency to accumulate and retain PSP toxins.** Often an area is closed to the harvest of butter clams only, while the harvest of other species is allowed.

The littleneck and particularly the manila clam may vary in colour and in patterns of markings. Butter, littleneck and manila clams can be distinguished in four ways:

All three species can withdraw their siphons into the shell. The butter clam gapes slightly at the posterior end.

Butter clams have only concentric sculpture; they grow to larger sizes; they have fused white siphons with black tips; they gape at the posterior end.

Littleneck and manila clams both have lattice sculpture; the manila has a stronger radial sculpture at the posterior end.

The siphon tip of a manila clams is split; on littlenecks the tip is fused.

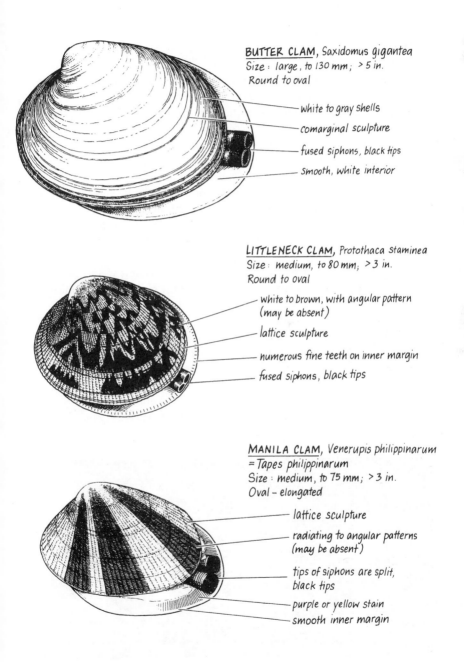

BUTTER CLAM, Saxidomus gigantea
Size : large , to 130 mm ; > 5 in.
Round to oval

— white to gray shells
— comarginal sculpture
— fused siphons, black tips
— smooth, white interior

LITTLENECK CLAM, Protothaca staminea
Size : medium, to 80 mm ; > 3 in.
Round to oval

— white to brown, with angular pattern
(may be absent)
— lattice sculpture
— numerous fine teeth on inner margin
— fused siphons, black tips

MANILA CLAM, Venerupis philippinarum
= Tapes philippinarum
Size : medium, to 75 mm ; > 3 in.
Oval - elongated

— lattice sculpture
— radiating to angular patterns
(may be absent)
— tips of siphons are split,
black tips
— purple or yellow stain
— smooth inner margin

*Figure 4: Comparative Features of Butter, Littleneck and
Manila (Japanese Littleneck) Clams*

BUTTER CLAM *(Illustration #B-77, #S-12)*

Species: *Saxidomus gigantea* (Deshayes, 1839).
Alternate names: Smooth Washington clam, *Saxidomus giganteus.*
Size: To 51/4" (130 mm) length.
Range: 60°N–37°N; Southeast Bering Sea, Alaska south to central California; rarely to southern California.
Habitat: Buried to 12" (30 cm) in the mid- to lower intertidal zone, to depths of 130' (40 m).
Description: Large oval to square shells only have comarginal lines or grooves. Typically white to grey; shells gape at posterior end. Interior smooth but not glossy; large, deeply marked muscle scars.
Comments: This clam forms abundant populations at the lower region of the intertidal zone. It grows to the BC minimum legal size of 21/2" (63 mm) in 4–5 years in southern areas, and in 8–9 years in northern areas. It can live 20 years or longer. Butter clams are typically harvested with a fork.
Some coast aboriginal groups used the white shells of this species in salmon traps, because a layer of white shell on the river bottom enabled fishers to see and spear their quarry more easily.
This species often hosts pea crabs.
Edibility: This clam is considered the very best chowder clam. All of the meat is edible, but **make sure to remove the black tips of the siphons where PSP toxin can accumulate**. The butter clam has long supported Native, recreational and commercial fisheries. Many canneries along the coast processed this species from the turn of the century to the 1950s. Peak commercial landings in BC occurred in 1938, when 2919 metric tonnes (nearly 6.5 million pounds) were reported.

Clam can label used at the Bag Harbour Cannery, Queen Charlotte Islands (see page 129). Courtesy Royal BC Museum.

JAPANESE LITTLENECK *(Illustration #B-78)*

Species: *Venerupis philippinarum* (A. Adams & Reeve, 1850).
Alternate names: Manila clam. The scientific Latin name has changed frequently. It has been included as *Venerupis, Tapes, Protothaca* and *Ruditapes*; and most recently named as *Tapes philippinarum* (A. Adams & Reeve, 1850); *Tapes japonica.*
Size: To 3" (75 mm) length.
Range: 54°N–37°N; Central northern coast of BC and south to Elkhorn Slough, California.
Habitat: In a variety of substrates from sand to mud to gravel. They have short siphons and are buried to only 4" (10 cm), high in the intertidal zone.
Description: Oval elongated shells have latticed sculpture with strong radial ribs; ribs stronger at posterior end. External colour variable: greys, browns, often with streaked patterns and occasionally angular pattern similar to native littleneck. Siphon tip is split. Interior often has purple or yellow coloration; inside edge of the shell is smooth to the touch.
Comments: The manila clam, first recorded in BC in 1936, was introduced to the Pacific coast of North America when it was inadvertently imported from Japan with Pacific oyster seed. The clams have since spawned and established wild populations. Because they live so high in the intertidal zone, they are not frequently attacked or drilled by moon snails (*Polinices lewisii*). This species can live as long as 14 years. It hosts pea crabs.
Edibility: This clam has been the main target species of the intertidal clam fishery in BC in the 1980s and 1990s. In fact it is the only clam that BC and Washington have developed extensively in recent years. It is ideal for the fresh steamer clam market: it stays fresh a long time after harvest and opens quickly when steamed. Some argue it is sweeter than the native littleneck. Manila clams are harvested with rakes, sometimes with long tines for gravel or rocky areas. Make sure to check with local fisheries offices for red tide and pollution closures before harvesting.

Geoduck clam harvesting at Sidney Island, off Victoria, 1940s.

PACIFIC LITTLENECK *(Illustration #B-79)*

Species: *Protothaca staminea* (Conrad, 1837).
Alternate names: Rock cockle, native littleneck.
Size: To 3" (75 mm) length.
Range: 54°N–23°N; Aleutian Islands, Alaska south to Baja California Sur.
Habitat: Buried to 4" (10 cm) or more in gravel, and in sand–mud bottoms in the mid-intertidal zone to 33' (10 m).
Description: Round to oval inflated shells; white to brown shell, sometimes with dark, angular patterns; latticed sculpture. Interior margin of shell has numerous fine teeth visible to the eye and easily felt. Short, fused siphons; external hinge ligament.
Comments: This species can live as long as 14 years. Shells that have been "drilled" by moon snails are often found. Some native littleneck specimens found in empty pholad holes, clay or shale have raised concentric ridges. They sometimes harbour small pea crabs and, on rare occasions, form small pearls.
Edibility: This is a fast-growing clam, often reaching a legal commercial fishery size of 11/2" (38 mm) in 3–4 years. It can live for 8–14 years. It is harvested as a steamer and for chowder-making. Littlenecks have been canned, but they are not as abundant as manila or butter clams and commercial landings have never reached the levels of other species. This clam does not live as long out of water as the manila and does not always open when steamed, making it less desirable in the commercial market.

MILKY VENUS *(Illustration #B-80)*

Species: *Compsomyax subdiaphana* (Carpenter, 1864).
Alternate names: Deep water littleneck.
Size: To 31/2" (85 mm) length.
Range: 59°N–30°N; Cook Inlet and northern Gulf of Alaska, south to Baja California Norte, and in the Gulf of California.
Habitat: Subtidal; 7–1800' (2–550 m), often in soft mud.
Description: Plump, thin shell with fine concentric lines; very light shiny periostracum.
Comments: There has been some commercial interest and small landings of this clam, which can be harvested using a towed dredge. It is very unusual in that it has coloured gonads. The male gonad is white and the female gonad red.

THIN-SHELL LITTLENECK *(Illustration #B-81)*

Species: *Protothaca tenerrima* (Carpenter, 1857).
Size: To 41/2" (110 mm).
Range: 50°N–28°N; Kyuquot Sound, Vancouver Island, BC and south to

Baja California Sur.
Habitat: Intertidal and subtidal to 33' (10 m), in gravel and sand.
Description: Large, thin to thick grey-white shells; fine latticed sculpture with stronger concentric lines. Interior margin of shell is smooth; no posterior gape.
Comments: This clam is sometimes dug and eaten by sea otters.

RIBBED CLAM *(Illustration #B-82)*

Species: *Humilaria kennerleyi* (Reeve, 1863).
Size: To 4" (100 mm) length.
Range: 60°N–34°N; Cook Inlet, Prince William Sound, south to Santa Rosa Island, California.
Habitat: In sand and gravel, intertidal to 150' (45 m). Common but not abundant.
Description: Thick shell with strong erect concentric ridges; inner margin of the shell finely notched.

LORD DWARF-VENUS *(Illustration #B-83)*

Species: *Nutricola lordi* (W. Baird, 1863).
Alternate names: Lord pebble shell. *Psephidia lordi.*
Size: To 1/2" (10 mm) length.
Range: 59°N–26°N; Bering Sea, Gulf of Alaska and south to Baja California Sur.
Habitat: In sand and mud, often in the roots of eelgrass, intertidal to 230' (70 m).
Description: Inflated thick shell, oval to triangular with rounded corners. Exterior glossy, smooth, yellowish with concentric growth lines.
Comments: The Latin *nutricola* means "little nurse." As in many small clams, the female broods young in the mantle.

PURPLE DWARF-VENUS *(Illustration #B-84)*

Species: *Nutricola tantilla* (A.A. Gould, 1853).
Alternate names: Little transennella, *Transennella tantilla.*
Size: To 1/4" (6 mm).
Range: 61°N–28°N; Prince William Sound, Alaska south to Isla Cedros, Baja California Norte.
Habitat: On sand–mud bottoms, often found among the roots of eelgrass; intertidal to 400' (120 m).
Description: Oval to elongated shell; posterior end bent. Exterior shiny white or yellow, purplish blotch on posterior end; low concentric ridges.
Comments: This species carries a brood of 30–40 all year, and releases the juveniles in the summer months.

PETRICOLA CLAMS Family Petricolidae

The members of this small family are nestlers or borers. As they grow larger they wear away the walls of the burrow by opening and closing the valves. Most species have radial sculpture.

HEARTY PETRICOLID *(Illustration #B-85, #S-17)*

Species: *Petricola carditoides* (Conrad, 1837).
Alternate names: Heart rock dweller.
Size: To 21/4" (55 mm) length.
Range: 57°N–26°N; Sitka, Alaska south to Baja California Sur.
Habitat: Nestling in empty pholad holes and crevices; low intertidal zone to 165' (50 m).
Description: Plump, generally oblong shell. Exterior white and chalky, concentric growth checks, fine radials may be eroded; interior white, continuous pallial line. Young stages attach by byssus, adults free. Partly fused siphons tipped with bright purple.
Comments: This clam secretes quantities of mucous.

Family Turtoniidae

LITTLE MULLET SHELL *(Illustration #B-86)*

Species: *Turtonia minuta* (Fabricius, 1780).
Alternate names: Minute turton.
Size: To 1/16" (2 mm).
Range: 60°N–49°N; Circumboreal; Bering Sea and south to Barkley Sound, Vancouver Island, BC.
Habitat: Intertidal, attached by byssus to coralline and other algae, sessile animals and rocks.
Description: Exterior glossy brown with purple or rose blotch at umbones.
Comments: This is the only species of the Family Turtoniidae that has been found.

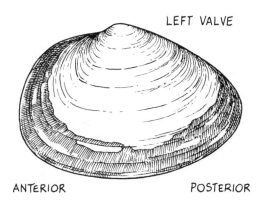

LEFT VALVE

ANTERIOR   POSTERIOR

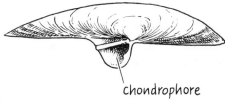

*Figure 5: Softshell-clam
Shell Features (Chondrophore)*

chondrophore

Subclass Asthenodonta

SOFTSHELL CLAMS Family Myidae

SOFTSHELL-CLAM *(Illustration #B-87)*

Species: *Mya arenaria* Linnaeus, 1758.
Alternate names: Mud clam.
Size: To 4" (100 mm).
Range: 70°N–37°N; Icy Cape, Alaska south to Elkhorn Slough, California.
Habitat: Intertidal, usually buried 4–8" (10–20 cm) below the surface in sand–mud, often in estuarine conditions.
Description: Thin, brittle, elongated shell; large spoon-shaped chondrophore at hinge of left valve. White to grey exterior, brown or yellow-orange periostracum obvious at edges of shell. Dark siphons.
Comments: This shell is not found in Native middens of the Northwest Coast. Evidence shows that it may have been introduced from the Atlantic coast in the late 1800s. The species hosts pea crabs.

TRUNCATED SOFTSHELL-CLAM *(Illustration #B-88, #S-3)*

Species: *Mya truncata* Linnaeus, 1758.
Alternate names: Blunt gaper.
Size: To 31/4" (80 mm) length.
Range: 71°N–47°N; Circumboreal; Panarctic; Beaufort Sea, Bering Sea and south to Neah Bay, Washington.
Habitat: Intertidal to 330' (100 m), in mud and sand of protected bays.
Description: Posterior abruptly truncated, flared and gaping; yellow-brown periostracum, thick at the edges; small, fused and wrinkled siphons exposed at the surface. Body of clam is buried a few cm in the substrate.
Comments: The shows and the clam can be confused with juvenile geoduck (see page 47).

BORING SOFTSHELL-CLAM *(Illustration #B-89, #S-18)*

Species: *Platyodon cancellatus* (Conrad, 1837).
Alternate names: Checked softshell-clam, checked borer, clay boring clam, chubby mya.
Size: To 3" (75 mm).
Range: 54°N–28°N; Tlell, Queen Charlotte Islands, BC and south to Isla Cedros, Baja California Sur.
Habitat: Burrowing in soft clay or rock, intertidal to 65' (20 m). Unlike most burrowing bivalves, this clam makes an elongated burrow, like the shape of its shell, rather than a round burrow.
Description: Rectangular shell, rounded posterior. Exterior with thin yellow-brown periostracum, fine concentric sculpture; interior white; left valve with a strong chondrophore. The siphons have 2 pointed pads.
Comments: This clam is believed to have been harvested occasionally for food by the Haida. They used stick wedges to break off chunks of clay to gather the clams.

CALIFORNIA SOFTSHELL-CLAM *(Illustration #B-90)*

Species: *Cryptomya californica* (Conrad, 1837).
Alternate names: Glass mya, false mya.
Size: To 11/16" (28 mm) length.
Range: 59°N–6°S; Gulf of Alaska south to Peru.
Habitat: Burrows in intertidal mud–sand, often in estuaries, and at depths to 265' (80 m). Sometimes found deep in the substrate (20"/50 cm or more) with its short (1/32"/1 mm) siphons, feeding from the burrows of the burrowing shrimps *Callianassa* and *Upogebia* and the echiurid worm, *Urechis capo*.

Description: Compressed, elliptical shell. Exterior white with fine concentric growth lines and faint radial lines on the posterior end; thin brown periostracum is fibrous at the hind end; interior white, chondrophore in left valve.

Comments: This clam broods its young. The commensal relationship with the burrowing shrimp and others allows this species, which has short siphons, to be buried deeper in the substrate where it is less vulnerable to predators. The clam feeds from the water or on food particles brought into the burrow by its host.

GIANT CLAMS – GEODUCKS – NESTLING CLAMS
Family Hiatellidae

These clams all gape; they cannot completely retract into the shell. Geoducks and false geoducks are buried deep in the substrate, to 30 cm or more. The smaller clams nestle in rock burrows or kelp holdfasts.

PACIFIC GEODUCK *(Illustration #B-91, #S-91)*

Species: *Panopea abrupta* (Conrad, 1849).
Alternate names: Geoduc, king clam, *Panope generosa.*
Size: To 7³/4" (195 mm) length.
Range: 58°N–34°N; Kodiak Island, Alaska south to Newport Bay, California.
Habitat: Buried in a variety of substrates from mud to sand to gravel, intertidal to 330' (100 m) or more.
Description: Shells are rounded anteriorly, truncated at siphon end, gaping at all sides due to large body and neck. Siphons and neck cannot be withdrawn into shell (see page 47). Exterior white; thin patches of periostracum at edges. Both shells have a cardinal tooth at the hinge, which may be broken off if torn apart by a sea otter. Interior white, with continuous pallial line (unlike false geoducks).
Comments: This is the largest intertidal clam in the world, weighing up to 10 lbs (4.5 kg). It is also among the oldest animals in the world with reported lifespans up to 146 years.
Edibility: Occasionally this clam has been harvested for food by Natives and recreational harvesters. It is found only at the lowest tides of the year, and its body is buried in the substrate to a depth of 1 metre, making it a challenge to capture. Geoducks support an important subtidal commercial fishery in Alaska, BC and Washington. Divers locate the clams by finding the siphons, and harvest each clam by loosening the substrate with a high pressure water jet.

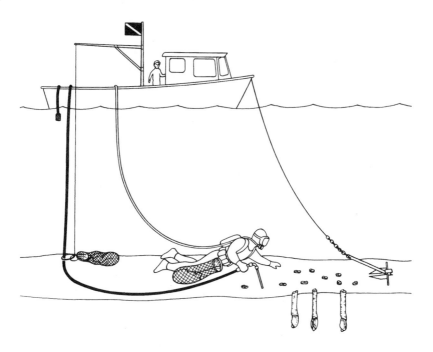

Figure 6: Technique of Commercial Geoduck Harvest

False Geoducks—Roughmya Clams

There are several species of what I have called "false geoducks" (*Panomya*) described from BC waters. Properly called "roughmya" clams, they are *P. ampla* (northern), *P. arctica* (intertidal), *P. berigiana* (deep water) and *P. chrysis* (shallow subtidal). Because *Panomya* are buried to 6" (15 cm) and more in the substrate, specimens are not commonly collected other than by geoduck harvesters. The divers often misidentify *Panoma* as juvenile geoducks (*Panopa*).

The taxonomy of the false geoducks, *Panomya*, is not consistent because of the variability of the shell shape. Few specimens are taken because they are buried so deep in the substrate. Kozloff (1987) lists two common species, *P. beringiana* (shell length to 23/4"/70 cm) and *P. chrysis* (shell length to 3"/75 mm). Bernard (1983) and Foster (1991) list an additional species in our waters, *P. ampla*.

The occurrence of *Panomya* in shallow subtidal waters in southern BC increases the ranges listed in Bernard's publication of 1983.

AMPLE ROUGHMYA *(Illustration #B-92, #S-2)*

Species: *Panomya ampla* Dall, 1898.
Alternate names: False geoduck, considered to include *P. chrysis.*
Size: To 2³/4" (70 mm).
Range: 71°N–47°N; Point Barrow, Alaska south to Puget Sound, Washington.
Habitat: Body is buried to 6" (15 cm) or more below surface of substratum, mud–sand to gravel.
Description: Hinge plate of both valves has small single tooth; square posterior and rounded anterior; 2 ridges radiating from the umbo; discontinuous pallial line; light brown to black periostracum covers much of the shell. Siphons are thick and fused (see page 59) and are sometimes mistaken for geoduck shows.

ARCTIC ROUGHMYA *(Illustration #B-93)*

Species: *Panomya norvegica* (Spengler, 1793).
Alternate names: Deepwater false geoduck, *P. arctica* (Lamarck, 1818).
Size: To 4¹/2" (110 mm).
Range: 71°N–45°N; Point Barrow, Alaska south to Tillamook, Oregon and occasionally Goleta, California.
Habitat: Has been found in mud, closer to the surface of the substrate, in Trincomali Channel and other locations in the Gulf Islands of BC.
Description: Shell quadrate but sometimes distorted; short, stubby black siphon.

Nestling Saxicaves
Due to variations in the shells, experts disagree on the taxonomy of the nestling saxicaves, *Hiatella* species. Some consider *Hiatella arctica* and *H. pholadis* to be the same species. Others (Foster, 1991; Bernard, 1983) consider them separate, *H. pholadis* being larger.

ARCTIC HIATELLA *(Illustration #B-94)*

Species: *Hiatella arctica* (Linnaeus, 1767).
Size: To 1¹/4" (33 mm).
Range: 71°N–10°N; Point Barrow, Alaska and south to Chile; considered to be found throughout the world.
Habitat: In algal holdfasts, mussel mats and burrows of other rock boring bivalves, attached by byssus; intertidal to 2650' (800 m).
Description: Elongated shells gape slightly; tips of siphons are bright red-orange.

NESTLING SAXICAVE *(Illustration #B-95, S-17)*

Species: *Hiatella pholadis* (Linnaeus, 1771).
Size: To 2" (50 mm).
Range: 68°N–48°N; Bering Sea and south to Puget Sound, Washington.
Habitat: In burrows of pholads (piddocks), mussel beds and kelp hold-fasts; intertidal to 33' (10 m).
Description: Irregular, elongated shell with smooth, sometimes slightly wrinkled exterior. Interior smooth, chalky with interrupted pallial line; tips of siphons are red-orange.

BORING CLAMS – PIDDOCKS Family Pholadidae

These medium to large clams gape at both ends and cannot retract com-pletely into the shell. All species burrow, some in very hard substrate such as limestone or hard clay. The shells have a conspicuous internal "myophore," a spoon-like projection reaching below the hinge. The exterior of the shell is divided by different patterns of sculpturing.

ROUGH PIDDOCK *(Illustration #B-96, #S-6)*

Species: *Zirfaea pisbryii* Lowe, 1931.
Alternate names: Pilsbry's piddock.
Size: To 53/4" (145 mm) length.
Range: 70°N–25°N; Arctic coast of Alaska south to Baja California Sur.
Habitat: Buried to 20" (50 cm), intertidal in limestone, shale or hard clay; sand, mud to 412' (125 m).
Description: Large white shells with unique sculpturing of two main areas separated by a groove; anterior edge has spines and teeth. Shells gape widely at both ends. Interior chalky white with distinctive hinge-myophore with a rounded end. Body of clam buries into the substrate with siphons extending to 6" (15 cm) above the bottom. Siphons are split when extended to or above the surface, rusty-red with white bumps at tip; lower siphon white with red spots.
Comments: May be found in high densities, to more than 50 individuals per square yard (m3) metre; sometimes mitaken for flat-tip piddock.

FLAT-TIP PIDDOCK *(Illustration #B-97, #S-16)*

Species: *Penitella penita* (Conrad, 1837).
Size: 1/8"–23/4" (3–72 mm) length.
Range: 60°N–26°N; Prince William Sound, Alaska south to Baja California Sur.
Habitat: In the mid-intertidal zone to 72' (22 m) in clay and soft rock. This is the most common piddock along the BC coast. It can be detected

by small siphon holes relative to the size of the siphon and shell.
Description: Shells gape at both ends; anterior is bulbous, followed by section of teeth and patterns of radial and concentric lines, posterior is smooth with a leathery extension. Smooth, white siphons; 2 heavy "leathery" (proteinaceous) pads. Leathery extension (siphonoplax) at end of each valve protects the siphons. Interior is white.

ABALONE PIDDOCK *(Illustration #B-98)*

Species: *Penitella conradi* Valenciennes, 1846.
Size: To 1/2" (10 mm) in shells; to 11/4" (33 mm) in rock.
Range: 50°N–28°N; Port Neville, BC, probably Queen Charlotte Islands and south to Baja California Sur.
Habitat: Found in soft rock and shells in the intertidal zone to 65' (20 m) depth. This piddock bores into the shells of abalone, California mussels and old specimens of the turban snail, *Astraea* and the jingle shell, *Pododesmus.*
Description: Oval shell; exterior white, rounded posterior with flaring extension of periostracum. Abalone secretes material inside the bore hole to form blisters inside the shell (see photograph). This activity weakens the shell of its host.

WOODBORERS – SHIPWORMS – TEREDOS
Family Teredinidae

The shipworm is a worm-like bivalve with a modified and reduced shell used for drilling in wood. Figure 7 (page 176) shows the burrows in the wood. This family of bivalves causes extensive damage to untreated wood in the marine environment, including wharves, pilings and the hulls of ships. Much study has gone into preventing shipworm larvae from settling on wood surfaces, because the larvae burrow immediately upon settling. A great many logs are stored in rivers or estuaries to prevent infestation.

SHIPWORM *(Illustration #B-99, #S-14)*

Species: *Bankia setacea* (Tryon, 1865).
Alternate names: Feathery shipworm.
Size: Shell to 1/4" (7 mm).
Range: 57°N–33°N; Bering Sea, Alaska south to San Diego, California.
Habitat: Found only in wood. Burrows are lined with a calcareous secretion. Intertidal to 300' (90 m).
Description: Worm-like body, posterior siphons separate, protected by feather-like "pallets" of cones that may stopper the burrow. Body tube to 1 m long. Boring is done by toothed shells with anterior cutting edge.

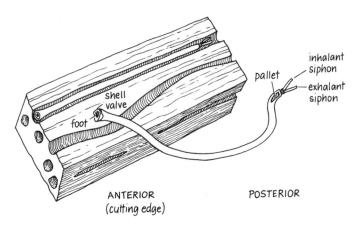

Figure 7: Many people believe the shipworm is a worm,
but it is actually a bivalve.

ATLANTIC SHIPWORM *(not illustrated)*

Species: *Teredo navalis* Linnaeus, 1758.
This is an introduced species, not a common one, whose established
populations attack floating wood in Pendrell Sound off the Strait of
Georgia (50°N), and in Willipa Bay, Washington (46°N) and San
Francisco Bay, California (38°N).

Subclass Anomalodesmata

PANDORAS Family Pandoridae

These clams have small, compressed shells, an interior ligament and interior
tooth-like ridges. The shells typically are not equal: one is flat and the other
inflated.

PUNCTATE PANDORA *(Illustration #B-100)*

Species: *Pandora punctata* Conrad, 1837.
Alternate names: Dotted pandora.
Size: To 2" (50 mm).
Range: 50°N–26°N; Esperanza Inlet, Vancouver Island south to Baja
California Sur.
Habitat: In sand–mud on exposed coasts, 7–165' (2–50 m), often washed
ashore.
Description: Compressed white shells, with anterior curved, upper mar-
gin has posterior ridge curving upward; right valve has fine, irregular

radial scratches. Interior dull, pearly white with pinprick markings; one long tooth in left valve and 2 long, diverging teeth in right valve.

THREADED PANDORA *(Illustration #B-101)*

Species: *Pandora filosa* (Carpenter, 1864).
Alternate names: Western pandora.
Size: To 1" (25 mm) length.
Range: 61°N–32°N; Northern Gulf of Alaska south to Ensenada, Baja California Sur.
Habitat: In gravel bottoms, 65–1000' (20–300 m).
Description: Compressed shell, both ends straight with rounded lower margin, posterior tip upturned and squared off. Exterior white, right valve with radiating lines; interior pearly.

BILIRATE PANDORA *(Illustration #B-102)*

Species: *Pandora bilirata* Conrad, 1855.
Size: To 5/8" (15 mm).
Range: 60°N–24°N; Prince William Sound, Alaska to Baja California Sur, and in the Gulf of California.
Habitat: In mud, subtidally in 16–825' (5–250 m).
Description: Oval-elongated shell; 1–3 strong radial ribs in left shell.

WARD PANDORA *(Illustration #B-103)*

Species: *Pandora wardiana* A. Adams, 1859.
Alternate names: Giant pandora, *Pandorella wardiana*, *Pandora grandis*.
Size: Largest of this family, to 21/4" (55 mm).
Range: 57°N–48°N; Point Barrow, Alaska, Bering Sea, Gulf of Alaska and south to Cape Flattery, Washington.
Habitat: At depths of 16–660' (5–200 m).
Description: Oval shell with conspicuous radial furrow.

LYONSIA CLAMS – PAPER SHELLS Family Lyonsiidae

The nomenclature of this group changes frequently.

ROCK ENTODESMA *(Illustration #B-104, #S-8)*

Species: *Entodesma navicula* (A. Adams & Reeve, 1850).
Alternate names: Northwest ugly clam, *Agriodesma saxicola*, *Entodesma saxicola*, *Lyonsia saxicola*.
Size: To 4" (100 mm) length.
Range: 56°N–34°N; Southern Bering Sea south to Government Point, California.

Habitat: Nestled in crevices or under rocks; intertidal to 65' (20 m).
Description: Shell gapes so that siphon cannot be completely retracted; thick, brown, rough periostracum; interior of shell pearly; shell typically cracks and breaks as it dries. Grains of sand often adhere to mucous produced by glands in the mantle.
Comments: The juvenile northwest ugly clam is distinctive. It grows to 3/4" (18 mm), with a tan to red periostracum, and a pronounced dorsal posterior groove that is less obvious in larger specimens. Interior of the shell is pearly. This species hosts pea crabs.

BLADDERCLAM *(Illustration #B-105, #S-13)*

Species: *Mytilimeria nuttalli* Conrad, 1837.
Alternate names: Bottle clam.
Size: To 13/4" (46 mm).
Range: 57°N–30°N; Sitka, Alaska to Baja California Norte.
Habitat: Found in the intertidal zone to 130' (40 m), protected in or under the thin mat of a compound ascidian such as *Aplidium* species or *Cystodes lobatus.*
Description: Thin shell is oval, higher than long. Exterior has thin yellow periostracum; interior is iridescent.
Comments: This shell cracks when dried.

Lyonsia Clams

SCALY LYONSIA *(Illustration #B-106)*

Species: *Lyonsia bracteata* (A.A. Gould, 1850).
Alternate names: Puget Sound Lyonsia, *Lyonsia pugetensis.*
Size: To 21/4" (55 mm).
Range: 56°N–48°N; Gulf of Alaska south to Cape Flattery, Washington.
Habitat: Sand bottoms, 165–925' (50–280 m).
Description: Elongated shell; grey-brown to green periostracum projects beyond shell margin. Fine, close radial lines.

CALIFORNIA LYONSIA *(Illustration #B-107)*

Species: *Lyonsia californica* Conrad, 1837.
Alternate names: There is some taxonomic confusion over this bivalve. There may be several species or variants of *L. californica.*
Size: To 11/2" (38 mm).
Range: 57°N–17°N; Kodiak Island to Prince William Sound, Alaska and south to Acupulco, Mexico.
Habitat: Found in sand; intertidal to 330' (100 m).
Description: Elongated shell; thin flattened valves with delicate radial

ribs; exterior slightly iridescent, interior smooth, almost iridescent.

Comments: The smaller specimens tend to have more sand adhering to the periostracum, which has led to the smaller specimens being named as different species or subspecies.

THRACIA SHELLS Family Thraciidae

This group usually has thin, brittle shells, with the right shell typically larger and the posterior gaping. There is a hole in the shell at the umbone.

PACIFIC THRACIA *(Illustration #B-108)*

Species: *Thracia trapezoides* Conrad, 1849.
Size: To 2¹/2" (65 mm).
Range: 57°N–28°N; Wide Bay, Alaska south to Isla Cedros, Baja California.
Habitat: In sand–mud, at 36–660' (11–200 m).
Description: Inflated, with right shell larger; anterior rounded, posterior truncated and gaping; periostracum dull brown. Depression or hole at the hinge, in the right shell.
Comments: This species has long, separate siphons.

DIPPER SHELLS Family Cuspidariidae

PECTINATE CARDIOMYA *(Illustration #B-109)*

Species: *Cardiomya pectinata* (Carpenter, 1864).
Alternate names: Ribbed dipper shell, *Cardiomya oldroydi.*
Size: ¹/2–1¹/2" (12–40 mm).
Range: 61°N–37°N; Prince William Sound, Alaska south to Monterey Bay, California.
Habitat: At 16–890' (5–270 m), in mud–sand.
Description: Thin, brittle shell; pear-shaped; anterior rounded, posterior drawn out to long narrow tip or "spout"; radiating ridges. Exterior white to tan.

This section was prepared with contributions from E. Coan, P. Scott and F. Bernard.

Brachiopods

Encased by two shells, the lamp shells appear to be bivalve mollusks but they are actually a different group of animals altogether, belonging to the Phylum Brachiopoda. The term "brachio/pod" translates to "arm/foot," referring to the food-gathering arm-like structures, once thought to be involved in locomotion.

There may be more than 30,000 fossil species but only about 325 living species, all marine.

LAMP SHELLS

A lamp shell remains fixed to by means of a fleshy stalk. Lamp shells cannot swim from site to site like the swimming scallops. They occur intertidally and to great depths, 600' (200m) and more. The only common intertidal species is *Terebratalia transversa.*

> **LAMP SHELL** *(Illustration #BR-1)*
>
> **Species:** *Terebratalia transversa* (Sowerby, 1846).
> **Size:** To 1¼" (30 mm) length.
> **Range:** 57°N–33°N; Kodiak Island, Alaska to San Diego, California.
> **Habitat:** Sometimes intertidal. Often abundant on subtidal rock faces.
> **Description:** Shell typically wider than long; broader anterior margin of the valves with pronounced waves or undulations. Shells are variable, from smooth to prominently ribbed; tan to brown periostracum.

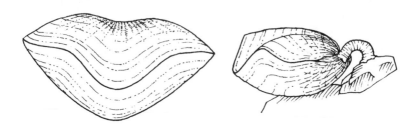

Figure 8: Lamp Shell

Gastropods

T he gastropods ("stomach foot" or "belly foot") comprise the class Gastropoda—the largest class of mollusks with as many as 37,500 living species and 15,000 fossil species worldwide. Gastropods enjoy the widest distribution of any animal, from land snails on mountaintops to marine snails in the ocean depths. About 1,000 marine gastropod species live in North American waters between Southern Alaska and central California.

A gastropod has a single shell (univalve), which may be conical, flattened, reduced, internal or absent depending on the species. Whatever its shape and size, in the larval stage the shell undergoes a twisting process that results in a coiled shell, unlike that of any other mollusk. The typical gastropod moves around on a large, soft "foot" which extends from the single opening (aperture) of the shell. It has a head and tentacles. Many gastropods also have scraping tooth-like radula, which can help identify a specimen.

The class Gastropoda is a diverse group which includes **abalone** (also called ear shells), **keyhole limpets, true limpets, Chinese-hat** or **cup-and-saucer shells, hoofshells, slippersnails,** a variety of **snails** and "bubble shells" or **opisthobranchs** (see Figure 9). Gastropods are usually viewed from the aperture side.

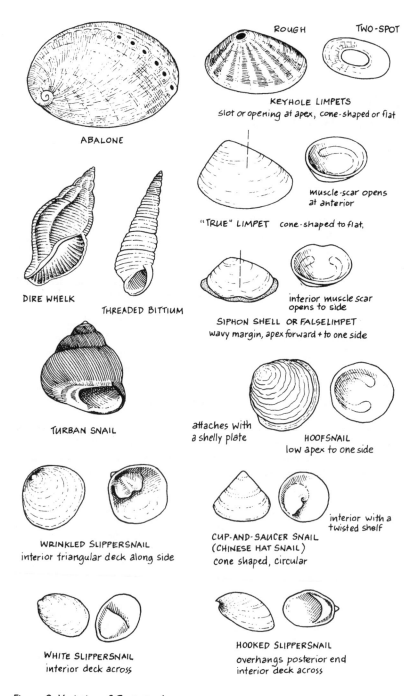

ROUGH   TWO-SPOT

KEYHOLE LIMPETS
slot or opening at apex, cone-shaped or flat

ABALONE

muscle-scar opens
at anterior

"TRUE" LIMPET   cone-shaped to flat,

DIRE WHELK

THREADED BITTIUM

interior muscle scar
opens to side

SIPHON SHELL OR FALSELIMPET
wavy margin, apex forward + to one side

TURBAN SNAIL

attaches with
a shelly plate

HOOFSNAIL
low apex to one side

WRINKLED SLIPPERSNAIL
interior triangular deck along side

CUP-AND-SAUCER SNAIL
(CHINESE HAT SNAIL)
cone shaped, circular

interior with a
twisted shelf

WHITE SLIPPERSNAIL
interior deck across

HOOKED SLIPPERSNAIL
overhangs posterior end
interior deck across

Figure 9: Varieties of Gastropods

Class
Gastropoda

Note: Latitude ranges are given here whenever specific distributions have been published in the scientific literature.

ABALONE Family Haliotidae

Like most gastropods, abalone live quietly. They cling to submerged rocks and eat algae that occur naturally in seawater. But anyone who has gathered abalone for food knows that they are tenacious—a strong prying tool and a quick, firm hand are required for harvesting. Abalone must be measured before harvesting, as the shell or body is often damaged when the abalone is pried off the rocks.

Male and female abalone spawn by broadcasting gametes into the water. The larvae are dispersed in the water column (from the surface to the sea bed), settle in 2 weeks or less, and then attach to a rock or hard surface on the sea bottom, where they spend the rest of their lives. They feed initially by rasping algae on rocks, and as they grow larger they begin to feed on drift algae. The shell grows about 1/2" (10 mm) each year, depending on the availability of food. Some abalone are believed to live as long as 15 years, or even more. The largest abalone measure about 7" (175 mm). Natural predators include sea otters, fishes, sea stars, crabs and octopus.

Native groups have used the colourful, iridescent abalone shells for centuries in making earrings, pendants and decorations on masks. To most people living today, abalone are better known for their shells than their potential in the kitchen. But for aboriginals, abalone was an important source of food as well as ornament. It was gathered mostly in the intertidal zone, and in the early 1900s a number of Japanese abalone canneries or drying plants operated in the Queen Charlotte Islands and other northern fishing areas. Commercial and recreational fisheries have expanded rapidly since the 1960s with the development of diving gear, scuba and surface supplied gear. But conservation concerns forced the closure of aboriginal, commercial and recreational fisheries in 1990. The stocks had not rebuilt at survey sites by 1994 and the closure has continued. Further research into abalone stocks and aquaculture alternatives is taking place.

NORTHERN ABALONE *(Illustration #G-1)*

Species: *Haliotis kamtschatkana* Jonas, 1845.
Alternate names: Japanese abalone, Pinto abalone.
Size: To 7" (175 mm) length.
Range: 58°N–34°N. Sitka, Alaska south to Point Conception, California.
Habitat: In kelp and rocks, lower intertidal zone to 50' (15 m).
Description: Thin shell, oval-elongated with irregular bumps and radial ridges over the spiral sculpture. Exterior mottled greenish and reddish-brown with areas of white and blue; 3–6 open holes on tubular projections. Interior iridescent white, lacking the prized colours of many abalone.
Comments: This species is the world's northernmost abalone. Has been fished commercially in BC and other locations.
Edibility: Abalone are prized food items. Some can be taken at low tide, but most are gathered by skin diving or scuba diving. Measure the abalone in place before attempting to remove it—abalone are easily damaged and may die later if the meat is cut or the shell broken. Pry the abalone off the rock with a blunt knife or ab tool. If undersized abalone are taken, they must be replaced upright in their original position on the bottom. This will reduce their vulnerability to sea stars and other nearby predators.
Abalone are marketed fresh and frozen in the shell, processed into steaks and frozen, canned in brine or made into soups. Abalone must be tenderized; it will be more tender if left overnight refrigerated or frozen. Clean and slice the body meat into 1/4" (6 mm) thick steaks and tenderize with a meat hammer. Then bread them and fry them, add them to soups or stir-frys, or check cookbooks for other ways to prepare them.

RED ABALONE *(Illustration #G-2)*

Species: *Haliotis rufescens* Swainson, 1822.
Size: To 10 1/2" (260 mm) length.
Range: Central BC to central Baja California.
Habitat: On rocks, intertidal to 545' (165 m); most abundant from 20–40' (6–12 m).
Description: Shell usually has 2–3 holes open. Exterior is brick red; interior has pinkish, blue or greenish iridescence.
Comments: This species is not found in BC waters, but Native people in BC traded for this prized abalone and used it for decoration and in masks and other art forms.

KEYHOLE LIMPETS Family Fissurellidae

This family of limpets is characterized by a hole at or near the top (apex) of the shell, which distinguishes them from the "true" limpets. Many feed on algae or detritus but a few are carnivorous, feeding on sponges and other animals.

Keyhole limpets are in the order Archaeogastropoda, which includes abalone, keyhole limpets, turban snails and margarite snails. The "true" limpets are in their own order, described later.

HOODED PUNCTURELLA *(Illustration #G-3)*

Species: *Cranopsis cucullata* (Gould, 1846).
Alternate names: *Puncturella cucullata.*
Size: To 1 1/2" (40 mm).
Range: 57°N–30°N; Alaska to Cabo San Quintin, Baja California.
Habitat: On and under rocks from the low tide to 660' (200 m).
Description: Shell peaked with a hooked apex, a small elongated slit behind the peak; shell has 13–23 (usually 16) strong radiating ribs, with smaller ribs between. Exterior and interior white. Margin irregular because of the ribs.

ROUGH KEYHOLE LIMPET *(Illustration #G-4)*

Species: *Diodora aspera* (Rathke, 1833).
Size: Shell to 2 3/4" (70 mm); body is larger than the shell.
Range: Alaska south to Baja California.
Habitat: Low intertidal and subtidal.
Description: Shell oval, narrow in front, grey-white with 12–18 radial colour bands of purple-brown. Shell has lattice sculpture. Circular opening to anterior of centre. An omnivore, feeding on encrusting bryozoans and algae.
Comments: This species has an escape response to predatory starfish (the painted star, *Orthasterias*, the sunflower star, *Pycnopodia*, and the six-ray star, *Leptasterias*,) in which the mantle is extended to cover over the shell. This keyhole limpet also hosts a commensal scale worm, *Arctonoe vittata*, which bites at the tube feet of the ray of the sea star and causes them to retreat.

This shell is often washed ashore and found on the beach, a prize for shell collectors.

The Latin *aspera* means "rough," referring to the rough surface of the shell.

TWO-SPOT KEYHOLE LIMPET *(Illustration #G-5)*

Species: *Fissurellidea bimaculata* Dall, 1871.
Alternate names: *Megatebennus bimaculatus.*
Size: To 3/4" (20 mm) shell length.
Range: Alaska to Baja California.
Habitat: On or under rocks on compound ascidians or sponges, and on holdfasts of kelp. Intertidal to shallow subtidal.
Description: Body elongated; shell reduced. Opening in shell is one-third of shell length or less. Soft body covers shell and is much larger than shell. Body is coloured red, yellow, brown to orange or white with dark spots or blotches.
Comments: Latin *megatebennus* translates to "large robe," referring to the fleshy mantle.

Snails

The Shell

The shell grows as the snail excretes calcareous material from its **mantle**. As the material collects, it winds around a central axis, the **columella**. (Most snail shells, when they are held with the **apex** pointing up, are dextral, or coiled from the right. Fewer shells are sinistral, or coiling from the left. A few species exhibit both forms of coiling.) The columella may be solid or hollow when it opens at the base of the shell, forming an **umbilicus**. The umbilicus is adjacent to the large opening, the **aperture**, where the soft body of the snail protrudes.

The lower **body whorl** is the most recently built shell part, and it contains most of the soft body of the animal; the original tiny larval shell, the **nuclear whorl**, is often still visible at the apex of the shell. The whorls above the body whorl are called the **spire**. The shell whorls are often defined by a shoulder and a line or **suture**.

The aperture may have a lower, anterior canal for the siphon called the **anterior** or **siphonal canal**. There may also be a canal at the top, the **posterior** or **anal canal**, for discharging water and wastes. The **inner lip** and **outer lip** may have folds or teeth. The shell grows as the secreted shell material is continually added to the outer lip. The aperture may be sealed off by a horny or calcareous **operculum**, a "trap door" on the foot of the snail that helps protect it from predators, heat and dryness when it withdraws into its shell. The bottom or base of the body whorl may be rounded or flattened.

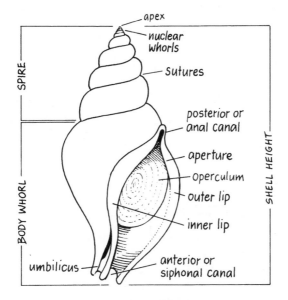

apex

nuclear whorls

Sutures

SPIRE

posterior or anal canal

aperture

operculum

outer lip

inner lip

SHELL HEIGHT

BODY WHORL

umbilicus

anterior or siphonal canal

SNAIL SHELL FEATURES

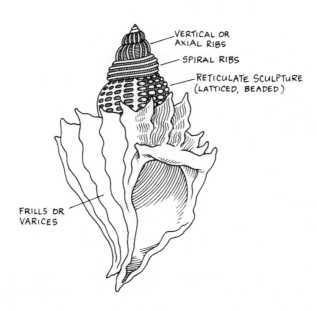

VERTICAL OR AXIAL RIBS

SPIRAL RIBS

RETICULATE SCULPTURE (LATTICED, BEADED)

FRILLS OR VARICES

Figure 10: Snail Shell Features and Measurements

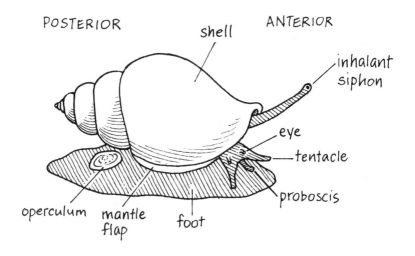

POSTERIOR   shell   ANTERIOR

inhalant siphon

eye

tentacle

proboscis

operculum   mantle flap   foot

Figure 11: Snail Body Features

The shell surface may be smooth or sculptured in any of a variety of ways. Sections of the shell may have spiral-lined chords, axial ribs, frills, varices, lamellae, spines, latticed sculpture or beaded sculpture. Like bivalves, some snails are covered with a skin-like layer, the periostracum.

The maximum size of snails found in the Pacific Northwest is 5 1/2–6" (140–150 mm). The largest species are the moonsnail (*Polinices lewisii*), the Oregon (hairy) triton (*Fusitriton oregonensis*), and the ridged whelk (common northwest Neptune) (*Neptunea lyrata*).

The Soft Body

The head of the snail has two simple **eyes** capable of detecting differences in light intensity, so that the snail can avoid predators. **Tentacles** act as feelers and receive chemical cues from the environment, detecting prey and predators. The mouth is at the end of the **proboscis** and has a file-tooth radula used to cut, tear and scrape food.

Many snails have anterior **siphons**, which are folded from the mantle, to circulate water over the interior gills. Some species also have a posterior siphon to discharge water and wastes. The siphons are protected by canals in the shell aperture.

The soft body of a snail is attached by muscles to the columella, so that even the massive moonsnail can withdraw its body completely into the shell.

Feeding

Snails can be herbivorous, carnivorous or omnivorous, feeding on a variety of plants, animals and organic material, or detritus. With its tooth-like radula, the snail can scrape material off rocks and other hard surfaces. The shape and structure of the radula is an identifying feature for many snails.

The carnivorous snails, including moonsnails, drills and whelks, feed on clams, mussels and barnacles. Typically a carnivorous snail engulfs its prey with its foot, and then uses its radula to drill into the shell and rasp out the soft flesh. Chemical secretions assist in the drilling and ingestion processes. Some whelks use the edges of their shells to pry open barnacles, mussels or clams.

Therefore, a common place to find some snails is on or near their prey. Drills are found feeding on oysters, many of the dogwinkles feed on barnacles and mussels in the intertidal zone, wentletraps are often found on anemones where they nip at the column and tentacles of their prey. The small lurid rocksnail, *Ocinebrina lurida,* is often found attacking the giant chiton, *Cryptochiton,* while clinging to the chiton's back.

Other snails, such as the olive snails and the dire whelk, are scavengers. The checkered hairysnail, *Trichotropis,* is a filter-feeder and rarely moves.

Reproduction

Snails usually have separate sexes but a few species are hermaphroditic (having both male and female reproductive organs). Fertilization is usually internal. Large numbers of snails are often seen clustered together as they spawn. The eggs are usually laid in the spring and summer in large numbers, often in protective egg cases—unique to each species—each of which contains some 25–80 eggs. In some species, the developing larvae feed on "nurse eggs" in the capsules and emerge as small snails. Many snail larvae have a free-swimming stage before they settle and grow. **Many egg cases are illustrated in the colour section (pp. 86, 88, 90, 92, 101).**

Predators

Octopus and starfish are common predators of snails, and a number of fish species dislodge and feed on them. Some species of snails are eaten by crabs as well, including *Nucella* and other larger snails, which are preyed upon by the red rock crab, *Cancer productus,* and some smaller species which are eaten by the graceful crab, *Cancer gracilis.*

Fisheries and Other Uses

In BC, the development of a sustainable snail fishery for food purposes has been limited, because there is so little information on the biology, abundance and distribution of many snail species. Some authorities believe some of the larger snails may live longer than 30 years, and few of the young survive to sustain a commercial fishery. Snails are not filter feeders, so they are rarely affected by PSP or other marine toxins. In exceptional cases they have accumulated some toxin from eating "hot" clams (clams that have already concentrated the toxin).

There are many traditional and contemporary uses of marine snails throughout the world. Some rare, prized specimens have been used as symbols of power or authority, and others have been used for money and collected for buttons, jewellery and other decorations. Large shells have taken on powerful religious or culture significance as horns or trumpets.

TURBAN SNAILS Family Turbinidae

This is a large family of shells found worldwide. Locally it is represented by only a few species. They are turban-shaped and have a calcareous operculum.

RED TURBAN *(Illustration #G-6)*

Species: *Astraea gibberosa* (Dillwyn, 1817).
Size: To 3" (75 mm) diameter, 2 1/4" (57 mm) height.
Range: SE Alaska, Queen Charlotte Islands south to Baja California; not common from Washington to northern California.
Habitat: On rocks on the open coast; sometimes shell is covered with coralline algae. Shallow subtidal to 200' (61 m) deep.
Description: Large, conical shell; flat base of shell is lined with furrows; whorls have prominent wavy, bumpy ridge. Reddish-brown shell; brown periostracum.
Comments: This species is eaten by sea stars. The thick, oval, white-pearly operculum was inset into bowls, masks and wooden bent-boxes made by the Haida and Natives of southeast Alaska, and there is evidence that the northern Natives traded with the Haida for these shells. Because this is a common and sometimes abundant species, there has been interest in harvesting this species commercially. It is not known whether populations could sustain a fishery.

DARK DWARF TURBAN *(Illustration #G-7)*

Species: *Homalopoma luridum* (Dall, 1885).
Alternate names: Northern or Dall's dwarf turban, often erroneously
noted as *H. carpenteri.*
Size: To 1/2" (10 mm) height.
Range: Sitka, Alaska to northern Baja California.
Habitat: On rocks, intertidal and in shallows.
Description: Small, squat shell with prominent, regularly spaced spiral
ridges. Shell is dull grey but reddish or purplish colour where worn. Has
a small, distinctive calcareous operculum.

TURBAN SNAILS – TOP SHELLS – MARGARITES
Family Trochidae

This is a large family found worldwide. Top shells are usually herbivores,
scraping algae and vegetable detritus. They are common and abundant in
many locations. Many have an iridescent mother-of-pearl finish inside the
shell.

BLACK TURBAN *(Illustration #G-8)*

Species: *Tegula funebralis* (A. Adams, 1855).
Size: To 11/4" (30 mm) diameter.
Range: Vancouver Island south to Point Conception, California, and
reports to central Baja California.
Habitat: Common and abundant aggregations under rocks in the intertidal zone.
Description: Thick shell with strong, low cone of 4 whorls; umbilicus
closed, 2 teeth in aperture. Shell is dark black-purple, often worn to
pearly white at the top; body black; interior of shell pearly.
Comments: Often has a black limpet, *Lottia asmi* or white slippersnails
growing on the shell. Researchers estimate this snail's life span to be as
long as 80–100 years.

BROWN TURBAN *(Illustration #G-9)*

Species: *Tegula pulligo* (Gmelin, 1791).
Alternate names: Dusky or Northern brown turban.
Size: To 11/2" (38 mm).
Range: Alaska south to Baja California; more common in the northern
range.
Habitat: On kelp on rocky shores on the open coasts, not as common as
black turbans. Intertidal to 10' (3 m).
Description: Strong, low cone with 7 flattened whorls; wide open

umbilicus. Brown with purple mottling and orange streaks; interior pearly.

There are conflicting reports in the literature on the identification of small, smooth olive- to tan-coloured *Margarites*. There appear to be two species with the same distribution: *M. helicinus* and *M. beringensis*. The Margarite *M. marginatus* is considered to be the same as *M. helicinus*.

BERING MARGARITE *(Illustration #G-10)*

Species: *Margarites beringensis* (E.A. Smith, 1899).
Size: To 1/2" (10 mm).
Range: Arctic to Alaska south to Hope Island, BC; also on Atlantic coast.
Habitat: On sand and mud.
Description: Small, thin, smooth, waxen, brownish periostracum.
Comments: The Pacific coast shells are sometimes classified as *M. beringensis*; often *M. marginatus*, from lower latitudes, is misidentified as this species.

HELICINA MARGARITE *(Illustration #G-11)*

Species: *Margarites helicinus* Phipps, 1874.
Alternate names: Smooth or spiral margarite; may be same species as *M. marginatus*.
Size: To 1/2" (10 mm).
Range: Aleutian Islands, Alaska south to Washington.
Habitat: On kelp or under rocks; shallow water to 100' (30 m).
Description: Smooth, occasionally faint low spiral ridges; white to tan or rose; interior of round aperture dull-iridescent. Small, deep umbilicus.
Comments: This is a common species. The distribution is the same as *M. helicinus*.

PUPPET MARGARITE *(Illustration #G-12)*

Species: *Margarites pupillus* (Gould, 1849).
Alternate names: Little margarite.
Size: To 3/4" (17 mm).
Range: Alaska south to southern California; more common in the northern range.
Habitat: On sand, mud and rubble on sheltered beaches; intertidal to 300' (90 m).
Description: 5–6 whorls; strong irregular spiral chords with fine, slanting axial threads. Exterior white to yellow-grey. Aperture with a rose to green iridescence.
Comments: This is a common species.

LOVELY PACIFIC SOLARELLE *(Illustration #G-13)*

Species: *Solariella peramabilis* Carpenter, 1864.
Alternate names: Lovely top shell.
Size: To 3/4" (20 mm).
Range: 55°N–18°N; Japan, and Forrester Island, Alaska south to Mexico.
Habitat: On offshore rocky and soft bottoms; 330–2000' (100–600 m).
Description: Thin, squat shell, with shell height equal to the width. Round aperture, wide deep umbilicus; 4–7 whorls. Tan to pinkish-grey exterior with light streaks and mottling.
Comments: The *Lirularia* snails resemble the Margarite snails, but are smaller and heavier. They are found in shallower water.

PEARLY TOPSNAIL *(Illustration #G-14)*

Species: *Lirularia lirulata* (Carpenter, 1864).
Alternate names: *Margarite lirulata.*
Size: To 1/4" (6 mm).
Range: Intertidal in BC and Washington; shallow subtidal species farther south to California.
Habitat: Under rocks and in gravel.
Description: Shell taller than diameter; turban-shaped with 5 whorls. Oblique aperture, slit umbilicus. Purplish-pink on a silver shell.

TUCKED TOPSNAIL *(Illustration #G-15)*

Species: *Lirularia succincta* (Carpenter, 1864).
Alternate names: Girdled lirularia, tucked lirularia, *Margarite succinatus* (Carpenter).
Size: To 1/4" (6 mm).
Range: Alaska south to northern Baja California.
Habitat: Intertidal to shallow subtidal.
Description: Shell height equal to diameter; spiral chords not prominent. Funnel-shaped umbilicus. Brown to dark purple-grey.

The following topsnails generally have a flat base without an umbilicus.

PURPLE-RING TOPSNAIL *(Illustration #G-16)*

Species: *Calliostoma annulatum* (Lightfoot, 1786).
Alternate names: Purple top shell, ringed top shell.
Size: To 11/4" (30 mm) height.
Range: Alaska south to Baja California.
Habitat: On the open coast, feeding on kelp and animals on rocks in the intertidal zone to 100' (30 m).
Description: Conical shell with 8–9 whorls; orange-yellow with bright purple-violet bands; soft body is pinkish orange with black.

BLUE TOPSNAIL *(Illustration #G-17)*

Species: *Calliostoma ligatum* (Gould, 1849).
Alternate names: Western ridged top shell, formerly Costate top shell, *C. costata.*
Size: To 1" (25 mm) diameter.
Range: Northern BC south to California.
Habitat: Rocky areas and kelp beds, intertidal to 100' (30 m) and deeper.
Description: Brown shell with light tan spiral ridges, worn patches show blue inner pearly layer. Round aperture. Snail body is black with cream patches and margin on foot.
Comments: This common and abundant species is known to eat compound tunicate *Cystodes lobatus.* Exhibits an escape response to the ochre sea star *Pisaster ochraceus.* Has also been observed feeding on sponges.

CHANNELLED TOPSNAIL *(Illustration #G-18)*

Species: *Calliostoma canaliculatum* (Lightfoot, 1786).
Size: To 1¹/₂" (35 mm) height.
Range: Alaska south to central California; not common north of California.
Habitat: In rocky areas and on kelp.
Description: Conical shell with low spiral ridges, flat-sided whorls, oval aperture. Flat base without umbilicus. White to grey-yellow with light brown grooves. Tan foot.

VARIABLE TOPSNAIL *(Illustration #G-19)*

Species: *Calliostoma variegatum* (Carpenter, 1864).
Size: To 1" (25 mm) height.
Range: 55°N–28°N; Forrester Island, Alaska south to Isla Cedros, Baja California.
Habitat: On rocks, subtidal in deep water.
Description: Light tan shell with red-brown speckles, yellowish or pale pink. 5–6 beaded chords on the top of the shell. Body of snail is cream with brown spots.
Comments: An uncommon species. It has been observed feeding on pink hydrocoral.

SILVERY TOPSNAIL *(Illustration #G-20)*

Species: *Calliostoma platinum* Dall, 1890.
Size: To 1" (25 mm) height.
Range: 53°N–33°N; Moresby Island, Queen Charlotte Islands south to San Diego, California.

Habitat: In deep waters on soft bottoms, 600–2300' (180–700 m).
Description: Smooth shell, white or yellowish to pinkish.
Comments: A beautiful and rare species.

SPINY TOPSNAIL *(Illustration #G-21)*

Species: *Cidarina cidaris* (Carpenter, 1864).
Alternate names: Adam's spiny Margarite, *Lischkeia cidaris* (Fischer 1879).
Size: To 1 1/2" (40 mm) height.
Range: 60°N–28°N; Prince William Sound, Alaska south to Isla Cedros, Baja California.
Habitat: On offshore rocky–rubble bottoms; moderately deep.
Description: Shell has rounded, beaded whorls with a deep suture line. Base with beaded spiral cords. Round aperture with pearly interior. Exterior grey with beads and ridges worn white.
Comments: A fairly common species.

"True" Limpets

These one-shelled animals are found in many habitats, on rocks, kelp, eelgrass and snail shells. They are classified under a separate order than keyhole limpets and snails. Several unrelated families, the siphon shells or falselimpets and the cup and saucer shells, produce uncoiled limpet-shaped shells.

Limpets range in size from a few small limpets, smaller than 5/8" (15 mm), to a few large limpets whose sizes may exceed 2" (50 mm). The largest BC limpet is likely the mask limpet, *Tectura persona*, which grows to 2" (50 mm) or more in length. A giant south African species grows to 6 1/2" (160 mm) long.

Biology of Limpets

Limpets are single-shelled animals, typically cone-shaped, found on rocks, kelp and other marine plants. Some species forage and move great distances, while others are highly territorial and defend their space aggressively. The territorial forms are typically intertidal, while subtidal species tend to wander. Most feed by scraping algae off rock surfaces.

Many limpets exhibit a "running" escape response to predatory sea stars and carnivorous snails. They are also preyed upon by a number of marine birds and small fish such as surf perch.

Limpets can often be found in aggregates because they gather together for protection from water loss when exposed by the tides to sun and wind. They move into crevices and shaded areas for the same reason. The finger limpet (*Lottia digitalis*) also secretes a mucous sheet that helps prevent water loss.

Limpets are believed to have a life span of 5–16 years.

Limpet Fisheries

In BC, aboriginal people have for centuries harvested larger limpets for food. The foot was scraped out and eaten raw, or the whole animal was steamed in a rock pit.

Hawaiians eat limpets raw and consider them a special or sacred food. Traditionally, they thought limpets were capable of calming heavy surf so fishermen could launch their boats and return to shore safely.

LIMPETS Family Acmaeidae

For almost 100 years, most of the limpets were named in this family. There remains only one species, with others being classified in a new family, Lottiidae.

WHITECAP LIMPET *(Illustration #G-22)*

Species: *Acmaea mitra* Rathke, 1833.
Alternate names: Dunce-cap limpet.
Size: To 1 1/2" (35 mm) length, 1 1/4" (30 mm) height.
Range: Aleutian Islands, Alaska south to Baja California.
Habitat: Intertidal and in shallow subtidal area, on rocks with encrusting coralline algae; shells often wash up on surf beaches.
Description: Round shell with smooth, thick margin. Apex is central. Exterior is white, usually covered by a pink, knobby coralline alga that is its major food.
Comments: This species is the tallest of limpets. The Latin name translates to "pointed cap."

LIMPETS Family Lottiidae

Accounts published of *Lottia* in the 1970s and earlier use the genera *Collisella*, *Acmaea* and *Notoacmaea*. The genera *Tectura* and *Discurria* are also members of this family. Several limpets can be identified on the basis of specific habitat preferences, such as substrate.

SHIELD LIMPET *(Illustration #G-23)*

Species: *Lottia pelta* (Rathke, 1833).
Alternate names: *Collisella pelta.*
Size: To 2 1/4" (54 mm) length, arched to 5/8" (15 mm) height.
Range: Aleutian Islands, Alaska south to Baja California.
Habitat: Often associated with brown algae, including the sea palm *Postelsia*, and common in mussel beds.
Description: Large, heavy shell with central apex, irregular ribbing; oval

outline. Exterior greyish with irregular white, radial stripes that form a net pattern. Interior bluish-white with brown spot.

Comments: This species exhibits a "running" escape response to predatory sea stars, the ochre star *Pisaster ochraceus*, the six-ray star *Leptasterias hexactis* and the mottled star *Evasterias troschelli*. The Latin *pelta* translates as "small shield."

PLATE LIMPET *(Illustration #G-24)*

Species: *Tectura scutum* (Rathke, 1833).
Alternate names: *Notoacmaea scutum*.
Size: To 2" (50 mm) length; arched to 5/8" (15 mm) height.
Range: Aleutian Islands, Alaska south to California.
Habitat: Mid- to low intertidal and shallow subtidal.
Description: Shell low and flattened with rounded off-centre apex; oval-smooth margin. Exterior green-grey with pattern of light and dark streaks or blotches or checkerboard; interior bluish with dark marginal rim, often spotted with white, and often a brown centre.
Comments: This common species is the only Pacific limpet with brown tentacles. It moves with the tide and exhibits running escape response to several sea stars. The Latin *scutum* translates to "shield," referring to the flattened profile.

RIBBED LIMPET *(Illustration #G-25)*

Species: *Lottia digitalis* (Rathke, 1833).
Alternate names: Finger limpet, *Collisella digitalis*.
Size: 5/8–11/4" (15–30 mm) length.
Range: Aleutian Islands, Alaska south to southern tip of Baja California.
Habitat: In cracks and crevices in the high intertidal and splash zones, on vertical or overhanging rock faces, sometimes on shells of goose barnacles, *Pollicipes (Mitella) polymerus*. It is tolerant to a variety of outer-coast habitats.
Description: Apex of shell is near anterior margin. Exterior usually olive-green to brown with white blotches or dots; interior with brownish central patch.
Comments: This species, one of the most common limpets, grazes on algae. The Latin *digitalis* refers to the finger-like ribbing of the shell.

MASK LIMPET *(Illustration #G-26)*

Species: *Tectura persona* (Rathke, 1833).
Alternate names: Speckled limpet, *Notoacmaea persona, Acmaea persona*.
Size: To 2" (50 mm) length; arched to 5/8" (15 mm) height.
Range: Alaska south to Monterey.

Habitat: In deep cracks and depressions, high on beach, often in area of fresh water seepage, and in shade of overhanging trees; sheltered from the heaviest wave action.

Description: Oval shell with a smooth margin; apex to front. Exterior mottled blue-grey with brown or black, speckled with white dots at the top. Interior bluish-white with a narrow dark margin, sometimes spotted with white and a dark mask-like stain behind the apex.

Comments: The Latin *persona* means "mask," referring to the dark interior stain.

FENESTRATE LIMPET *(Illustration #G-27)*

Species: *Tectura fenestrata* (Reeve, 1855).
Alternate names: *Notoacmaea fenestrata, Acmaea fenestrata.*
Size: To 1" (25 mm) length.
Range: Alaska south to California.
Habitat: On smooth boulders and rocks in the mid- and lower intertidal.
Description: Solid oval arched shell, apex ahead of the centre. Exterior brown-olive with white speckles. Interior variable, bluish-white with a narrow brown border to an interior of dark solid brown.
Comments: The Latin *fenestrata* refers to the marginal checkerboard pattern.

UNSTABLE LIMPET *(Illustration #G-28)*

Species: *Lottia instabilis* (Gould, 1846).
Alternate names: *Collisella instabilis, Acmaea instabilis.*
Size: To 1 1/2" (35 mm) length.
Range: Alaska south to San Diego.
Habitat: On the stipes of kelp and on holdfasts.
Description: Oval shell with smooth margin. Apex just forward of centre. Margins curved upwards at both ends so that it rocks on a flat surface. Exterior dark brown, sometimes lighter at the top; interior bluish-white with a central brownish blotch. The shell is shaped to hold on to stipes of kelp and on holdfasts, upon which the limpet feeds.
Comments: The Latin *instabilis* refers to the shell's shape.

BLACK LIMPET *(Illustration #G-29)*

Species: *Lottia asmi* (Middendorff, 1847).
Alternate names: *Collisella asmi, Acmaea asmi.*
Size: To 1/2" (10 mm).
Range: Northern Vancouver Island south to Mexico.
Habitat: On black turban snail, *Tegula funebralis*, and sometimes on California mussels, *Mytilus californianus*.

Description: Grey to black exterior; uniform black interior.
Comments: This limpet grazes on the fine film of algae growing on snail or mussel shells.

SEAWEED LIMPET *(Illustration #G-30)*

Species: *Discurria insessa* (Hinds, 1842).
Alternate names: *Notoacmaea insessa.*
Size: To 3/4" (20 mm).
Range: Southern Alaska south to Baja California.
Habitat: On algae at low tide, especially found feeding on and eroding the brown feathery kelp, *Egregia menziesii.*
Description: Elliptical shell with apex toward front. Exterior shiny, smooth, brown with fine striations; interior brown with a white ring.

SURFGRASS LIMPET *(Illustration #G-31)*

Species: *Tectura paleacea* (Gould, 1853).
Alternate names: Chaffy limpet, *Notoacmaea paleacea.*
Size: To 1/2" (10 mm) length.
Range: Vancouver Island south to northern Baja California.
Habitat: Found on the blades of open coast surfgrass, *Phyllospadix.*
Description: Apex near front of shell; parallel sides with notch in anterior right margin. Exterior light brown with darker margins; interior bluish-white.

EELGRASS LIMPET *(Illustration #G-32)*

Species: *Lottia alveus* (Conrad, 1831).
Alternate names: Bowl limpet, *Collisella alveus, Acmaea alveus.*
Size: To 1/2" (12 mm).
Range: Alaska south to California, not common south of Washington.
Habitat: On the blades of eelgrass in protected waters.
Description: Small, narrow; exterior brown with light radial or checkerboard patterns. Interior blue with dark stain at the top.

PERIWINKLES LITTORINES Family Littorinidae

The periwinkles are common small intertidal snails that scrape algae growing on the rocks.

SITKA PERIWINKLE *(Illustration #G-33)*

Species: *Littorina sitkana* Philippi, 1846.
Size: To 7/8" (22 mm).
Range: Alaska south to Puget Sound.

Habitat: In sheltered waters on rocks among rockweed and other algae; in eelgrass from high to low intertidal.
Description: Small, squat shell with diameter almost equal to height; sculpture and colour variable; some with strong spiral threads, others smooth. Colours vary from light brown to red-brown, grey or black, some with yellow, orange or white bands. Aperture large and circular; interior of shell brown or orange.

CHECKERED PERIWINKLE *(Illustration #G-34)*

Species: *Littorina scutulata* Gould, 1849.
Size: To 5/8" (15 mm) height.
Range: Alaska south to Baja California.
Habitat: In sheltered waters on rocks in the intertidal zone.
Description: Somewhat slender shell with height greater than diameter. About 4 whorls, thick shell, no umbilicus. Exterior dark brown to black-purple, often checkered with white. Some have spiral bands of orange crossed with bars or white spots. Interior purplish.
Comments: The egg capsules are unique, with one rim projecting much farther than the other.

LACUNA SHELLS Family Lacunidae

These small intertidal snails resemble periwinkles. They are generally thin and smooth and are often found on eelgrass and algae. Eggs are laid in a jelly-like mass or ring. They have a slit or "chink" above the aperture and between the aperture and the first whorl. Several species live along the Pacific coast.

VARIABLE LACUNA *(Illustration #G-35)*

Species: *Lacuna variegata* Carpenter, 1864.
Alternate names: Variegated chink-shell.
Size: To 5/8" (16 mm) height.
Range: Alaska south to Puget Sound, some in California.
Habitat: On algae and conspicuous on eelgrass.
Description: Plump shell; about 4 whorls. Aperture about half the height or slightly greater. Umbilicus is a wide slit or "chink" above the aperture and between the aperture and the first whorl. Exterior smooth brown with chevron markings.
Comments: This snail often deposits yellow rings of eggs on the blades of eelgrass.

WIDE LACUNA *(Illustration #G-36)*

Species: *Lacuna vincta* (Montagu, 1803).
Alternate names: Common northern chink-shell, wide chink-shell, *Lacuna carinata*.
Size: To 5/8" (16 mm).
Range: Circumpolar; Alaska south to Puget Sound, some in California.
Habitat: Intertidal on algae on rocky shores. Sometimes abundant.
Description: Shell aperture wide and flaring, umbilical chink is deep and white. Exterior dark brown often with narrow brown bands.
Comments: The Latin *vincta* means "wound about," referring to the winding bands of colour.

WORMSNAILS Family Vermetidae

This is a family of colonies of twisted and compact tubes. They resemble tube worms but they are actually a family of snail-like animals.

NORTHERN COMPACT WORMSNAIL *(Illustration #G-37)*

Species: *Petalaconchus compactus* (Carpenter, 1864).
Size: Diameter of each small tube 1/8" (3 mm); mass of short, coiled tubes to 1" (25 mm) height.
Range: Vancouver Island south to California.
Habitat: On or under rocks, shallow subtidal to 165' (50 m).
Description: Tangled mass of tubes, coiling of the shell is not obvious. Exterior of tube white with faint lines, almost smooth. Operculum seals off the tube.
Comments: This species has been found in Barkley Sound, BC. It has been estimated that there are as many as 100,000 individual wormsnails per square metre. Another small snail, *Odostomia*, can often be seen feeding on the fleshy mantle of the wormsnail mass.

BITTIUM-SNAILS Family Cerithiidae

These small, elongated snails are found on sheltered rocky beaches, and often on sandy areas and in eelgrass. They feed on algae and detritus. The most abundant snail with a slender drill shape is the threaded bittium or cerith. Some have been called hornsnails when they were considered to be in a larger family.

THREADED BITTIUM *(Illustration #G-38)*

Species: *Bittium eschrichtii* (Middendorff, 1849).
Alternate names: Giant Pacific hornsnail, threaded cerith.

Size: To 3/4" (20 mm), largest of the *Bittium* species.
Range: From Alaska south to central California.
Habitat: Common under rocks and oyster beds, sometimes on coralline algae in tidepools and sometimes on eelgrass. Intertidal to 180' (55 m).
Description: Elongated shell with about 9 rounded whorls, tapering to sharp apex; smooth flattened spiral chords with square grooves. Exterior dull grey to red-brown. Short canal at base of ovate aperture.
Comments: Empty shell is frequently taken over by small hermit crabs.

SLENDER BITTIUM *(Illustration #G-39)*

Species: *Bittium attenuatum* Carpenter, 1864.
Alternate names: Slender hornsnail.
Size: To 5/8" (15 mm) height.
Range: Southern Alaska south to northern Baja California.
Habitat: Rocky beaches, common and abundant among the roots of eelgrass. Intertidal to 230' (70 m).
Description: Elongated shell more slender than threaded bittium; spiral ridges only faintly beaded. Short canal at base of aperture is not pronounced. Exterior grey, pale to dark brown, sometimes with white bands.

HORNSNAILS Family Batillariidae (formerly Potamididae)

This family of snails usually inhabits brackish waters. They are known as hornsnails or false-cerith snails.

MUDFLAT SNAIL *(Illustration #G-40)*

Species: *Batillaria cumingi* (Crosse, 1862).
Alternate names: False-cerith snail, *B. zonalis*, *B. attramentaria*.
Size: To 11/4" (30 mm) length.
Range: Introduced from Japan along with oyster seed, British Columbia south to California.
Habitat: Sand–mud shores, mid- to high intertidal.
Description: Shell has 8–9 whorls with beaded spiral ridges. Teeth on inner margin of outer lip of aperture; short canal twisted to the left. Grey with brown beads.

HOOFSNAILS Family Hipponicidae

A hoofsnail resembles a limpet, but it attaches itself permanently to a hard surface by secreting a shelly plate from its foot. Hoofsnails are found intertidally under rocks or often on other shells. They brood their young in the mantle cavity.

FLAT HOOFSNAIL *(Illustration #G-41)*

Species: *Hipponix cranioides* Carpenter, 1864.
Alternate names: Horse's hoofsnail, *Hipponix antiquatus, Antisabia cranioides.*
Size: To 3/4" (20 mm).
Range: BC south to California and possibly farther south, most common in California.
Habitat: Common in groups, intertidal and subtidal on the open coast, often overgrown with algae and other organisms.
Description: Flattened, circular, limpet-like shell; exterior white with brownish periostracum. Comarginal striations. The animal sits on a calcareous slab, not part of the shell but secreted by the foot.
Comments: A second species, the sculptured or ribbed hoofsnail, *Hipponix tumens* Carpenter, 1864, has only been recorded from Table Island, north of Vancouver Island. The small shell grows to 5/8" (15 mm), the apex is hooked and there are coarse axial ribs. The white shell has a yellow-brown periostracum that is hairy at the margin.

CUP-AND-SAUCER SNAILS – SLIPPERSNAILS
Family Calyptraeidae

The sessile slipper shells are filter-feeders with specialized gills. They eat small plankton and organic detritus carried in the water. Slipper shells are often found stacked several high, with the larger, older individuals on the bottom.

CUP-AND-SAUCER SNAIL *(Illustration #G-42)*

Species: *Calyptraea fastigiata* Gould, 1846.
Alternate names: Pacific Chinese-hat snail.
Size: To 1" (25 mm).
Range: Alaska south to California.
Habitat: Sometimes intertidal, usually subtidal, 60–450' (18–137 m) deep, on rocks, on dead shells or sometimes attached to crabs.
Description: Shell is conical with circular outline; central apex. Exterior white; interior pearly with a twisted shelf.

HOOKED SLIPPERSNAIL *(Illustration #G-43)*

Species: *Crepidula adunca* Sowerby, 1825.
Size: To 1" (25 mm).
Range: Queen Charlotte Islands south to Baja California.
Habitat: Often stacked up on snail shells, especially the black turban, *Tegula funebralis,* and top shells, *Calliostoma.* Intertidal and deeper.
Description: Oval shell with hooked apex. Exterior brown; interior with a white shelf curved forward. Filter feeders.

WRINKLED SLIPPERSNAIL *(Illustration #G-44)*

Species: *Crepipatella dorsata* (Broderip, 1834).
Alternate names: *Crepipatella lingulata*, Pacific half-slipper.
Size: To 1" (25 mm) length.
Range: 60°N–14°S; Bering Sea, Alaska south to Peru.
Habitat: On rocks and snail shells. Intertidal and deeper.
Description: Low shell, irregular outline almost circular; apex near margin. Interior has small cup attached along one side. Exterior wrinkled, white shell with yellowish to brown periostracum. Interior white with tan to mauve blotches.
Comments: This shell is a filter feeder.

WESTERN WHITE SLIPPERSNAIL *(Illustration #G-45)*

Species: *Crepidula perforans* (Valenciennes, 1846).
Size: To 1 1/2" (38 mm).
Range: Vancouver Island south to Baja California.
Habitat: On rocks, but often on insides of shells, or in holes of boring clams. Intertidal and deeper.
Description: Small, elongated shell almost flat to concave. Exterior white, sometimes with thin, brown periostracum; sometimes strong scaly comarginal ridges.

NORTHERN WHITE SLIPPERSNAIL *(Illustration #G-46)*

Species: *Crepidula nummaria* Gould, 1846.
Size: To 1 1/2" (40 mm).
Range: Alaska to Panama.
Habitat: Intertidal and in shallow water on rocks and dead shells, sometimes in holes of boring clams.
Description: Elongated, almost flat shell; flatter and broader than *C. perforans*. May have several growth forms. Exterior white, often with heavy, shaggy yellow-tan periostracum. Interior shiny white.
Comments: This species is a sedentary filter feeder. Some authorities consider it to be a variation of *Crepidula perforans* (above).

HAIRYSNAILS Family Trichotropididae and Family Ranellidae (Cymatiidae) (Tritonidae)

Two unrelated "hairysnails," so called because of their shaggy periostracum, are commonly encountered: the checkered hairysnail, which is small, and the Oregon hairy triton, which is the largest intertidal snail in the Northwest Coast region.

Family Trichotropididae

CHECKERED HAIRYSNAIL *(Illustration #G-47)*

Species: *Trichotropis cancellata* Hinds, 1843.
Alternate names: Cancellate hairysnail.
Size: To 1¼" (30 mm) height.
Range: Alaska south to Oregon.
Habitat: Subtidal in rocky areas, often among sea squirts and tube worms, and overgrown with other organisms. Found on tube worms up off the bottom, where currents are stronger and more food is carried by.
Description: Shell with 6–7 whorls, latticed or checkered sculpture; aperture is nearly round. Exterior yellow-white covered by a yellow, bristly periostracum.
Comments: This snail is unusual in that it is a filter feeder, so it moves very little. It often hosts another small white snail, *Odostomia columbiana*.

Family Ranellidae (=Cymatiidae)

OREGON TRITON *(Illustration #G-48)*

Species: *Fusitriton oregonensis* (Redfield, 1848).
Alternate names: Hairy Oregon triton.
Size: Largest intertidal snail, to 6" (150 mm) height.
Range: Bering Sea, Alaska south to San Diego, California.
Habitat: Intertidal to 300' (90 m).
Description: Shell has about 6 whorls; axial riblets crossed by spiral pairs of threads. Long siphon canal is about one-third the length of the aperture. Exterior with thick, shaggy, grey-brown periostracum.
Comments: This carnivorous snail, common and abundant in some areas, feeds on tunicates and even sea urchins. Sea urchins sometimes bear black scars where they were attacked by the hairy triton. The eggs are laid in distinctive coils of translucent egg capsules attached to the sea bed. The egg capsules look like grains of corn.
The large shells of the hairy triton are in demand by the largest of the hermit crabs, such as *Pagurus granosimanus*.

VELUTINA SNAILS Family Velutinidae

These snails resemble sea slugs or nudibranchs. They are known to feed on compound and solitary tunicates, and often lay their eggs on tunicates as well.

SMOOTH VELVET SNAIL *(Illustration #G-49)*

Species: *Velutina prolongata* Carpenter, 1864.
Alternate names: Elongate lamellaria.
Size: Shell to 3/4" (20 mm) length.
Range: Aleutian Islands, Alaska south to central California.
Habitat: On rocks in the intertidal and shallows to 330' (100 m).
Description: Shell a low spiral with large body whorl. Pink shell with smooth brown periostracum. Soft white slug-like body extends over the shell; large, round aperture has no operculum. Orange margin on foot.
Comments: This shell lacks sculpturing.

SPIRAL VELVET SNAIL *(Illustration #G-50)*

Species: *Velutina velutina* O.F. Müller, 1776.
Alternate names: Smooth velutina, smooth lamellaria, *Velutina laevigata, Velutina plicatilis.*
Size: Shell to 3/4" (20 mm).
Range: Aleutian Islands, Alaska south to central California.
Habitat: On rocks, often associated with the solitary stalked tunicate, *Styela gibbsii,* in shallow waters to 65' (20 m).
Description: Thin shell has spiral ridges that diverge; thick brown periostracum. Large, nearly circular aperture.
Comments: The nomenclature for this species has been inconsistent. The species has a circumpolar distribution, from the Arctic to California on the Pacific coast.

MOONSNAILS Family Naticidae

Several hundred moonsnail species are found throughout the world, on sandy bottoms, feeding on clams. In England the snails are called "necklace shells" because they leave sand collars of eggs. Each species has its own characteristic egg collar shape. The operculum may be horny or calcareous. Most of the shells are smooth.

ALEUTIAN MOONSNAIL *(Illustration #G-51)*

Species: *Cryptonatica aleutica* (Dall, 1919).
Alternate names: *Natica clausa,* Closed moonsnail.

Size: To 1¼" (30 mm) height.
Range: Circumpolar; Arctic south to northern California.
Habitat: In or on the sand; shallow subtidal to 1650' (500 m).
Description: Medium, squat, cream-coloured shell with thin brown periostracum; umbilicus closed with glossy white callus; calcareous operculum. Snail body is translucent-cream with dark brown spots and blotches.
Comments: This snail may live deeper in the sand than Lewis moonsnail. Egg sand-collar has tiny protuberances. The Latin *clausa* ("closed") refers to the umbilicus.

LEWIS'S MOONSNAIL *(Illustration #G-52)*

Species: *Euspira lewisii* (Gould, 1847).
Alternate names: *Lunatia lewisii.*
Size: To 5½" (140 mm) height.
Range: Southeastern Alaska to southern California.
Habitat: On sand, intertidal to 165' (50 m).
Description: Large, round shell, cream exterior with thin brown periostracum; wide and flaring aperture, umbilicus open, brown horny operculum. Interior brown. Soft body is translucent-brown, without spots or blotches.
Comments: The moonsnail lays its eggs in a distinctive sand collar, which is moulded by the shell curvature as it is released from the snail's body. Many small eggs are distributed in a central jelly layer, covered on both sides by a sand coat. They are found in the intertidal zone and deeper, generally from April to September, with a peak in May–June. The eggs take 6 weeks to hatch out of the collar.
The moonsnail burrows and feeds on clams; it drills into clam shells and actively cuts up the flesh of its prey with its tooth-like radula. An adult moonsnail consumes about one clam every 4 days. A variety of clam species can be found with characteristic holes in their shells, drilled by the moonsnail. Shown in the illustration are the littleneck clam, butter clam, truncated mya and Pacific horse clam. Even though cockles are at the surface of the sand, they are rarely drilled by moonsnails.
Large hermit crabs such as *Pagurus armatus* are fortunate to find empty moonsnail shells, as few species are as large as these.
Edibility: This species is massive but not particularly edible. It was seldom eaten by aboriginal peoples.

WENTLETRAPS Family Epitoniidae

These snails are carnivorous, feeding on sea anemones, corals and probably other cniderians. Some species of wentletraps are known to release a purple dye when they are disturbed, to confuse predators. All have a rounded aperture with a horny operculum. The genus *Epitonium* is currently favoured over *Nitidiscala*. "Wentletreppe" is a Danish term for a winding staircase.

TINTED WENTLETRAP *(Illustration #G-53)*

Species: *Epitonium tinctum* (Carpenter, 1864).
Alternate names: Painted wentletrap, *Nitidiscala tincta*.
Size: To 5/8" (15 mm).
Range: 55°N–25°N; Forrester Island, Alaska south to Magdalena Bay, Baja California.
Habitat: Found near or feeding on the tentacles of sea anemones, *Anthopleura elegantissima*, and giant green anemone, *A. xanthogrammica*. Intertidal to 150' (45 m). When exposed at low tide, the snail burrows into the sand.
Description: Small, slender shell with 8–14 angled, sometimes spiny, axial ribs. Exterior white with brown-purple band below suture.
Comments: May be found in aggregations of up to 15 snails. This shell is favoured by the small hermit crab, *Pagurus hirsutiusculus*. Sand-encrusted egg capsules are laid in the sand between anemones; the capsules are joined by a single thread.

MONEY WENTLETRAP *(Illustration #G-54)*

Species: *Epitonium indianorum* (Carpenter, 1865).
Alternate names: *Nitidiscala indianorum*.
Size: To 11/2" (35 mm).
Range: 55°N–25°N; Alaska south to Baja California.
Habitat: Often found associated with and feeding on tealia anemones, *Urticina crassicornis* and *U. lofotensis*, this snail is attracted by the "scent" of the anemone. Intertidal and subtidal to 400' (120 m).
Description: Slender shell, 10 rounded whorls with deep sutures and 10–17 axial ribs; rounded flaring aperture. Exterior pure white.

BOREAL WENTLETRAP *(Illustration #G-55)*

Species: *Opalia borealis* Keep, 1881.
Alternate names: Wroblewski's wentletrap, *Opalia wroblewskii, O. chacei*.
Size: To 1" (25 mm).
Range: Aleutian Islands, Alaska south to Puget Sound, Washington.
Habitat: Intertidal and subtidal.

Description: Has a spiral ridge near the base of the body whorl, usually with 7 axial ribs. Soft body of snail is white with pearly bumps.

SHINING BALCIS SNAILS
Family Eulimidae (=Melanellidae)

The snails in this family are often parasitic on sea stars, sand dollars and sea urchins. Some species are bent at the top.

SHINING BALCIS *(Illustration #G-56)*

Species: *Balcis micans* (Carpenter, 1864).
Alternate names: *Eulima micans.*
Size: To 1/2" (13 mm) height.
Range: 57°N–27°N; Kodiak Island, Alaska south to Baja California.
Habitat: Subtidal, 100–330' (30–100 m).
Description: Straight, slender shell with sharp spire. Shiny white, often with shading near the apex.

ROCKSNAILS – DWARF TRITONS – WHELKS AND DOGWINKLES Family Muricidae

This large, diverse family of snails found worldwide includes the murex shells decorated with spines and ridges. Locally it includes drills, rock snails, the leafy hornmouth, whelks, dogwinkles and trophons.

LEAFY HORNMOUTH *(Illustration #G-57)*

Species: *Ceratostoma foliatum* (Gmelin, 1791).
Alternate names: Leafy or foliated thorn purpura.
Size: To 31/2" (85 mm).
Range: Alaska south to San Pedro, California.
Habitat: On barnacles and bivalves, intertidal to 200' (60 m).
Description: Large tooth projecting from aperture; 3 wing-like projections or frills; canal closed, and turned and twisted at the end.
Comments: These snails feed on barnacles and bivalves. In late February and March, they cluster to lay yellow egg cases, each containing 25–80 eggs, and sometimes guard the eggs while they hatch. The larvae emerge from the egg cases as small snails.
The frills of a leafy hornmouth help it to land with the aperture or "face" down when dislodged by a fish. In this way it can protect itself from being picked.

LURID ROCKSNAIL *(Illustration #G-58)*

Species: *Ocinebrina lurida* (Middendorff, 1849).
Alternate names: Dwarf triton, formerly *Ocenebra lurida, Urosalpinx lurida.*
Size: To 1¹/2" (38 mm) height.
Range: 57°N–32°N; Sitka, Alaska south to northern Baja California.
Habitat: On rocky beaches in the intertidal and to 180' (55 m); found on and known to attack the giant chiton, *Cryptochiton.*
Description: Small, solid shell with up to 6 whorls; fine, close spiral threads crossing 6–10 axial ribs; oval aperture with 6–7 teeth or more within outer lip. Exterior pale, white-yellow-brown.
Comments: Often confused with larger rock snail, *Ocinebrina sclera.* The giant chiton, *Cryptochiton stelleri,* is often attacked by the lurid rock snail, *Ocinebrina lurida.* Egg cases are attached to rocks.

SCULPTURED ROCKSNAIL *(Illustration #G-59)*

Species: *Ocinebrina interfossa* Carpenter, 1864.
Alternate names: Carpenter's dwarf triton, *Ocenebra interfossa.*
Size: To ³/4" (20 mm) height.
Range: Alaska south to northern Baja California.
Habitat: On rocks in sheltered areas, intertidal to 20' (6 m).
Description: Shells vary considerably, whorls typically with flattened shoulders, 8–11 coarse axial ribs crossed by strong spiral cords. Exterior dull grey to yellow.

JAPANESE ROCKSNAIL *(Illustration #G-60)*

Species: *Ceratostoma inornatum* (Recluz, 1851).
Alternate names: Japanese oyster drill, *Ocenebra japonica.*
Size: To 1¹/4" (30 mm) height.
Range: Introduced to BC and Puget Sound.
Habitat: Gravel, mud and sand beaches.
Description: Smaller and less conspicuously ornamented than the leafy hornmouth.
Comments: This species, introduced with the Japanese oyster in the 1930s and 1940s, is a pest to oyster farmers. It feeds by drilling a hole in an oyster and rasping out the soft body. Eggs are deposited in egg cases.

ATLANTIC OYSTER DRILL *(Illustration #G-61)*

Species: *Urosalpinx cinerea* Say, 1822.
Alternate names: Eastern oyster drill.
Size: To ³/4" (20 mm).

Range: Found at Boundary Bay, BC along with a small population of Atlantic oysters; also found from Washington south to California in areas of oyster culture.

Habitat: In oyster beds and among barnacles, on which it feeds; buried in mud during the winter.

Description: Shell has 5–6 whorls with 10 strong axial ribs and fine spiral lines. Exterior grey, interior of aperture stained with purple.

Comments: This snail drills a hole into the oyster, inserts its proboscis, rasps and feeds on the meat of the oyster. It is a pest to oyster farmers.

WHELKS – DOGWINKLES Family Muricidae (continued)

The names of families and genera of these snails have been revised by authorities several times, because they are extremely variable in shape. They are found drilling and feeding on barnacles in the intertidal zone, to the extent that they are determining factors in the vertical distribution of barnacles. Most recently, the Pacific northeast snails have been assigned to the genus *Nucella* in the family Muricidare, and the genus *Thais* in the family Thaisidae appears to contain exclusively tropical species.

FRILLED DOGWINKLE *(Illustration #G-62)*

Species: *Nucella lamellosa* (Gmelin, 1791).
Alternate names: Wrinkled dogwinkle, *Thais lamellosa.*
Size: 2–31/4" (50–80 mm) height.
Range: Aleutian Islands, Alaska south to central California.
Habitat: On rocks and in crevices, intertidal to shallow subtidal.
Description: Shells vary in colour, banding, sculpture and thickness. Those found in exposed areas may be smooth; those in sheltered areas, may be ornamented with up to a dozen axial frills. Uniform colour, grey to white to pale brown, sometimes banded. Outer lip broadly flared with 3 rounded teeth.
Comments: A large number of snails aggregate in the winter and lay stalked yellow egg cases in the spring and summer. Smooth-shelled animals have been observed by researchers at Bamfield, BC to grow axial frills when in the presence of their major predator, the red rock crab, *Cancer productus.*

CHANNELLED DOGWINKLE *(Illustration #G-63)*

Species: *Nucella canaliculata* (Duclos, 1832).
Alternate names: *Thais canaliculata.*
Size: To 11/2" (40 mm).
Range: Aleutian Islands, Alaska south to central California.

Habitat: On rocks and barnacles.
Description: Shell may be slightly more slender than other whelks; short spire, 14–16 spiral ridges separated by deep furrows. Exterior white-grey; interior tan to orange.
Comments: Not considered common in BC. Found feeding on barnacles.

STRIPED DOGWINKLE *(Illustration #G-64)*

Species: *Nucella emarginata* (Deshayes, 1839).
Alternate names: Emarginate or ribbed dogwinkle, *Thais emarginata.*
Size: To 1¹/16" (28 mm).
Range: Bering Sea, Alaska south to northern Baja California.
Habitat: Feeds on mussels on semi-protected and exposed rocky beaches.
Description: Plump, thick shell, sculptured with alternating thick and thin ribs, often with white bands on the ribs. Exterior variable, grey to black, brown or yellow. Interior of aperture often purple; width of opening is less than one-half diameter of shell.
Comments: This snail is common and widespread in BC. There may be two or more species of striped dogwinkles, lumped under *N. emarginata.* These small shells are often favoured by hermit crabs.

FILE DOGWINKLE *(Illustration #G-65)*

Species: *Nucella lima* (Gmelin, 1791).
Alternate names: Rough purple whelk, *Thais lima.*
Size: To 1¹/4" (30 mm).
Range: Aleutian Islands, Alaska and BC; not common south of the northern end of Vancouver Island.
Habitat: On rocky beaches.
Description: White to orange-brown shell, thinner than emarginate dogwinkle and squarer than channelled dogwinkle, with more (17–20) and finer spiral cords on the body whorl, often crossed by fine, sometimes frilled ridges. Width of aperture about half diameter of shell.
Comments: The Latin *lima* means "file," from the rough file-like cords.

SANDPAPER TROPHON *(Illustration #G-66)*

Species: *Scabrotrophon maltzani* (Kobelt and Küster, 1878)
Alternate names: *Trophonopsis lasius.*
Size: To 1" (25 mm).
Range: Bering Sea, Alaska south to Baja California.
Habitat: Intertidal in Alaska; on rocky bottoms to 1000' (330 m).
Description: Elongated, with height more than twice the diameter. Siphonal canal is an open trough, not tube. Strong axial and about 12 spiral ridges, shell grey or white.

STUART'S TROPHON *(Illustration #G-67)*

Species: *Boreotrophon stuarti* (E.A. Smith, 1880)
Alternate names: *Trophon stuarti.*
Size: To 2¹/2" (60 mm).
Range: 58°N–33°N; Pribilof Islands, Bering Sea south to Newport Beach, California.
Habitat: Rocky bottoms, intertidal in Alaska, to depths of 330' (100 m).
Description: Shell white to cream with a waxy appearance. Shouldered whorls with strong, projecting axial frills, 7–11 per whorl. Body whorl with 5 faint spiral threads.
Comments: Beautiful and uncommon.

CORDED TROPHON *(Illustration #G-68)*

Species: *Boreotrophon orpheus* (Gould, 1849)
Alternate names: *Trophonopsis macouni* (Dall & Bartsch, 1910).
Size: To 1" (25 mm).
Range: Gulf of Alaska south to Washington.
Habitat: Subtidal, 0 to 165' (50 m), gravel and rock bottoms.
Description: Light tan; moderately long canal, numerous spiral cords and stronger axial varices.
Comments: This uncommon trophon was taken by a dredge in BC. It is similar in appearance to *Boreotrophon pedroanus* (Arnold, 1903).

WHELKS Family Buccinidae

This is a family of large snails, known in England as buckies and whelks and sold there in fish markets. In Alaska and BC there has been some commercial fishing of the larger species.

DIRE WHELK *(Illustration #G-69)*

Species: *Lirabuccinum dirum* (Reeve, 1846).
Alternate names: Spindle whelk, *Searlesia dira.*
Size: To 2" (50 mm) height.
Range: Alaska south to central California; particularly abundant in Washington.
Habitat: Intertidal on wave-washed rocks.
Description: Thick, strong shell with 9–11 low, rounded axial ribs; numerous unequal-size spiral threads. Tan-coloured aperture, more than half the length of the shell. Exterior dull grey. Soft body of animal is white.
Comments: The spindle whelk is mostly a scavenger, specializing in injured animals including snails, barnacles and worms. The Latin *dira* means "ominous" and likely refers to the dull grey color.

LYRE WHELK *(Illustration #G-70)*

Species: *Buccinum plectrum* Stimpson, 1865.
Alternate names: Plectrum whelk, sinuous whelk.
Size: To 2½" (60 mm).
Range: Circumpolar; Alaska south to Puget Sound.
Habitat: Common offshore, 100–2000' (30–600 m).
Description: Strong, thin shell; rounded axial ribs or "wrinkles"; numerous fine spiral chords. Exterior grey to white to brown. Snail body is white with brown-black patches.
Comments: A similar species, the waved whelk, *Buccinum undatum*, is harvested commercially in the Atlantic.

NEPTUNE SNAILS included in the Family Buccinidae

The *Neptunea*, which some authorities include in the Family Neptuneidae, are large snails with thick shells. Most live offshore, but some are found in the shallows by divers or the shells get carried into the shallows by hermit crabs. There have been fisheries in Alaska for some *Neptunea* species.

Generally these snails feed on bivalves and polychaetes in sand to mud bottoms. They are capable of extending their proboscis a great distance, some species to 14" (35 cm), to feed on buried animals.

RIDGED WHELK *(Illustration #G-71)*

Species: *Neptunea lyrata* (Gmelin, 1791).
Alternate names: Common northwest neptune, lyre whelk.
Size: To 6½" (165 mm) height.
Range: Alaska south to northern California.
Habitat: On sand and mud, from shallow shores, occasionally intertidal, to 330' (100 m).
Description: Thick shell with 5–6 whorls; unevenly spaced raised spiral ridges. Exterior whitish-brown.
Comments: Deposits flattened oval egg cases with short stalks to form a dome-shaped mass of 15–40 cases.

PHOENICIAN WHELK *(Illustration #G-72)*

Species: *Neptunea phoenicia* (Dall, 1891).
Size: To 4½" (110 mm) height.
Range: Alaska south to Oregon.
Habitat: In deep water, on soft and rocky bottoms. This snail is commonly taken in prawn traps.
Description: Shell has evenly spaced spiral ridges, with alternating ridges

on the lower section. It often has a brown periostracum that dries and peels when the shell dries.

TABLED WHELK *(Illustration #G-73)*

Species: *Neptunea tabulata* (Baird, 1863).
Size: To 41/2" (110 mm).
Range: 57°N–33°N; Petersburg, Southeast Alaska south to San Diego, California.
Habitat: On mud, subtidal.
Description: Shell has flattened shoulders on upper portion of whorls; close, thin spiral ridges; exterior yellowish-white.

CHOCOLATE WHELK *(Illustration #G-74)*

Species: *Neptunea smirnia* (Dall, 1919).
Size: To 41/2" (110 mm).
Range: Japan and Alaska south to Puget Sound, Washington.
Habitat: Common soft-bottom species; shallows to 1000' (300 m).
Description: Shell has 5–6 whorls, sometimes with very faint spiral ridges; brown-purple colour; body is white with brown blotches.
Comments: This species has been observed by divers in shallow waters, less than 33' (10 m).

AMPHISSA SHELLS – DOVE SHELLS
Family Columbellidae (=F. Pyrenidae)

Small dove shells are found worldwide, usually in large colonies. They are aggressive carnivores.

WRINKLED AMPHISSA *(Illustration #G-75)*

Species: *Amphissa columbiana* Dall, 1916.
Size: To 1" (25 mm).
Range: Alaska south to Oregon; not common in California.
Habitat: On rocky beaches and mud, in shallows.
Description: Shell has 20–24 weak, vertical ridges; thin yellowish-brown periostracum.

JOSEPH'S COAT AMPHISSA *(Illustration #G-76)*

Species: *Amphissa versicolor* Dall, 1871.
Alternate names: Variegate amphissa.
Size: To 5/8" (15 mm) height.
Range: BC to Baja California.
Habitat: Intertidal to 65' (20 m).

Description: Shell has oblique axial ribs; outer lip of aperture has small, white teeth. Often coloured with distinctive light and dark markings.

DOVESNAIL *(Illustration #G-77)*

Species: *Astyris gausapata* (Gould, 1850).
Alternate names: *Alia gausapata, Mitrella gouldii.*
Size: To 1/2" (13 mm).
Range: 55°N–33°N; Alaska south to San Diego, California.
Habitat: On rocks, subtidal to 660' (200 m).
Description: Shell has spiral ridges limited to lower portion; aperture thickened with several teeth inside. Exterior yellowish-brown, sometimes with red-brown spots.

CARINATE DOVESNAIL *(Illustration #G-78)*

Species: *Alia carinata* (Hinds, 1844).
Size: To 1/2" (10 mm).
Range: Southern Alaska south to Baja California.
Habitat: Among eelgrass and algae, often on giant kelp, *Macrocystis.* Intertidal to 16' (5 m).
Description: Smooth shell except for a few spiral lines at base; elongated aperture with pinkish-white interior; aperture has dark brown outer lip and strong elongated teeth within.

DOGWHELKS – NASSA MUD SNAILS
Family Nassariidae

These common snails live buried in mud and sand and sometimes on inter-tidal rocks. The upturned canal notch is a feature of this family.

WESTERN LEAN NASSA *(Illustration #G-79)*

Species: *Nassarius mendicus* (Gould, 1850).
Alternate names: Western lean dogwhelk, lean basketsnail.
Size: To 7/8" (22 mm).
Range: Alaska south to central Baja California.
Habitat: On sand, mud and rocks, intertidal to 60' (18 m). Seen more often on sand or rocks than other Nassas, which often burrow.
Description: Elongated shell has spiral ridges with about 12 pronounced axial ridges, forming numerous small beads. Grey-brown, occasionally white, with one or more spiral bands of brown; white interior.

GIANT WESTERN NASSA *(Illustration #G-80)*

Species: *Nassarius fossatus* (Gould, 1850).
Alternate names: Giant western dogwhelk, basket shell, channelled dog-whelk or Nassa.
Size: To 2" (50 mm).
Range: Queen Charlotte Islands, BC south to Baja California.
Habitat: On sand–mud, intertidal to 60' (18 m), buried in sand.
Description: Plump shell. Inner lip of aperture has broad orange callus, wound with about 20 spiral chords with faint axial ribs. Notch canal turns up. Exterior orange-brown to grey.
Comments: Abundant on many sheltered beaches. Will feed on clams using a long proboscis, which can extend more than 1" (25 mm).

OLIVE SHELLS Family Olividae

These glossy shells have been highly prized for much of human history. Coastal Natives made necklaces of them and used them to decorate their clothing, as the early Spanish explorers documented in illustrations. Two similar species are found in BC. Snails in this family are carnivorous scavengers.

PURPLE OLIVE *(Illustration #G-81)*

Species: *Olivella biplicata* (Sowerby, 1825).
Size: To 1 1/4" (30 mm) height.
Range: Vancouver Island, BC south to Baja California.
Habitat: In sand, on open coast. They burrow into the sand quickly when the tide goes out.
Description: Elongated, somewhat globular, highly polished shell. Exterior blue-grey with violet around lower part of aperture.
Comments: This shell was used by Native peoples for jewellery and ornaments.

BAETIC OLIVE *(Illustration #G-82)*

Species: *Olivella baetica* Carpenter, 1864.
Size: To 3/4" (20 mm); smaller than pirple olive, *O. biplicata*, above.
Range: Alaska south to Baja California.
Habitat: In sandy bays and beaches, often in same areas as purple olive. Also found in more protected waters.
Description: Shell is more slender than purple olive; glossy tan colour, sometimes with brown angular patterns; white around the aperture.

TURRID SNAILS Family Turridae

This is the largest family of mollusks, comprising as many as 20,000 species (many of these species names are for fossils) in 150–200 genera. Not surprisingly, the family is under review. These are small snails—few of them are longer than 3/4" (20 mm)—but common ones, abundant in some locations. There are more than 50 species described from the Northwest Coast region.

The turrid snails kill their prey (usually marine worms) by injecting a toxin with a hypodermic-like radular tooth. Fortunately the small representatives of the family in our region have teeth that are too small to pierce human skin. Snails in the tropical genus *Conus*, which have similar but larger teeth, have been known to cause serious injury and even death to humans.

This section was prepared with contributions from Ron Shimek.

LORA *(Illustration #G-83)*

Species: *Oenopota levidensis* (Carpenter, 1864).
Size: To 3/4" (20 mm) shell length.
Range: East Bering Sea south to northern California.
Habitat: Common in the shallows, in brown kelp (*Agarum*) beds, and on muddy sands to 660' (200 m).
Description: Exterior body whorl violet with apical whorls coloured grey, brown, violet, pinkish violet or maroon. Spiral sculpture of grooves.
Comments: This snail is found in high densities—20 per square yard (m3) in some locations in the San Juan Islands, Washington. Its shell colour is not white, and does not have spiral bands of colour.

TABLE LORA *(Illustration #G-84)*

Species: *Oenopota tabulata* (Carpenter, 1864).
Size: To 5/8" (15 mm) height.
Range: Sitka, Alaska south to Puget Sound, Washington.
Habitat: In sand–shell mix, on rocks in the shallows, under the broad-bladed kelp canopy of *Agarum.*
Description: Upper portion of each whorl is flattened or "tabulate." Exterior body whorl may be bright pink when animal is alive.
Comments: This snail feeds on polychaete worms.

CANCELLATE SNAKESKIN-SNAIL *(Illustration #G-85)*

Species: *Ophiodermella cancellata* (Carpenter, 1865).
Alternate names: *Pleurotoma vancouverensis.*
Size: To 1/2" (13 mm).
Range: Outer coast of BC and San Juan Islands to Puget Sound, Washington.

Habitat: Sandy to silty areas, 165–1650' (50–500 m).
Description: White shell with fine cancellate appearance from crossing of axial and spiral sculpture.
Comments: This snail feeds on polychaete worms.

GRAY SNAKESKIN-SNAIL *(Illustration #G-86)*

Species: *Ophiodermella inermis* (Reeve, 1843).
Size: To 1 1/2" (40 mm); largest of local species.
Range: Northern BC to central California.
Habitat: Sometimes intertidal, to 230' (70 m) and more feeding on polychaete worms, usually in shallow water.
Description: Slender shell; anal notch at widest part of aperture. Exterior of shell grey, with thin black incised lines.

VIOLET-BAND MANGELIA *(Illustration #G-87)*

Species: *Kurtziella crebricostata* (Carpenter, 1864).
Alternate names: *Kurtziella plumbea.*
Size: Seldom over 3/8" (10 mm); maximum recorded 3/4" (20 mm).
Range: Cook Inlet, Alaska south to northern Washington.
Habitat: Sandy areas in shallow subtidal, and deeper in sand–mud. Intertidal to 280' (85 m).
Description: Exterior white with tan, brown or violet spiral band.
Comments: In spite of their small size, these snails are often easy to detect on the sediment because of their coloration. They feed on polychaete tube worms, using their dagger-shaped teeth.

Subclass Opisthobranchia

PYRAMID SHELLS Family Pyramidellidae

The taxonomy of this group has not been studied fully. There are 12 or more species in Northwest Coast waters.

PYRAMID SNAIL *(Illustration #G-88)*

Species: *Turbonilla* species.
Size: To 1/2" (12 mm) height.
Range: Alaska south to California; often dredged.
Habitat: Soft bottoms.
Description: Small, slender shell with more than 7 whorls, fine spiral lines and axial ribs. Squarish aperture, less than one-fourth the total height. Brown with darker bands.

ODOSTOME *(not illustrated)*

Species: *Odostomia columbiana* (Dall & Bartsch, 1907).
Size: To 3/8" (8 mm).
Range: Gulf of Alaska south to Puget Sound, Washington.
Habitat: Often found on sedentary checkered hairysnail, *Trichotropis cancellata* (#G-47); often feeds on northern compact wormsnail (#G-37).
Description: Elongated, body whorl at least half the total height.

Bubble Shells

These single-shelled, slug-like animals have shells that vary from being prominent, such as the barrel shell, to being thin and partially or completely covered by the soft body.

Family Haminoeidae

WHITE BUBBLE SHELL *(Illustration #G-89)*

Species: *Haminoea vesicula* Gould, 1855.
Alternate names: Blister glassy-bubble.
Size: Body to 3/4" (20 mm) length.
Range: Ketchikan, Alaska south to Magdalena Bay, Gulf of California.
Habitat: In bays, on mudflats and on eelgrass.
Description: Brown slug-like body almost completely covers internal shell.
Comments: The two species, *H. vesicula* and the green bubble shell, *H. virescens*, sometimes can be distinguished only by the body colour and shell measurements. The white bubble shell was observed in July, congregating on a sandy bottom laying egg ribbons.

Family Acteonidae

BARREL SHELL *(Illustration #G-90)*

Species: *Rictaxis punctocaelatus* (Carpenter, 1864).
Alternate names: Baby's bubble, *Acteon punctocaelatus*.
Size: Shell to 3/4" (20 mm) height.
Range: Alaska south to central Baja California.
Habitat: In tidepools or on sand among eelgrass, feeding on sand-dwelling worms; to 300' (90 m).
Description: Barrel-shaped shell with aperture more than half the length of the shell. Exterior white with grey, grey-brown or black bands with pitted grooves. Shell is large enough to accommodate the animal when it retracts; no operculum. Soft body is translucent to opaque white.

INTERNAL BUBBLE SHELL Family Aglajidae

SPOTTED AGLAJA *(Illustration #G-91)*

Species: *Aglaja ocelligera* (Bergh, 1894).
Alternate names: Eyespot aglaja.
Size: To 1" (25 mm).
Range: Sitka, Alaska south to Santa Barbara, California.
Habitat: On mud–sand bottoms, shallow subtidal to 65' (20 m).
Description: Shell is completely covered by the mantle and not visible externally. Dark brown-black body with numerous yellow spots and yellow lines bordering it.
Comments: This species leaves a small, gelatinous egg case attached to the bottom by a stalk, in June–August.

Subclass Pulmonata

SIPHON SHELL or FALSELIMPET Family Siphonariidae

These are air-breathing mollusks, living on rocks close to the high tide. They are hermaphroditic.

CARPENTER'S FALSELIMPET *(Illustration #G-92)*

Species: *Siphonaria thersites* (Carpenter, 1864).
Alternate names: Siphon shell, *Liriola thersites* (Carpenter, 1864).
Size: To 1 1/4" (31 mm).
Range: Not commmon; Aleutian Islands, Alaska south to Puget Sound, Washington; more common in northern range.
Habitat: Mid-intertidal, on rocky ocean beaches, often among rockweed, *Fucus*.
Description: Limpet-like shell, low, oval-irregular with light ribbing; body is much larger than shell. Margin has a slight wave for the siphon. An interior muscle scar opens on one side, differing from limpets where the scar opens at one end. Exterior dark brown; interior shiny dark brown.
Comments: The Latin *sipho* translates to "pipe" and refers to the siphon. *Thersites*, after a Greek mythological character who was deformed, refers to the misshapen shell.

Tuskshells

The class Scaphopoda comprises about 500 living species of burrowing mollusks commonly known as tuskshells or toothshells. The common name comes from the tusk-like appearance of the single curved and tapered shell, which is open on both ends. Tuskshells, or scaphopods, are found buried in the top few inches down to 16" (40 cm) deep in marine mud–sand, from the shallows to great depths in the ocean.

They remain buried in mud–sand, only rarely with their tips protruding (less than 1 percent visible at the surface of the sediment). They draw and expel water through the open posterior end of the shell. Illustrations in much of the literature show tuskshells regularly protruding from the sediment, an error that can be traced back through the history of scaphopod study. Some early workers put the specimens in shallow bowls to study their behaviour, and as hard as the animals tried, there wasn't enough sediment to bury them completely and their shells stuck out of the sand. So begins a "legend."

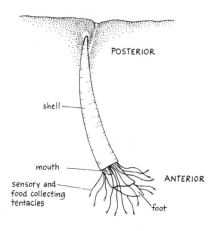

POSTERIOR

shell

mouth

ANTERIOR

sensory and food collecting tentacles

foot

Figure 12: Tuskshell

The Shell

Local species have a tubular shell that grows to 4" (100 mm), but some foreign species attain lengths of 10" (250 mm). The shells are usually white but some tropical species are coloured. The shell exterior may be smooth, dull or chalky and sometimes longitudinally ribbed. Identification is based on the slits at the tapered **posterior end** and the presence or absence and nature of the shell ribbing.

The Body

Tuskshells in the Northwest Coast region live and feed totally within the sediment. The **head end** is continually buried in the sand and the animal gathers microscopic food particles mostly by using sticky **tentacles** to transfer food to its **mouth**. Digested food is circulated by the blood. The animal both takes in and expels water through the **apex opening**, and fluids are circulated in the body by muscular action. A tuskshell absorbs oxygen through the **mantle** (scaphopods do not have gills).

Tuskshells are eaten by the ratfish, *Hydrolagus colliei*, and a variety of crabs, among other marine creatures. The hermit crab *Orthopagurus minimus* often takes up residence in empty tuskshells of the more robust *Antalis*.

Reproduction

Reproduction has not been studied or observed for any of our local species. For European species it has been described that at spawning time, the male and female tuskshells back up to the surface of sand and discharge gametes (eggs and sperm) into the water, where they are fertilized. It has been estimated that the larvae develop quickly, in 5–6 days, and settle in the sand.

Fisheries

North American aboriginal people traditionally used tuskshells for decoration and for currency in trade. The tuskshells were considered very valuable, as populations were limited mostly to the west coast of Vancouver Island. Shells were harvested in a number of ways, including the use of a pole as long as 70' (21 m) equipped with a special broom-like head.

Class
Scaphopoda

TUSKSHELLS Family Dentaliidae

WAMPUM TUSKSHELL *(Illustration #T-1)*

Species: *Antalis pretiosum* (Sowerby, 1860).
Alternate names: Indian money tusk, Dentalia, *Dentalium pretiosum*.
Size: To 2" (50 mm) length.
Range: Alaska south to Baja California.
Habitat: Common offshore in coarse shell–gravel.
Description: Solid, moderately curved shell, smooth and tapering to a point at apex; narrow slit at posterior aperture (may be broken off).
Comments: This species occurs from Alaska to Baja California but its common name comes from the tradition of the Nuu-chah-nulth Indians of Vancouver Island, who harvested the tusks with pronged spears or a dredge-like apparatus. The Latin term *pretiosum* means "precious" or "valuable."

WESTERN STRAIGHT TUSKSHELL *(Illustration #T-2)*

Species: *Rhabdus rectius* (Carpenter, 1865).
Alternate names: *Laevidentalium rectius, Dentalium rectius.*
Size: To 5 1/4" (130 mm) length.
Range: Alaska south to Panama.
Habitat: Offshore in mud and silt.
Description: Smooth, thin, fragile shell; no slit at posterior apex. White to clear with flecks. Males have white gonads and females have yellow gonads, showing through the shell in some specimens.
Comments: This species is moderately common.

This section was prepared with contributions from Ronald L. Shimek.

Chitons

Chitons (pronounced *KY-tons*), also known as "sea cradles," are members of the class Polyplacophora ("bearing many plates"). They are slow-moving marine animals that have lived on earth for some 500 million years. Scientists have identified as many as 500–600 species of chitons worldwide. In BC there are some 20 intertidal species of chitons in as many as 8 families, and more than 100 intertidal and subtidal species can be found along the Pacific coast from the Aleutian Islands, Alaska, south to Baja California.

The black Katy chiton, *Katharina tunicata,* and the giant Pacific chiton, *Cryptochiton stelleri,* were important foods to Native groups, who had several rituals that revolved around collecting, preparing and eating chitons. Chitons also play a part in stories and legends.

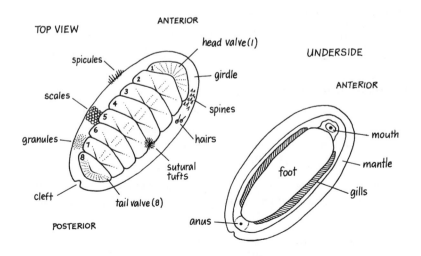

Figure 13: Chiton Features

The Shell

Chitons are oval, flattened creatures with coat-of-mail shells that have eight overlapping plates or "valves" bound together by a leathery girdle. The valves are jointed so that the chiton can roll up into a ball when disturbed, hence the name sea cradle. When a chiton dies, its valves are often washed up on the beach. They are called "butterfly shells."

The Body

A chiton has a small head with a mouth on the underside, but no tentacles or eyes. It travels slowly along the sea bottom, scraping algae and animal life from rocks with its tooth-like radula. Chitons are said to have "teeth of iron," because the radula contains so much magnetite (an iron oxide) that it can be picked up by a magnet.

A chiton also has a muscular foot much like the foot of a snail, which it uses to attach itself to surfaces and to travel along, hugging the contours of the sea bottom. But these animals do not move quickly. Some of them are so sedentary they wear depressions into the rocks as they slowly grow. Marine life watchers have reported seeing chitons at the same site for 25 years.

A chiton has gills on its underside, along the foot. It also has light-sensitive organs in the shell plates, and species that are sensitive to light are found only in crevices, on the underside of rocks, or even embedded in the sand under rocks. Chitons are typically more active at night, when many of them feed. They are preyed upon by several species of sea stars.

Reproduction

Male and female chitons spawn by releasing gametes into the water, where fertilization occurs. A few species brood their eggs in grooves along the foot.

Identifying Chitons

Most chitons can be identified by external characteristics: length, shape, girdle characteristics (scales, beads, smooth, hairy), valve characteristics (colour, line patterns), habitat and distribution. Sometimes the interior colour of the valves is another useful identifying feature.

However, only a few species can be identified easily in the field. Most require examination with a hand lens or microscope to distinguish features of the girdle and markings on the plates.

Only a few common names have been identified and accepted by the American Fisheries Society (1988).

Class
Polyplacophora

Family Lepidochitonidae

LINED (Red) CHITON *(Illustration #C-1)*

Species: *Tonicella lineata* (Wood, 1815).
Size: To 2" (50 mm).
Range: 60°N–34°N; Aleutian Islands, Gulf of Alaska south to central California.
Habitat: Often on rocks, grazing on encrusting coralline algae, *Lithothamnion*, and others. Often in depressions under purple sea urchins, *Strongylocentrotus purpuratus*.
Description: Smooth, dark girdle, often banded with whitish, yellowish or orange blotches; valves are red to orange-red to pink with dark zigzag lines edged with white.
Comments: A relatively common chiton, noticeable because of its bright colour patterns. This chiton is often eaten by the ochre star, *Pisaster ocraceus* and the six-ray star, *Leptasterias hexactis*.

BLUE-LINE CHITON *(Illustration #C-2)*

Species: *Tonicella undocaerulea* (Sirenko, 1973).
Alternate names: Often misidentified as the lined chiton, *T. lineata*.
Size: To 2" (50 mm).
Range: 57°N–34°N; Kodiak Island, Alaska south to central California.
Habitat: Often on rocks, grazing on coralline algae, from intertidal to shallow subtidal.
Description: Similar to *Tonicella lineata*, but valves are light orange to pink, with concentric white zigzag lines; brilliant blue zigzag lines in live specimens.

WHITE-LINE CHITON *(Illustration #C-3)*

Species: *Tonicella insignis* (Reeve, 1847).
Size: To 2" (50 mm).
Range: 60°N–43°N; Alaska south to Oregon.
Habitat: Intertidal but mostly subtidal, to 170' (52 m).
Description: Maroon-red valves with wavy white lines in live specimens; smooth dark brown girdle with subdued green blotches.

Family Ischnochitonidae

MERTEN'S CHITON *(Illustration #C-4)*

Species: *Lepidozona mertensii* (Middendorff, 1847).
Size: To 1 1/2" (38 mm).
Range: 59°N–28°N; Cook Inlet, Alaska south to northern Baja California.
Habitat: Often under rocks, intertidal to 300' (90 m).
Description: Elliptical shape; girdle with alternating yellow and reddish bands and low, smooth scales. Valves are variable in colour, usually reddish, sometimes green-purple, with strong white longitudinal lines and smaller cross ridges. Interior of valves is whitish.
Comments: Females release egg cases.

THREE-RIB CHITON *(Illustration #C-5)*

Species: *Lepidozona trifida* (Carpenter, 1864).
Size: To 2 1/2" (60 mm).
Range: 60°N–47°N; Aleutian Islands, Gulf of Alaska south to Puget Sound, Washington.
Habitat: On rocks, intertidal to 365' (110 m).
Description: Valves reddish-brown to orange brown.
Comments: This chiton has been found in the stomachs of wolf eels.

Family Mopaliidae

More than 10 *Mopalia* species live in Northwest Coast waters. Three large hairy or mossy species, *Mopalia muscosa*, *M. lignosa* and *M. ciliata*, are most commonly encountered in our region.

HAIRY CHITON *(Illustration #C-6)*

Species: *Mopalia ciliata* (Sowerby, 1840).
Size: To 3" (75 mm).
Range: 60°N–28°N; Gulf of Alaska south to northern Baja California.
Habitat: Protected areas, under rocks or sometimes in mussel beds, mid- to low intertidal.
Description: Elongated-oval shape, wide girdle variable in colour from dark to light, bristly with soft hairs and clearly notched at the rear end. Valves, reduced in size, are variable in colour, often with brilliant colour patterns of blotches and streaks.
Comments: The hairy chiton feeds on algae, sponges, hydroids and bryozoans.

MOSSY CHITON *(Illustration #C-7)*

Species: *Mopalia muscosa* (Gould, 1846).
Size: To 2³/4" (70 mm).
Range: 57°N–28°N; Alaska south to Isla Cedros, northern Baja California.
Habitat: Often in tidepools and on top of rocks; not affected by accumulations of silt.
Description: Oval shape; girdle has small, shallow notch at rear, stout stiff hairs. Head valve has ten beaded ribs; valves are dull, dark brown, grey to black sometines with white stripes. Interior of valves is light blue.
Comments: This is a common species. It often has barnacles, seaweeds or other growths on the valves. This chiton only moves at night when it is wet or submerged. It feeds on algae.

WOODY CHITON *(Illustration #C-8)*

Species: *Mopalia lignosa* (Gould, 1846).
Size: To 2³/4" (70 mm).
Range: 59°N–34°N; Alaska south to Point Conception, California.
Habitat: Intertidal and deeper. Found feeding on algae, especially sea lettuce, *Ulva.*
Description: Oval shape; grey, blue, brown, green or white valves with streaks of brown to purple brown, sometimes white; girdle has scattered stout, stiff hairs that grow from the centres of light spots; it is difficult to distinguish posterior cleft in girdle.

HIND'S MOPALIA *(Illustration #C-9)*

Species: *Mopalia hindsii* (Sowerby, in Reeve, 1847).
Size: To 4" (100 mm).
Range: 57°N–34°N; Kodiak, Alaska south to Ventura County, California.
Habitat: In shallow bays, protected waters, often on pilings and rocks with deposits of silt.
Description: White to dark green girdle. Short, fine hairs on girdle do not branch. Broad posterior cleft. Valve colour is variable, often dark olive to brown. Some specimens have white markings along tops of valves. Interior of valves is white.
Comments: Feeds on algae, bryozoans and young barnacles.

SWAN'S MOPALIA *(Illustration #C-10)*

Species: *Mopalia swanii* Carpenter, 1864.
Size: To 2¹/2" (60 mm).
Range: 55°N–34°N; Aleutian Islands, Alaska south to Malibu, California.

Habitat: On bottoms of rocks, in crevices or under ledges; intertidal.
Description: Broad girdle is light brown mottled with dark brown. It has a distinct posterior cleft. Many small, fine bristles. Valves green to brown.

RED-FLECKED MOPALIA *(Illustration #C-11)*

Species: *Mopalia spectabilis* Cowan and Cowan, 1977.
Size: To 2³/4" (70 mm).
Range: 60°N–32°N; Prince William Sound, Alaska south to Ensenada, northern Baja California.
Habitat: On bottoms of rocks, in crevices and under ledges; intertidal to 33' (10 m).
Description: Broad, hairy girdle with posterior cleft; valves olive, almost always with bright turquoise, orange or reddish-brown marks, especially plate 2.
Comments: This species is often found with and feeding on red social tunicates, *Metandrocarpa taylori*.

SMOOTH MOPALIA *(Illustration #C-12)*

Species: *Mopalia vespertina* (Gould, 1852)
Size: To 3¹/4" (80 mm).
Range: 57°N–35°N; Sitka, Alaska south to Morro Bay, central California.
Habitat: Common subtidal species.
Description: Smooth valves with fine central pitting. Colour from olive to dark brown with green markings. Girdle with banded margin which extends between valves. Small fine hairs on the girdle.

BLACK KATY CHITON *(Illustration #C-13)*

Species: *Katharina tunicata* (Wood, 1815).
Alternate names: Leather chiton, black chiton. Natives referred to it as "small Chinese slippers" or sea prune.
Size: To 3" (75 mm).
Range: 57°N–37°N; Alaska south to Monterey, California.
Habitat: Mid-intertidal, in exposed wave-swept situations.
Description: Oval to elongated shape; smooth, black to brownish black girdle covers about two-thirds of the white plates. The foot on the underside is pink-red.
Comments: This chiton is not extremely sensitive to light and can often be found in the open, feeding on algae. The female lays greenish eggs in the summer.
Edibility: These chitons were eaten by Native peoples and are the subjects of many legends. The Haida believed they originated from the black beetle while the Manhousat on the west coast of Vancouver Island told

how a land slug was transformed into the black chiton. The chitons were soaked, cleaned and eaten raw or thrown whole onto hot coals. "The world was different then." —Luke Swan, Manhousat.

RED VEILED-CHITON *(Illustration #C-14)*

Species: *Placiphorella rufa* Berry, 1917.
Alternate names: Red hooded-chiton.
Size: To 2" (50 mm).
Range: 60°N–43°N; Aleutian Islands to Prince William Sound, Alaska, south to southern Oregon.
Habitat: Common subtidal species, to 150' (45 m). In areas of strong currents.
Description: Valves red in colour, oval girdle much wider at the head than elsewhere. There are long, slender setae at the periphery of the girdle.
Comments: Veiled-chitons are the only chiton genus adapted to capturing active animal prey. The animal raises its "hood" to trap food. This species is the largest and most common of a variety of hooded-chitons in our waters.

VEILED-CHITON *(not illustrated)*

Species: *Placiphorella velata* (Carpenter, in Dall, 1897).
Alternate names: Hooded-chiton.
Size: To 21/2" (60 mm).
Range: 60°N–24°N; Prince William Sound, Alaska south to central Baja California; rare north of Vancouver Island.
Habitat: More commonly found in intertidal, but to 65' (20 m), on tops, sides and bottoms of rocks and cobble, in areas of current flow. Also in depressions of the open coast purple sea urchin, *Stronglyocentrotus purpuratus.*
Description: Valves are streaked with brown pink, blue and olive. The girdle has hairs throughout.

Family Acantitochitonidae

GIANT PACIFIC CHITON *(Illustration #C-15)*

Species: *Cryptochiton stelleri* (Middendorff, 1847).
Alternate names: Gumboot chiton, giant red chiton, moccasin chiton, butterfly shells.
Size: To 13" (330 mm). This is the largest chiton in the world.
Range: 60°N–34°N; Alaska south to Channel Islands, California.

Habitat: Intertidal to 65' (20 m).

Description: Oval-elongated; brown to reddish brown granular girdle completely covers the plates. Underside is yellow, with a large broad foot. Juveniles, less than 1/2" (10 mm), are yellow and a tiny portion of the valves may be exposed.

Comments: The shell plates (butterfly shells) often wash ashore and are found in beach drift. This species' radular teeth are covered with magnetite. The rocksnail, *Ocinebrina lurida,* eats the giant Pacific chiton, and leaves yellow pits in the upper body surface.

Chief Skidegate, after whom the village of Skidegate, Queen Charlotte Islands (Haida Gwaii) is named, in turn received his name from this chiton. The Haida name for large specimens, SG̲IÍDAA, translates to "lying face down forever."

Edibility: Because of its size and high profile, this species is easily dislodged. It is a traditional source of food, and plates are often found in local middens. When chitons were eaten, the plates were first removed one by one and counted. This ensured that all eight were removed and no plates were left to hurt the mouth of the person eating the chiton. The giant Pacific chiton has the appearance of a wandering meatloaf, but do not be deceived. The common name "gumboot chiton" gives a clue to the toughness of this chiton's meat! Even careful preparation and pounding of the chiton do not necessarily mean a tender meal.

This section was prepared with contributions from Roger N. Clark.

Acknowledgements

This book is dedicated to my wife Heather and to my children Jennifer, Michael and Amy.

Scientific editing was graciously undertaken by numerous experts. My thanks to Ronald L. Shimek, Paul H. Scott, Eugene V. Coan, James H. McLean, Roger N. Clark and William Merilees. The book benefitted from the interest and assistance provided by William C. Austin, Marine Ecology Station, Cowichan Bay; Phillip Lambert, Kelly Sendall, Gordon Green, Nancy Romaine, Robert Griffin, John Viellette, Grant Keddie, Alan Hoover and Dan Savard at the Royal British Columbia Museum, Victoria; Calvor Palmateer at the Sidney Museum; Natalie MacFarlane at the Skidegate Museum; and Gordon Miller and Pam Olsen at the Pacific Biological Station library. Many individuals provided advice, specimens, or assistance in collecting specimens, including Frank R. Bernard, Dan B. Quayle, Neil Bourne, Graham Gillespie, Bruce Clapp, Dwight Heritage, Alan Campbell, Glen Jamieson, Bruce Adkins, Steve Heizer, Neil McDaniel, Guy Martel, Bill Heath, Lou Barr and Ed Andrusiak.

My thanks to Mary Schendlinger who patiently edited many drafts of the text, Susan Mayse who reviewed final drafts, and Peter Robson and Howard White who provided direction in the development of the book. Martin Nichols contributed his skill in the design and layout of the book.

Photograph credits

Lou Barr: wide lacuna G-36; Carpenter's falselimpet in situ G-92.

Edward S. Curtis: Native woman wearing tuskshell dress, p. 103.

Neil McDaniel: variable topsnail G-19; checkered hairysnail G-47; boreal wentletrap G-55; northern compact wormsnail G-37; lined chiton (middle) C-1; woody chiton C-8; Hind's mopalia (top) C-9; Swan's mopalia C-10.

William Merilees: dredge haul, p. 12; oystercatcher B-18; weathervane scallops B-25; burrows of boring softshell-clam (chubby mya), p 59; bladderclam S-13; shipworm in fir log S-14; boring softshell-clam S-18; two-spot keyhole limpet G-5; underside of limpet G-25; Merten's chiton C-4.

Martin Nichols: Cox Point, Vancouver Island, p. 8.

Ronald L. Shimek: money wentletrap in-situ G-54; baetic olive G-82; lora G-83; table lora G-84; violet-band mangelia G-87.

Archie Wills: geoduck harvesting, p. 165.

Archival photograph credits

Sidney Museum: Butter clam cannery, Sidney, BC, p. 54.

Skidegate Museum: clam cannery, Bag Harbour, p. 129; clam diggers, p. 149.

Department of Fisheries and Oceans: Indian clam digger's canoe, p. 145; Indian woman digging for cockles, p. 150 (from W. F. Thompson, 1913, Report of the clam-beds of British Columbia, British Columbia Fisheries Department, Report of the Commissioner of Fisheries for the year ending December 31, 1912).

All other photographs by Rick Harbo.

Checklist

Phylum Mollusca

There are two groups of animals with two shells: the lampshells of the Phylum Brachiopoda and the bivalves of the Phylum Mollusca. All of the single-shell animals and chitons presented are members of the Phylum Mollusca.

Alternate common names appear after the species name in parentheses.

Key: **E** Edible species; **I** Intertidal species; ***** Introduced species.

BIVALVES

CLASS BIVALVIA

Subclass PROTOBRANCHIA (=PALEOTAXODONTA)
Order Solemyidae
Family Solemyidae
❑ GUTLESS AWNING-CLAM, *Solemya reidi* Bernard, 1980
Order Nuculoida
Family Nuculidae
❑ DIVARICATE NUTCLAM, *Acila castrensis* (Hinds, 1843)
Family Sareptidae (=Yoldiidae)
❑ AXE (Broad) YOLDIA, *Megayoldia thraciaeformis* (Storer, 1838)
❑ CRISSCROSS YOLDIA, *Yoldia seminuda* Dall, 1871

Subclass PTERIOMORPHIA
Order Arcoida
Family Glycymerididae
❑ I WESTERN BITTERSWEET, *Glycymeris septentrionalis* (Middendorff, 1849)
Family Philobryidae
❑ I HAIRY PHILOBRYA, *Philobrya setosa* (Carpenter, 1864)

Order Mtilioida
Family Mytilidae
❑ E PACIFIC BLUE MUSSEL, *Mytilus edulis* complex, Linnaeus, 1758
❑ E MEDITERRANEAN MUSSEL, *Mytilus galloprovincialis* Lamarck, 1819
❑ E FOOLISH MUSSEL, *Mytilus trossulus* A.A. Gould, 1850
❑ E I CALIFORNIA (Sea, Ribbed) MUSSEL, *Mytilus californianus* Conrad, 1837
❑ I STRAIGHT (FAN) HORSEMUSSEL, *Modiolus rectus* (Conrad, 1837)
❑ I NORTHERN HORSEMUSSEL, *Modiolus modiolus* (Linnaeus, 1758)
❑ I CALIFORNIA DATEMUSSEL, *Adula californiensis* (Philippi, 1847)
❑ I DISCORDANT MUSSEL, *Musculus discors* (Linnaeus, 1767)
❑ BLACK MUSSEL, *Musculus niger* (Gray, 1824)
❑ I TAYLOR'S DWARF-MUSSEL, *Musculus taylori* (Dall, 1897)
❑ * I JAPAN MUSSEL, *Musculista senhousia* (Benson, 1842)
❑ BRITISH COLUMBIA CRENELLA, *Solamen columbianum* (Dall, 1897)

Order Ostreoida
Family Ostreidae
❑ * E I OLYMPIA OYSTER, *Ostrea conchaphila* Carpenter, 1857
❑ * E I PACIFIC (Japanese) OYSTER, *Crassostrea gigas* (Thunberg, 1793)
❑ * E I AMERICAN (Eastern, Atlantic) OYSTER, *Crassostrea virginica* (Gmelin, 1791)
❑ * E I EDIBLE (European) FLAT OYSTER, *Ostrea edulis* Linnaeus, 1758
Suborder Pectinina
Family Anomiidae
❑ I GREEN FALSE-JINGLE, *Pododesmus macroschisma* (Deshayes, 1839)
Family Pectinidae
❑ E SMOOTH PINK (Reddish) SCALLOP, *Chlamys rubida* (Hinds, 1845)
❑ E I SPINY PINK SCALLOP, *Chlamys hastata* (Sowerby, 1842)
❑ E I GIANT ROCK (Purple-hinged) SCALLOP, *Crassadoma gigantea* (Gray, 1825) =*Hinnites giganteus* (Gray, 1825)
❑ E WEATHERVANE (Giant Pacific) SCALLOP, *Patinopecten caurinus* (A.A. Gould, 1850)
❑ * E JAPANESE WEATHERVANE SCALLOP, *Mizuhopecten yessoensis* (Jay, 1857) =*Patinopecten yessoensis*
❑ VANCOUVER (Transparent) SCALLOP, *Delectopecten vancouverensis* (Whiteaves, 1893)
Subclass HETERODONTA
Order Veneroida
Family Lucinidae
❑ I WESTERN RINGED LUCINE, *Lucinoma annulatum* (Reeve, 1850)
❑ FINE-LINED LUCINE, *Parvalucina tenuisculpta* (Carpenter, 1864)
Family Ungulinidae
❑ I ROUGH (Orb) DIPLODON, *Diplodonta impolita* S.S. Berry, 1953
Family Thyasiridae
❑ GIANT CLEFTCLAM, *Conchocele bisecta* (Conrad, 1849)
❑ FLEXUOSE (Gould's) CLEFTCLAM, *Thyasira flexuosa* (Montagu, 1803)
❑ I NORTHERN AXINOPSID, *Axinopsida serricata* (Carpenter, 1864)
Family Astartidae
❑ ELLIPTICAL (Alaska) TRIDONTA, *Astarte elliptica* (Brown, 1827)
❑ I ESQUIMALT ASTARTE, *Astarte esquimalti* (Baird, 1863)
Family Carditidae
❑ I CARPENTER'S CARDITA, *Glans carpenteri* (Lamy, 1922) =*Cardita carpenteri*
Family Lasaeidae
❑ I ADANSON'S LEPTON (Red Lasaea), *Lasaea adansoni* (Gmelin, 1791)
❑ I KELLYCLAM, *Kellia suborbicularis* (Montagu, 1803) =*Kellia laperousi*
❑ I NETTED KELLYCLAM, *Rhamphidonta retifera* (Dall, 1899)
❑ I WRINKLED MONTACUTID, *Neaeromya rugifera* (Carpenter, 1864) =*Neaeromya* =*Orobitella rugifera*
❑ I ROBUST MYSELLA, *Rochefortia tumida* (Carpenter, 1864)
Family Cardiidae
❑ E I NUTTALL'S COCKLE, *Clinocardium nuttallii* (Conrad, 1837)

❑ SMOOTH COCKLE, *Clinocardium blandum* (Gould, 1850)

❑ ALEUTIAN (California) COCKLE, *Clinocardium californiense* (Deshayes, 1839)

❑ HAIRY COCKLE, *Clinocardium ciliatum* (Fabricius, 1780)

❑ FUCAN COCKLE, *Clinocardium fucanum* (Dall, 1907)

❑ **I** GREENLAND COCKLE, *Serripes groenlandicus* (Mohr, 1786)

❑ HUNDRED LINE COCKLE, *Nemocardium centifilosum* (Carpenter, 1864)

Family Mactridae

❑ **E I** FAT GAPER, *Tresus capax* (Gould, 1850)

❑ **E I** PACIFIC GAPER, *Tresus nuttallii* (Conrad, 1837)

❑ **I** HOOKED SURFCLAM, *Simomactra falcata* (A. A. Gould, 1850)

❑ **E I** ARCTIC SURFCLAM, *Mactromeris polynyma* (Stimpson, 1860)

❑ **I** CALIFORNIA SURFCLAM, *Mactrotoma californica* (Conrad, 1837)

Family Solenidae

❑ **I** SICKLE JACKKNIFE-CLAM, *Solen sicarius* A.A. Gould, 1850

Family Pharidae

❑ **E I** PACIFIC RAZOR-CLAM, *Siliqua patula* (Dixon, 1789)

Family Tellinidae

❑ **I** BODEGA TELLIN, *Tellina bodegensis* Hinds, 1845

❑ **I** CARPENTER'S TELLIN, *Tellina carpenteri* Dall, 1900

❑ **I** PLAIN TELLIN, *Tellina modesta* (Carpenter, 1864)

❑ **I** SALMON TELLIN, *Tellina nuculoides* (Reeve, 1854) =*T. salmonea*

❑ **I** BALTIC MACOMA, *Macoma balthica* (Linnaeus, 1758)

❑ **I** POINTED MACOMA, *Macoma inquinata* (Deshayes, 1855)

❑ **I** BENT-NOSE MACOMA, *Macoma nasuta* (Conrad, 1837)

❑ **I** WHITE-SAND MACOMA, *Macoma secta* (Conrad, 1837)

❑ HEAVY MACOMA (Pacific brota), *Macoma brota* Dall, 1916

❑ **I** CHALKY MACOMA, *Macoma calcarea* (Gmelin, 1791)

❑ CHARLOTTE MACOMA, *Macoma carlottensis* Whiteaves, 1880

❑ FILE MACOMA, *Macoma elimata* Dunhill & Coan, 1968

❑ **I** EXPANDED MACOMA, *Macoma expansa* Carpenter, 1864

❑ **I** ALEUTIAN MACOMA, *Macoma lama* Bartsch, 1929

❑ SLEEK MACOMA, *Macoma lipara* Dall, 1916

❑ FLAT (Doleful) MACOMA, *Macoma moesta* (Deshayes, 1855)

❑ OBLIQUE MACOMA, *Macoma obliqua* (Sowerby, 1817)

❑ **I** YOLDIA SHAPE MACOMA, *Macoma yoldiformis* Carpenter, 1864

Family Semelidae (includes Scrobiculariidae)

❑ **I** ROSE-PAINTED CLAM, *Semele rubropicta* Dall, 1871

Family Psammobiidae (=Garidae)

❑ **I** CALIFORNIA SUNSETCLAM, *Gari californica* (Conrad, 1849)

❑ * **I** DARK MAHOGANY-CLAM (Varnish clam), *Nuttallia obscurata* (Reeve, 1857)

Family Veneridae

❑ **E I** BUTTER (Smooth Washington) CLAM, *Saxidomus gigantea* (Deshayes, 1839) =*Saxidomus giganteus*

❑ * **E I** JAPANESE LITTLENECK (Manila clam), *Venerupis philippinarum* (A. Adams & Reeve, 1850) =*Tapes philippinarum* (A. Adams & Reeve, 1850)

❑ **E I** PACIFIC LITTLENECK, *Protothaca staminea* (Conrad, 1837)
❑ **E** MILKY VENUS (Deep water littleneck), *Compsomyax subdiaphana* (Carpenter, 1864)
❑ **I** THIN-SHELL LITTLENECK, *Protothaca tenerrima* (Carpenter, 1857)
❑ **I** RIBBED CLAM, *Humilaria kennerleyi* (Reeve, 1863)
❑ **I** LORD DWARF-VENUS, *Nutricola lordi* (W. Baird, 1863)
❑ **I** PURPLE DWARF-VENUS, *Nutricola tantilla* (A.A. Gould, 1853)

Family Petricolidae
❑ **I** HEARTY PETRICOLID, *Petricola carditoides* (Conrad, 1837)

Family Turtoniidae
❑ **I** LITTLE MULLET SHELL, *Turtonia minuta* (Fabricius, 1780)

Subclass ASTHENODONTA
Order Myoida
Family Myidae
❑ **E I** SOFTSHELL-CLAM (Mud clam), *Mya arenaria* Linnaeus, 1758
❑ **I** TRUNCATED SOFTSHELL-CLAM (Blunt gaper), *Mya truncata* Linnaeus, 1758
❑ **I** BORING SOFTSHELL-CLAM, *Platyodon cancellatus* (Conrad, 1837)
❑ **I** CALIFORNIA SOFTSHELL-CLAM, *Cryptomya californica* (Conrad, 1837)

Family Hiatellidae
❑ **E I** PACIFIC GEODUCK (King clam), *Panopea abrupta* (Conrad, 1849)
❑ AMPLE ROUGHMYA (False geoduck), *Panomya ampla* Dall, 1898 =includes *Panomya chrysis*
❑ ARCTIC ROUGHMYA (Deepwater false geoduck), *Panomya norvegica* (Spengler, 1793)
❑ **I** ARCTIC HIATELLA, *Hiatella arctica* (Linnaeus, 1767)
❑ **I** NESTLING SAXICAVE, *Hiatella pholadis* (Linnaeus, 1771)

Family Pholadidae
❑ **I** ROUGH (Pilsbry's) PIDDOCK, *Zirfaea pisbryii* Lowe, 1931
❑ **I** OVAL (Richardson's) PIDDOCK, *Penitella richardsoni* G.L. Kennedy, 1989 =*P. gabbii* (Tyron, 1863)
❑ **I** FLAT-TIP PIDDOCK, *Penitella penita* (Conrad, 1837)
❑ **I** ABALONE PIDDOCK, *Penitella conradi* Valenciennes, 1846

Family Teredinidae
❑ **I** SHIPWORM (Feathery shipworm), *Bankia setacea* (Tryon, 1865)
❑ *** I** ATLANTIC SHIPWORM, *Teredo navalis* Linnaeus, 1758

Subclass ANOMALODESMATA
Order Pholadomyoida
Family Pandoridae
❑ PUNCTATE PANDORA, *Pandora punctata* Conrad, 1837
❑ THREADED PANDORA, *Pandora filosa* (Carpenter, 1864)
❑ BILIRATE PANDORA, *Pandora bilirata* Conrad, 1855
❑ WARD (Giant) PANDORA, *Pandora wardiana* A. Adams, 1859 =*P. grandis*

Family Lyonsiidae
❑ **I** ROCK ENTODESMA (Northwest ugly clam), *Entodesma navicula* (A. Adams & Reeve, 1850) =*Agriodesma saxicola*
❑ **I** BLADDERCLAM, *Mytilimeria nuttallii* Conrad, 1837

❑ **I** SCALY LYONSIA, *Lyonsia bracteata* (A.A. Gould, 1850)
❑ **I** CALIFORNIA LYONSIA, *Lyonsia californica* Conrad, 1837

Family Thraciidae
❑ PACIFIC THRACIA, *Thracia trapezoides* Conrad, 1849

Order Septibranchida
Family Cuspidariidae
❑ PECTINATE CARDIOMYA (Ribbed dipper shell), *Cardiomya pectinata* (Carpenter, 1864)

Phylum Brachiopoda

Order Terebratulida
Family Laqueidae
❑ LAMP SHELL, *Terebratalia transversa* (Sowerby, 1846)

GASTROPODS
CLASS GASTROPODA

Subclass PROSOBRANCHIA (PALEOTAXODONTA)
Order Archaeogastropoda
Suborder Pleurotomarina
Family Haliotidae
❑ **E I** NORTHERN (Pinto) ABALONE, *Haliotis kamtschatkana* Jonas, 1845
❑ **E I** RED ABALONE, *Haliotis rufescens* Swainson, 1822

Family Fissurellidae
❑ **I** HOODED PUNCTURELLA, *Cranopsis cucullata* (Gould, 1846)
❑ **I** ROUGH KEYHOLE LIMPET, *Diodora aspera* (Rathke, 1833)
❑ **I** TWO-SPOT KEYHOLE LIMPET, *Fissurellidea bimaculata* Dall, 1871
=*Megatebennus bimaculatus*

Suborder Trochina
Family Turbinidae
❑ **E** RED TURBAN, *Astraea gibberosa* (Dillwyn, 1817)
❑ **I** DARK (Northern) DWARF TURBAN, *Homalopoma luridum* (Dall, 1885)

Family Trochidae
❑ **I** BLACK TURBAN, *Tegula funebralis* (A. Adams, 1855)
❑ **I** BROWN (Dusky) TURBAN, *Tegula pulligo* (Gmelin, 1791)
❑ **I** BERING MARGARITE, *Margarites beringensis* (E.A. Smith, 1899)
❑ **I** HELICINA (Smooth, Spiral) MARGARITE, *Margarites helicinus* Phipps, 1874
❑ **I** PUPPET (Little) MARGARITE, *Margarites pupillus* (Gould, 1849)
❑ LOVELY PACIFIC SOLARELLE, *Solariella perambilis* Carpenter, 1864
❑ **I** PEARLY TOPSNAIL, *Lirularia lirulata* (Carpenter, 1864) =*Margarite lirulata*
❑ **I** TUCKED TOPSNAIL (Girdled lirularia), *Lirularia succincta* (Carpenter, 1864)
❑ **I** PURPLE-RING TOPSNAIL, *Calliostoma annulatum* (Lightfoot, 1786)
❑ **I** BLUE (Western ridged) TOPSNAIL, *Calliostoma ligatum* (Gould, 1849)
❑ CHANNELLED TOPSNAIL, *Calliostoma canaliculatum* (Lightfoot, 1786)
❑ VARIABLE TOPSNAIL, *Calliostoma variegatum* (Carpenter, 1864)

❑ SILVERY TOPSNAIL, *Calliostoma platinum* Dall, 1890
❑ SPINY TOPSNAIL, *Cidarina cidaris* (Carpenter, 1864)

Order Patellogastropoda
Suborder Nacellna
Family Acmaeidae
❑ ı WHITECAP LIMPET, *Acmaea mitra* Rathke, 1833

Family Lottiidae
❑ ı SHIELD LIMPET, *Lottia pelta* (Rathke, 1833) =*Collisella pelta*
❑ ᴇ ı PLATE LIMPET, *Tectura scutum* (Rathke, 1833) =*Notoacmaea scutum*
❑ ı RIBBED (Finger) LIMPET, *Lottia digitalis* (Rathke, 1833)
❑ ᴇ ı MASK (Speckled) LIMPET, *Tectura persona* (Rathke, 1833)
❑ ı FENESTRATE LIMPET, *Tectura fenestrata* (Reeve, 1855)
❑ ı UNSTABLE LIMPET, *Lottia instabilis* (Gould, 1846)
❑ ı BLACK LIMPET, *Lottia asmi* (Middendorff, 1847)
❑ ı SEAWEED LIMPET, *Discurria insessa* (Hinds, 1842) =*Notoacmaea insessa*
❑ ı SURFGRASS LIMPET, *Tectura paleacea* (Gould, 1853)
=*Notoacmaea paleacea*
❑ ı EELGRASS (Bowl) LIMPET, *Lottia alveus* (Conrad, 1831)

Order Mesogastropoda
Suborder Taeniogrossa
Family Littorinidae

The periwinkle is sometimes called a "littorine" and the "lacuna" is often called a "chink-shell," referring to the slit or chink above the aperture and between the first whorl.
❑ ı SITKA PERIWINKLE, *Littorina sitkana* Philippi, 1846
❑ ı CHECKERED PERIWINKLE, *Littorina scutulata* Gould, 1849

Family Lacunidae
❑ ı VARIEGATE LACUNA (Chink-shell), *Lacuna variegata* Carpenter, 1864
❑ ı WIDE LACUNA (Northern chink-shell), *Lacuna vincta* (Montagu, 1803)
=*Lacuna carinata*

Family Vermetidae
❑ NORTHERN COMPACT WORMSNAIL, *Petalaconchus compactus*
(Carpenter, 1864)

Family Cerithiidae

The common names are sometimes listed as batillaria, cerith or hornsnails. For example, the common names threaded bittium, threaded cerith and threaded horn-snail all appear in the literature.
❑ ı THREADED BITTIUM (Giant Pacific hornsnail), *Bittium eschrichtii*
(Middendorff, 1849)
❑ ı SLENDER BITTIUM (Hornsnail), *Bittium attenuatum* Carpenter, 1864

Family Batillariidae (formerly Potamididae)
❑ * ı MUDFLAT SNAIL, *Batillaria cumingi* (Crosse, 1862) =*B. attramentaria;*
=*B. zonalis*

Family Hipponicidae
❑ ı FLAT HOOFSNAIL, *Hipponix cranioides* Carpenter, 1864

Family Calyptraeidae

The members of this family have been commonly called "Chinese-hat" snails or "cup-and-saucer" snails and slippersnails or slipper-shells.

❏ ∎ CUP-AND-SAUCER SNAIL (Pacific Chinese-hat), *Calyptraea fastigiata* Gould, 1846

❏ ∎ HOOKED SLIPPERSNAIL, *Crepidula adunca* Sowerby, 1825

❏ ∎ WRINKLED (Half) SLIPPERSNAIL, *Crepipatella dorsata* (Broderip, 1834)

❏ ∎ WESTERN WHITE SLIPPERSNAIL, *Crepidula perforans* (Valenciennes, 1846)

❏ ∎ NORTHERN WHITE SLIPPERSNAIL, *Crepidula nummaria* Gould, 1846

Family Trichotropididae

❏ CHECKERED (Cancellate) HAIRYSNAIL, *Trichotropis cancellata* Hinds, 1843

Family Ranellidae (=Cymatiidae)

❏ ∎ OREGON TRITON, *Fusitriton oregonensis* (Redfield, 1848)

Family Velutinidae

These snails have been commonly called "velvet," "velutina" or "lamellaria" snails.

❏ ∎ SMOOTH VELVET SNAIL, *Velutina prolongata* Carpenter, 1864

❏ SPIRAL VELVET SNAIL, *Velutina velutina* O.F. Müller, 1776

Family Naticidae

❏ ALEUTIAN MOONSNAIL, *Cryptonatica aleutica* (Dall, 1919) =*Natica clausa*

❏ E ∎ LEWIS'S MOONSNAIL, *Euspira lewisii* (Gould, 1847)

Family Epitoniidae

❏ ∎ TINTED (Painted) WENTLETRAP, *Epitonium tinctum* (Carpenter, 1864)

❏ ∎ MONEY WENTLETRAP, *Epitonium indianorum* (Carpenter, 1865)

❏ ∎ BOREAL WENTLETRAP, *Opalia borealis* Keep, 1881

Family Eulimidae

❏ SHINING BALCIS, *Balcis micans* (Carpenter, 1864)

Order Neogastropoda
Suborder Rachiglossa
Family Muricidae

A variety of common names are used for members of this family: hornmouth=purpura, rocksnail=dwarf triton, drills, dogwinkles (different from dogwhelks) and trophons.

❏ ∎ LEAFY HORNMOUTH, *Ceratostoma foliatum* (Gmelin, 1791)

❏ ∎ LURID ROCKSNAIL (Dwarf triton), *Ocinebrina lurida* (Middendorff, 1849)

❏ ∎ SCULPTURED ROCKSNAIL (Carpenter's dwarf triton), *Ocinebrina interfossa* Carpenter, 1864

❏ * ∎ JAPANESE ROCKSNAIL (Oyster drill), *Ceratostoma inornatum* (Recluz, 1851) =*Ocenebra japonica*

❏ * ∎ ATLANTIC OYSTER DRILL, *Urosalpinx cinerea* Say, 1822

❏ ∎ FRILLED (Wrinkled) DOGWINKLE, *Nucella lamellosa* (Gmelin, 1791) =*Thais lamellosa*

❏ ∎ CHANNELLED DOGWINKLE, *Nucella canaliculata* (Duclos, 1832)

❏ ∎ STRIPED (Emarginate) DOGWINKLE, *Nucella emarginata* (Deshayes, 1839)

❏ ∎ FILE (Rough purple) DOGWINKLE, *Nucella lima* (Gmelin, 1791)

❏ SANDPAPER TROPHON, *Scabrotrophon maltzani* (Kobelt and Küster, 1878)

❑ STUART'S TROPHON, *Boreotrophon stuarti* (E.A. Smith, 1880)
❑ CORDED TROPHON, *Boreotrophon orpheus* (Gould, 1849)

Family Buccinidae

All members of this family are commonly referred to as whelks. The Neptunea are often called neptunes rather than whelks and are sometimes described as having their own family.

❑ DIRE (Spindle) WHELK, *Lirabuccinum dirum* (Reeve, 1846)
❑ **E** LYRE (Plectrum) WHELK, *Buccinum plectrum* Stimpson, 1865
❑ **I** RIDGED WHELK (Common northwest neptune), *Neptunea lyrata* (Gmelin, 1791)
❑ PHOENICIAN WHELK, *Neptunea phoenicia* (Dall, 1891)
❑ TABLED WHELK, *Neptunea tabulata* (Baird, 1863)
❑ CHOCOLATE WHELK, *Neptunea smirnia* (Dall, 1919)

Family Columbellidae (Pyrenidae)

❑ **I** WRINKLED AMPHISSA, *Amphissa columbiana* Dall, 1916
❑ **I** JOSEPH'S COAT AMPHISSA, *Amphissa versicolor* Dall, 1871
❑ **I** DOVESNAIL, *Astysis gausapata* (Gould, 1850)
❑ **I** CARINATE DOVESNAIL, *Alia carinata* (Hinds, 1844)

Family Nassariidae

These snails are commonly called "dogwhelks" or "nassas."

❑ **I** WESTERN LEAN NASSA, *Nassarius mendicus* (Gould, 1850)
❑ **I** GIANT WESTERN (Channelled) NASSA, *Nassarius fossatus* (Gould, 1850)

Family Olividae

These snails are often called dwarf olives.

❑ **I** PURPLE OLIVE, *Olivella biplicata* (Sowerby, 1825)
❑ **I** BAETIC OLIVE, *Olivella baetica* Carpenter, 1864

Suborder Conacea (Toxoglossa)
Family Turridae

Many of these snails do not have common names.Many Oenopota are commonly called "lora" or "mangelia," which were earlier names of the genus, and some, Ophiodermella, as "snakeskin-snail."

❑ LORA, *Oenopota levidensis* (Carpenter, 1864)
❑ TABLE LORA, *Oenopota tabulata* (Carpenter, 1864)
❑ CANCELLATE SNAKESKIN-SNAIL, *Ophiodermella cancellata* (Carpenter, 1865)
❑ GRAY SNAKESKIN-SNAIL, *Ophiodermella inermis* (Reeve, 1843)
❑ VIOLET-BAND MANGELIA, *Kurtziella crebricostata* (Carpenter, 1864)

Subclass OPISTHOBRANCHIA
Order Pyramidellacea
Family Pyramidellidae

❑ PYRAMID SNAIL (Turbonilla), *Turbonilla* species
❑ ODOSTOME, *Odostomia columbiana* (Dall & Bartsch, 1907)

Order Cephalasida
Family Haminoeidae

❑ **I** WHITE BUBBLE SHELL (Blister, Glassy-bubble), *Haminoea vesicula* Gould, 1855

Family Acteonidae
❑ **I** BARREL SHELL (Baby's bubble), *Rictaxis punctocaelatus* (Carpenter, 1864) =*Acteon punctocaelatus*
Family Aglajidae
❑ SPOTTED (Eyespot) AGLAJA, *Aglaja ocelligera* (Bergh, 1894)
Subclass PULMONATA
Order Basommatophora
Family Siphonariidae
❑ **I** CARPENTER'S FALSELIMPET (Siphon shell), *Siphonaria thersites* (Carpenter, 1864)

TUSKSHELLS
CLASS SCAPHOPODA

Order Dentaliida
Family Dentaliidae
❑ WAMPUM (Indian money) TUSKSHELL, *Antalis pretiosum* (Sowerby, 1860)
Family Laevidentalidae
❑ WESTERN STRAIGHT TUSKSHELL, *Rhabdus rectius* (Carpenter, 1865)

CHITONS
CLASS POLYPLACOPHORA

Order Neoloricata
Suborder Lepidopleurina
Family Lepidochitonidae
❑ **I** LINED (Red) CHITON, *Tonicella lineata* (Wood, 1815)
❑ **I** BLUE-LINE CHITON, *Tonicella undocaerulea* (Sirenko, 1973)
❑ **I** WHITE-LINE CHITON, *Tonicella insignis* (Reeve, 1847)
Suborder Chitonina
Family Ischnochitonidae
❑ **I** MERTEN'S CHITON, *Lepidozona mertensii* (Middendorff, 1847)
❑ **I** THREE-RIB CHITON, *Lepidozona trifida* (Carpenter, 1864)
Family Mopaliidae
❑ **I** HAIRY CHITON, *Mopalia ciliata* (Sowerby, 1840)
❑ **I** MOSSY CHITON, *Mopalia muscosa* (Gould, 1846)
❑ **I** WOODY CHITON, *Mopalia lignosa* (Gould, 1846)
❑ **I** HIND'S MOPALIA, *Mopalia hindsii* (Sowerby, in Reeve, 1847)
❑ **I** SWAN'S MOPALIA, *Mopalia swanii* Carpenter, 1864
❑ **I** RED-FLECKED MOPALIA, *Mopalia spectabilis* Cowan and Cowan, 1977
❑ **I** SMOOTH MOPALIA, *Mopalia vespertina* (Gould, 1852)
❑ **E I** BLACK KATY (Leather) CHITON, *Katharina tunicata* (Wood, 1815)
❑ **I** RED VEILED-CHITON (Red hooded-chiton), *Placiphorella rufa* Berry, 1917
❑ **I** VEILED-CHITON (Hooded-chiton), Placiphorella velata (Carpenter, in Dall, 1897)
Suborder Acanthochitonina
Family Acanthochitonidae
❑ **E I** GIANT PACIFIC CHITON, *Cryptochiton stelleri* (Middendorff, 1847)

Common and scientific names have been assigned to species of Class Bivalvia primarily according to E.V. Coan, P.H. Scott and F.R. Bernard (in press, 1996). Other publications consulted include Bernard (1983), Quayle (1940, 1960), Quayle and Bourne (1972), Kozloff (1987) and the American Fisheries Society's Common and Scientific Names of Aquatic Invertebrates from the United States and Canada: Mollusks (1988).

The choice of current scientific names for species of the **Class Gastropoda** was aided by advice from Jim McLean and Rom Shimek, and recent publications (McLean, 1966; Kozloff, 1987). Many of the common names were chosen to be consistent with the *The Intertidal Univalves of British Columbia* (Griffith, 1967) and the American Fisheries Society common and scientific lists of mollusks. Other references with common names include Abbott (1990) and Rehder (1981).

Common and scientific names have been assigned to species of **Class Polyplacophora** (Chitons) according to the work of Roger Clark, and several publications (e.g. Kozloff, 1987). The chitons listed are the most common chitons and the largest of the Pacific coast chitons, many of which grow to a length exceeding 2" (50 mm).

Further Reading

General

Austin, W.C., 1985. *An Annotated Checklist of Marine Invertebrates in the Cold Temperate Northeast Pacific.* Cowichan Bay BC: Khoyatan Marine Laboratory.

Borrer, D.J., 1960. *Dictionary of Root Words and Combining Forms.* Mountain View CA: Bayfield Publishing Co.

Harbo, R.M., 1980. *Tidepool and Reef: Marinelife Guide to the Pacific Northwest Coast.* Surrey BC: Hancock House.

_____, 1988. *Guide to the Western Seashore: Introductory Guide to the Pacific Coast.* Surrey BC: Hancock House.

Kozloff, E.N., 1983. *Seashore Life of the Northern Pacific Coast: An illustrated guide to Northern California, Oregon, Washington, and British Columbia.* Vancouver: Douglas & McIntyre.

_____, 1987. *Marine Invertebrates of the Pacific Northwest.* Seattle: University of Washington Press.

Morris, R.H., D.P. Abbott and E.C. Haderlie. *Intertidal Invertebrates of California.* Stanford CA: Stanford University Press.

Snively, G., 1978. *Exploring the Seashore in British Columbia, Washington and Oregon: A guide to shorebirds and intertidal plants and animals.* Vancouver: Gordon Soules.

Seashells (Mollusks)

Abbott, R.T., 1990. *Canadian Nature Series: Seashells.* New York: W.H. Smith Publishers/Gallery Books.

Behrens, D.W., 1991. *Pacific Coast Nudibranchs.* 2nd edition, A Guide to the Opisthobranchs, Alaska to California. Monterey CA: Sea Challengers.

Bernard, F.R., 1983. *Catalogue of the Living Bivalvia of the Eastern Pacific Ocean: Bering Strait to Cape Horn.* Canadian Special Publication of Fisheries and Aquatic Sciences, No. 61.

Coan, E.V., P.H. Scott and F.R. Bernard, in press. *Bivalve Seashells of Western North America: Marine Bivalve Mollusks from Arctic Alaska to Baja California.* Santa Barbara CA: Santa Barbara Museum of Natural History.

Foster, N.R., 1991. *Intertidal Bivalves: A Guide to the Common Marine Bivalves of Alaska.* University of Alaska Press.

Griffith, L.M., 1967. *The Intertidal Univalves of British Columbia.* BC Provincial Museum Handbook 26. Victoria: Royal British Columbia Museum.

McLean, J.H. and T.M. Gosliner, 1996. *Taxonomic Atlas of the Benthic Fauna of the Santa Maria Basin and Western Santa Barbara Channel.* Vol. 9, The Mollusca: Part 2,

The Gastropoda. Santa Barbara CA: Santa Barbara Museum of Natural History.

Morris, P.A., 1996. *A Field Guide to Pacific Coast Shells.* 2nd edition, Peterson Field Guide Series. Boston: Houghton Mifflin.

Quayle, D.B., 1960. *The Intertidal Bivalves of British Columbia.* BC Provincial Museum Handbook 17. Victoria: Royal British Columbia Museum.

Rehder, H.A., 1981. *The Audubon Society Field Guide to North American Seashells.* New York: Alfred A. Knopf/Chanticleer Press.

Rice, T., 1972. *Marine Shells of the Pacific Northwest.* Ellis Robinson Publishing.

Stewart, H., 1996. *Stone, Bone, Antler & Shell Artifacts of the Northwest Coast.* Vancouver: Douglas & McIntyre.

Turgeon, D.D., A.E. Bogan, E.V. Coan, W.K. Emerson, W.G. Lyons, W.L. Pratt, C.F.E. Roper, A. Scheltema, F.G. Thompson and J.D. Williams, 1988. *Common and Scientific Names of Aquatic Invertebrates from the United States and Canada: Mollusks.* American Fisheries Society Special Publication 16.

Recreational and Commercial Fishing

Cheney, D.P. and T.F. Mumford, Jr., 1986. *Shellfish and Seaweed Harvests of Puget Sound.* Seattle: University of Washington Press/Puget Sound Books.

Dore, I., 1991. *Shellfish: A Guide to Oysters, Mussels, Scallops, Clams and Similar Products for the Commercial User.* New York: Van Nostrand Reinhold.

Jamieson, G.S. and K. Francis, eds., 1986. *Invertebrate and Marine Plant Fishery Resources of British Columbia.* Canadian Special Publication, *Fish. Aquat. Sci.* 91:8. Ottawa: Canadian Government Publishing Centre.

Quayle, D.B. and N. Bourne, 1972. *The Clam Fisheries of British Columbia.* Bulletin 179, Fisheries Research Board of Canada. Nanaimo BC: Biological Station.

Cookbooks

Harbo, R.M., 1988. *The Edible Seashore: Pacific Shores Cookbook and Guide.* Surrey BC: Hancock House.

Hardigree, P.A., 1977. *The Free Food Seafood Book.* Harrisburg, PA: Stackpole Books.

Pill, V. and M. Furlong, 1985. *Edible? Incredible.* Seattle: Andover Printing and Graphics.

Introduced Species

Carl, G.C. and C.J. Guiget. *Alien Animals in British Columbia.* British Columbia Handbook 14. Victoria: Royal British Columbia Museum.

Quayle, D.B., 1964. "Distribution of Introduced Marine Mollusca in British Columbia Waters," *Journal of the Fisheries Research Board, Canada* 21 (5).

Recreational Harvest Information, Licensing Requirements and Regulations (1996)

ALASKA
Alaska Department of Fish and Game, Sport Fish Division
P.O. Box 95526, Juneau AK 99802-5526
(907) 465-4180

BRITISH COLUMBIA
Department of Fisheries and Oceans, Recreational Fisheries Division
555 West Hastings Street, Vancouver BC V6B 563
Recreational Fisheries Ombudsman: (604) 666-2768
North Coast, BC: (250) 624-0409
South Coast, BC: (250) 756-7222

WASHINGTON
Washington Department of Fish and Wildlife
600 Capitol Way North, Olympia WA 98501-1091
(360) 902-2200

OREGON
Oregon Department of Fish and Wildlife, Marine Region
2040 Marine Science Drive, Newport OR 97365
(503) 867-4741

CALIFORNIA
California Department of Fish and Game
P.O. Box 944209, Sacramento CA 94244-2090
(916) 653-7664

PSP (Red Tide) Marine Toxin Hotlines (1996)

ALASKA
Check with the local Department of Environmental Conservation office.

BRITISH COLUMBIA
Fisheries and Oceans, Shellfish and Red Tide Update, (604) 666-3169

WASHINGTON
Washington State Department of Health, PSP Hotline, (800) 562-5632

CALIFORNIA
California Department of Health Services, Shellfish Information Line,
(510) 540-2605

Glossary of Terms

Adductor muscles. Large muscles, separate or joined, that open and close the shells of a bivalve.

Anterior canal. In snails: the base of the aperture where the foot extends sometimes forms a narrow, extended canal.

Anterior end. The end where the "foot" extends from the shell; in gastropods the head end that moves forward.

Aperture. In snails and gastropods: the opening from which the soft body extends from the shell.

Apex. In snails, limpets and other gastropods: the top of the shell.

Axial sculpture or threads. Shell sculpture that follows the axis of the shell.

Beak. See umbo.

Body whorl. In gastropods: the last and largest of the shell whorls containing the major portion of the body.

Byssus or byssal material. In bivalves: organic threads or material that attaches the bivalve to a hard surface, rocks or other substrates. The byssus is attached at the front end.

Centi/filosum. Hundred/line.

Chondrophore. In bivalves: shelf-like, spoon-like or socket-like part of the hinge.

Circumboreal. Found in the cool water regions south of the Arctic. On the west coast of North America, this includes the area from the Bering Strait south to Point Conception, California.

Cirrus (plural cirri). Soft finger-like projection; tentacle.

Columella. In coiled snails and gastropods: the axis around which the shell whorls are formed as the shell grows.

Comarginal. Refers to concentric lines or sculpture parallel to the margin of the shell; in bivalves the beak is at the centre.

Commensal. Refers to the relationship between one animal or plant living harmlessly with another and sharing its food.

Compressed. Flattened.

Concentric growth lines, ribs or ridges. See comarginal.

Concave. Surface curved inwards, like interior of a circle or sphere.

Convex. Surface curved outwards, like exterior of a circle or sphere.

Detritus. Debris containing organic material for food.

Dextral. Turning from left to right, opposite of sinistral. The snail aperture is most commonly found on the right of the axis.

Dira. Ominous (refers to dark grey colour).

Dorsal. Back or upper surface of the body; the shells of a bivalve are attached or hinged to one another dorsally and grow outwards.

Escutcheon. In bivalve shells: an indentation in the hinge area, posterior to the umbo.

Fenestrata. Refers to the marginal checkerboard pattern.

Foot. Muscular part of soft body used for digging, and sometimes for locomotion (e.g. jackknife clam) or attachment (e.g. scallop). A large, muscular foot is obvious in some clams such as razorclams, surfclams and butter clams. Some attached bivalves such as oysters and rock scallops lack a foot in the adult, sedentary stage. The foot is generally compressed and blade-like, hence the name Class Pelecypoda—"hatchet-foot"—sometimes used to describe bivalves.

Gaping shells. In bivalves: the shells do not close tightly and do not completely contain the body of the bivalve (e.g. geoduck or horse clams).

Gills. Serve primarily in food sorting and gathering as water is pumped through the body of a filter-feeder. The mantle is important in respiration.

Girdle. In chitons: muscular tissue that holds the plates together and forms the margin.

Growth rings or lines. Lines that can help age a bivalve shell. The growth of a shell is rapid in the spring and summer but slows and virtually stops in the winter, leaving a "check" or growth ring.

Height. Standard measurement of a shell from the hinge to the lower ventral margin. Few bivalves are higher than wide, except for scallops which are usually measured in shell height. Fishery regulations often refer to shell height for scallops.

Herbivorous. Feeding on seaweeds and other plant materials.

Hermaphroditic. Having the functioning organs of both sexes.

Hinge ligament. In bivalves: the ligament that springs the shells open when the adductor muscles relax. The external hinge ligaments are found posterior to the umbo (beak), at the siphon end, along the dorsal margin.

Incisus. Incised or cut-in grooves in a shell.

Inequivalve. Having two shells (right and left) that are significantly different from each other in size or shape.

Inflated. Expanded, not flattened.

Iridescent. Having a rainbow-like shine.

Left valve. In bivalves: the left shell when the bivalve is positioned with the hinge or beak facing, and the anterior (foot) end up, posterior (siphon) end down.

Lineata. Lined.

Lunule. Bivalve shell depression, usually heart-shaped, located in front of the umbo hinge (see also escutcheon).

Length. Measurement of the longest diameter across the shell (anterior to posterior), usually at 90 degrees to the height.

Mantle. An interior sheet of tissue that encloses the soft body of the mollusk. The shell is secreted from the edge of the mantle and has sensory perception, sometimes small tentacles and eyes in the case of scallops. The mantle is important in respiration.

Mendicus. Beggarly, needy (refers to "lean" elongated shell).

Myophore. In bivalves: spoon-shaped structure inside the hinge, projecting downwards (e.g. piddocks), used for muscle attachment.

Neck. In bivalves: a term used for the thickened, fused siphons of many clams.

Nest. In bivalves: a protective mat made of byssal threads and sand–mud (e.g. mussels, Musculus species).

Nuclear whorl. In gastropods: the earliest or first whorl of the snail, a small whorl at the top or apex of the shell.

Operculum. In snails: the "trap door" which covers the aperture to seal and protect the soft body parts within the shell. May be a horny or calcareous material.

Orbicular. Having a circular outline.

Ovate. Egg-shaped or oval.

Pallial line. In bivalves: a continuous or discontinuous scar where mantle flesh attached. May be present or absent.

Pallial sinus. In bivalves: an indentation in the pallial line, open toward the posterior (siphon) end where the siphons are attached.

Panarctic distribution. Found throughout the Arctic.

Periostracum. Coloured, sometimes glossy, thick or thin skin-like layer covering the exterior of the shell. It may have short hairs. This layer is often worn off by abrasion and may peel off when the shell is dried.

Posterior or siphonal. In bivalves: the end of the shell where the siphon protrudes, taking in and expelling water; opposite to the head end of snails, limpets and other mollusks.

Pretiosum. Precious or valuable.

Quadrate. Squarish or rectangular.

Radial lines or ribs. Lines that project toward the margin of a shell from a central point.

Radula. In snails, limpets and other gastropods: a tooth-like file located in the animal's mouth, used to rasp materials off hard surfaces for food. The radula is a unique identifying feature of many species.

Resilifer. In bivalves: the pit for an internal elastic hinge ligament, also termed "chondrophore" when shelf-like or spoon-like.

Reticulate sculpture. Squarish patterns formed from radial and axial sculpture.

Right valve. In bivalves: the right shell when viewing the hinge anterior end up, posterior end down.

Rufa. Red.

Sessile. Attached, fixed, not freely moving.

Sinistral. Turning from right to left, opposite of dextral.

Siphons. In bivalves: tube-like folds of the mantle that take in water and food (inhalant siphon) and expel water and waste products (exhalant siphon). The inhalant siphon is typically larger.

Spat. The newly settled bivalve larvae.

Spire. In snails: all the whorls above the body whorl.

Sub. Nearly.

Subovate. Nearly ovate.

Subquadrate. Nearly square or rectangular.

Subtrigonal. Nearly trigonal or triangular.

Suture. In snails: a line, ridge or channel where the spiral whorls touch.

Taxodont dentition. In bivalves: a series of teeth along the interior margin of the shell.

Teeth, cardinal. In bivalves: the largest two or three ridges in the hinge.

Teeth, lateral. In bivalves: smaller long, narrow ridges in the hinge below the cardinal teeth.

Tentacles. In bivalves: long, thin projections from the mantle and siphon tips that are sensitive to stimuli; cirri.

Thickness. In bivalves: width or distance, measured at the thickest part of the shell when facing the hinge.

Trigonal. Triangular in shape.

Truncate. Having a cut-off appearance; often abrupt.

Tunicata. Cloaked (refers to the mantle covering much of the plates).

Type specimens. The specimens used by authors to describe a species or subspecies. For example, holotype refers to a single-type specimen; paratype refers to each specimen of a type series other than the holotype.

Umbo or umbone. In bivalves: the beak or prominent part above the hinge, the earliest juvenile start of the shell. The umbo is usually anteriorly inclined.

Umbilicus. In snails: opening or hole in the shell visible from below, at the base of a hollow columella surrounded by the body whorl as it grows. The umbilicus is common on globular shells.

Valve. A term for shell. It refers to a gastropod shell; one of the two shells of a bivalve; one of the eight shell plates of a chiton.

Varices. Lengthwise or axial ridges, frills.

Ventral margin. The lower side or underside of the body; in bivalves opposite from the hinge and usually rounded.

Vinctu. Wound about (refers to bands of colour).

Width. In shell measurement, same as thickness.

Whorl. In gastropods: turning or coiling of a single shell. See also body whorl; nuclear whorl.

Glossary of Approximate Meanings of Scientific Names

Acmaea. Entire, no indentations.

Acteon. A huntsman.

Adunca. Hooked.

Amphissa. Double or round about.

Annulatum. Ringed.

Antiquatus. Old.

Arenaria. Sandy.

Aspera. Rough.

Astraea. Starry.

Attenuatum. Weakened or reduced.

Baetica. Slim, small.

Bimaculatus. Two-spotted.

Biplicata. Double-folded.

Bivalvia. Two-shelled (class name).

Bodegensis. After the Spaniard Bodega.

Californianus. Of California.

Californica. Of California.

Callio/stoma. More beautiful/mouth or opening.

Cancellata(us). Latticed.

Canaliculata. Channelled.

Capax. Roomy, spacious.

Carinata. Keeled.

Carpenteri. After P.P. Carpenter, a noted taxonomist of mollusks who prepared checklists of mollusks in 1857–64 and a full description later in the 1860s.

Centi/filosum. Hundred/line.

Cerato/stoma. Horned/mouth.

Clausa. Closed space.

Columbiana. Of British Columbia.

Conradi. After T.A. Conrad, who published in the 1830s–1860s.

Cranioides. Helmet-like.

Crassodoma. Thick house (referring to rock scallop shell).

Crassostrea. Thick oyster.

Cryptochiton. Concealed chiton (referring to the "hidden" plates).

Cryptomya. Hidden mya.

Dalli. After William H. Dall, US Geological Survey, US National Museum, who began to collect specimens in the Northwest Coast area (northeastern Pacific) in 1865, and later published several checklists and full descriptions, into the 1920s.

Dentalium. Tooth-like.

Digitalis. Pertaining to a finger or toe, referring to shell ribbing.

Diodora. With a passage through.

Dira. Ominous, referring to the dark grey colour.

Edulis. Edible.

Emarginata. Without a border.

Entodesma. Ligament within.

Eu/lima. True/rasp or file.

Falcata. Hook-shaped.

Fastigiata. Exalted.

Fenestrata. Referring to the marginal checkerboard pattern.

Flabellatus. Fan-like.

Fossatus. Pierced.

Funebralis. Funereal (probably referring to dark colour).

Fusi/triton. Spindle (shaped)/demigod of the sea.

Gastropoda. Stomach-foot (class name).

Gaus/apata. Crooked/illusion.

Generosa. Created.

Gibberosa. Hunched.

Gigantea(eus). Large.

Gigas. Large.

Glycymeris. Sweet-part (referring to bittersweet clams).

Gouldi. After A.A. Gould, who published from the 1830s to the 1870s.

Granti. After U.S. Grant, who catalogued the mollusks of California and the adjacent region in 1931.

Hali/otus(otidae). Of the sea/ear.

Haminoea. Hooked.
Helicinus. Twisted.
Hiatella. Small cleft.
Hindsii. After R.B. Hinds, who published several papers on mollusks in the 1840s.
Hinnites. Hinny-mule (referring to tenacious attachment).
Hipp/onix. Horse/hoof.
Homalo/poma. Smooth/cover.
Inter/fossa. Between/ditch.
Instabilis. Unstable.
Ischnochitonidae. Slender chitons (chiton subclass name).
Japonica. Of Japan.
Kamtschatkana. Of Kamtschatka.
Lacuna. Pitted or hollowed out.
Laevigata. Slippery, smooth.
Lamellosa. Thinly layered.
Lepidopleuridae. Scaly vales (chiton subclass name).
Lepidozona. Scaly girdle.
Lewisii. After Captain Meriwether Lewis of the Lewis and Clark expedition.
Ligatum. With bands.
Lima. Rasp or file.
Lineata. Lined.
Lirulatus. Ridged.
Littorina. Belonging to the seashore.
Lordi. After J.K. Lord, naturalist on the British North American Boundary Commission.
Lurida. Pale yellow.
Machroschisma. Long split.
Margarites. A pearl.
Mega/tebennus. Large/robe or toga (referring to the fleshy mantle covering the shell).
Mendicus. Beggarly, needy, referring to the "lean" elongated shell.
Minuta. Tiny.
Mitra. Headdress or cap.
Mitrella. Headdress or cap.
Mya. Sea mussel.
Mytilus. Mussel.
Nassarius. Like a narrow-necked fish basket.

Nasuta. Pertaining to the nose.
Natica. Swimmer.
Nummaria. Like money.
Nuttalli(ii). After Thomas Nuttall, a botanist who collected shell material from Oregon and California, 1834–36, later described by Conrad (1837).
Odo/stomia. Way/mouth.
Oldroydi. After I.S. Oldroyd. who published from 1918 to the 1930s; during 1925–27 a four-part compilation of illustrations and original descriptions of mollusks, *Marine Shells of the West Coast of North America.*
Olivella. Like a little olive.
Opisthobranchia. Behind gills (gastropod subclass name).
Oregonensis. Of Oregon.
Panope. Sea-nymph.
Patula. Open.
Pelecypoda. Hatchet foot (another class name for bivalves).
Pelta. A small shield.
Persona. A mask.
Pholadis. Lurking in a hole.
Pilsbryi. After H.A. Pilsbry, am eminent conchologist who catalogued mollusks from 1895 into the 1930s.
Placyphorella. Bearing many plates (referring to chiton class name).
Platydon. Flat tooth.
Pododesmus. Fettered foot.
Polinices. A Greek mythological character.
Polyplacophora. Bearing many plates (chiton class name).
Pretiosum. Precious, valuable.
Prosobranchia. Forward gills (gastropod subclass name).
Psephidia. Pebble.
Pulligo. Dark-coloured.
Pulmonata. With "lungs" (gastropod subclass name).
Puncto/caelatus. Spotted/carved in relief.
Pupillus. Doll-like.
Rectius. Straight.
Rhabdus. Rod-like.

Rubropicta. Painted red.
Rufa. Red.
Rugifera. Wrinkled.
Salmonea. Salmon-coloured.
Saxicola. Rock dwelling.
Saxidomus. Rock house.
Scaphopod. Shovel foot (tuskshell class name).
Scutulata. Checkered.
Scutum. An oblong shield.
Secta. Cleft.
Semele. Daughter of Cadmus and Hermione.
Semidecussata. Half-divided.
Setacea. Brittle.
Sicarius. Assassin.
Siliqua. Pod.
Siphon/aria. Tube/like, referring to the siphon.
Sitkana. Of Sitka.
Solen. Channel-pipe.
Staminea. Thread.
Stelleri. After Georg Wilhelm Steller, a German naturalist on Bering's early expedition to Alaska in 1741.
Subobsoleta. Somewhat worn.
Succinctus. Short or tucked up.
Tantilla. So little.
Taras. Son of Neptune.
Tegula. A roof or covering.
Tenerrima. Most delicate.
Thais. Celebrated courtesan of Athens.
Thersites. The audacious, reviling one.
Transennella. Tiny trap.
Tricho/tropis. Hairy; keel.
Truncata. Shortened.
Tumida. Swollen.
Tunicata. Cloaked, referring to the covering of the chiton's plates.
Turbonilla. Cone-shaped.
Variegata. Changing colours.
Velata. Veiled.
Velutina. Velvety.
Venerupis. Rock.
Vesicula. A little bladder.
Vincta. Wound about, referring to the bands of colour.
Virginica. Of Virginia.

Many of these approximate meanings have been taken from Borror (1960), Griffith (1967) and Quayle (1960).

Index

A

abalone (Family Haliotidae), 70, 182, 183-4

abalone piddock (*Penitella conradi*), 49, 175

aboriginals, *see* Native North Americans

Acantitochitonidae, 111, 231

Acila castrensis (divaricate nutclam; tent nutshell; nut clam), 14, 132

Acmaea alveus (*Lottia alveus, Collisella alveus*) (eelgrass limpet; bowl limpet), 81, 199

Acmaea asmi (Lottia asmi; Collisella asmi) (black limpet), 80, 198

Acmaea fenestrata (*Tectura fenestrata; Notoacmaea fenestrata*) (fenestrate limpet), 79, 198

Acmaea instabilis (*Lottia instabilis; Collisella instabilis*) (unstable limpet), 80, 198

Acmaea mitra (whitecap limpet; dunce-cap limpet), 77, 196

Acmaea persona (*Tectura persona; Notoacmaea persona*) (mask limpet; speckled limpet), 79, 197

Acteon punctocaelatus (*Rictaxis punctocaelatus*) (barrel shell; baby's bubble), 101, 220

Acteonidae (bubble shells), 101-2, 220-21

Adam's spiny Margarite (spiny topsnail) (*Cidarina cidaris*), 77, 195

Adanson's lepton (red lasaea) (*Lasaea adansoni; Lasaea subviridis, Lasaea rubra*), 28, 148

Adula californiensis (California datemussel; pea-pod borer), 18, 137

age of bivalves, 119

Aglaja ocelligera (spotted aglaja), 102, 221

Aglajidae (internal bubble shell; eyespot aglaja), 102, 221

Agriodesma saxicola (*Entodesma navicula; Entodesma saxicola; Lyonsia saxicola*) (rock entodesma; Northwest ugly clam), 51, 62, 66, 177

Alaska astarte (elliptical tridonta) (*Astarte elliptica; Tridonta alaskensis, Astarte alaskensis*), 27, 147

Alaskan gaper (fat gaper; horse clam; summer clam; otter clam) (*Tresus capax*), 32, 60, 67, 153

Aleutian cockle (California cockle) (*Clinocardium californiense*), 30, 151

Aleutian macoma (*Macoma lama*), 39, 160

Aleutian moonsnail (closed moonsnail) (*Cryptonatica aleutic;, Natica clausa*), 87, 206

Alia carinata (carinate dovesnail), 97, 216

Alia gausapata (*Astysis gausapata; Mitrella gouldii*) (dovesnail), 97, 216

American oyster (Atlantic oyster; eastern oyster) (*Crassostrea virginica*), 21, 140

Amphissa columbiana (wrinkled amphissa), 96, 215

amphissa shells (Family Columbellidae [=Pyrenidae]), 96-97, 215-16

Amphissa versicolor (Joseph's coat amphissa; variegate amphissa), 97, 216

ample roughmya (false geoduck) (*Panomya ampla*), 47, 59, 173

Anomiidae (rock/jingle oysters), 22, 140-1

Antalis pretiosum (*Dentalium pretiosum*) (wampum tuskshell; Indian money tusk; dentalia), 104, 224

Antisabia cranioides (*Hipponix cranioides; Hipponix antiquatus*) (flat hoofsnail; horse's hoofsnail), 84, 203

Arctic hiatella (*Hiatella arctica*), 48, 173

Arctic roughmya (deepwater false geoduck) (*Panomya norvegica; Panomya arctica*), 48,173

Arctic surfclam (northern clam; Stimpson surfclam) (*Mactromeris polynyma; Spisula polynyma*), 33, 154

Astarte alaskensis (*Astarte elliptica; Tridonta alaskensis*) (elliptical tridonta; Alaska astarte), 27, 147

Astarte elliptica (*Tridonta alaskensis; Astarte alaskensis*) (elliptical tridonta; Alaska astarte), 27, 147

Astarte esquimalti (Esquimalt astarte), 27, 147

Astartida, 27, 147

Astraea gibberosa (red turban), 72, 190

Astyris gausapata (*Alia gausapata; Mitrella gouldii*) (dovesnail), 97, 216

Atlantic oyster (American oyster; eastern oyster) (*Crassostrea virginica*), 21, 140